In The Presence of the Sensuous

CONTEMPORARY STUDIES IN PHILOSOPHY AND THE HUMAN SCIENCES

Series Editor: John Sallis, Loyola University of Chicago

Associate Editors: Hugh J. Silverman, SUNY-Stony Brook, David Farrell Krell, University of Essex

EDITORIAL BOARD

This new international book series explores recent developments in philosophy as they relate to foundational questions in the human sciences. The series stresses fundamental and pervasive issues, alternative methods, and current styles of thought. It constitutes a response to the emergence in England and America of widespread interest in the domains, intersections, and limits of questions arising from the human sciences within a climate inspired chiefly by Continental thought. Although primarily philosophical in orientation, the series cuts across the boundaries of traditional disciplines and will include volumes in such areas as phenomenology, structuralism, semiotics, post-structuralism, critical theory, hermeneutics, and contemporary cultural (literary and artistic) criticism.

In the Presence of the Sensuous: Essays in Aesthetics

Mikel Dufrenne

edited and translated by

Mark S. Roberts

and

Dennis Gallagher

Humanities Press International, Inc.
Atlantic Highlands, NJ

First published in 1987 in the United States of America by HUMANITIES
PRESS INTERNATIONAL, INC., Atlantic Highlands, NJ 07716

© 1987 Humanities Press International, Inc.

Library of Congress Cataloging-in-Publication Data
Dufrenne, Mikel.
In the presence of the sensuous.

(Contemporary studies in philosophy and the
human sciences)
Bibliography: p.
Includes index.
1. Aesthetics.   2. Arts—Philosophy.   3. Criticism.
I. Roberts, Mark S.   II. Gallagher, Dennis.   III. Title.
IV. Series.
BH39.D82 1987   111'.85   86–4700
ISBN 0–391–03369–7

MANUFACTURED IN THE UNITED STATES OF AMERICA

Contents

Author's Preface

My *Phénoménologie de l'expérience esthétique* (*The Phenomenology of Aesthetic Experience*) was able to cross the Atlantic thanks to the excellent translation by my friend Edward S. Casey and his collaborators. Today the same opportunity is afforded some of my later writings under the title *In the Presence of the Sensuous: Essays in Aesthetics.* I am most happy about it, and must express my gratitude to its editors, Dennis Gallagher and Mark S. Roberts.

They have themselves chosen the articles to be presented in this anthology, and their judicious selection clearly indicates the movement of a certain philosophical reflection covering approximately thirty years and that is attuned to the vicissitudes of what is known in the United States as continental philosophy.

I feel that in fact aesthetics has an inherent right to be considered part of philosophy, even if the philosophical vocation is mainly to reflect on Being. For this meditation must be a human concern, and man must show himself capable of it through his acts and works. Among these works, and alongside the sciences, technologies, and institutions, we find the arts, that is, the object of aesthetics. This object is ambiguous, and its contours are indistinct, being precise only for the institution that authoritatively determines the domain of the Fine Arts, whereas today we have to take into account all the marginal or subversive practices disrupting these limits. Yet this object is a privileged one, precisely if, in order to define it, reflection is less attached to it than to the experience it implies, that is, the dual experience of the creator producing the object and the spectator welcoming and appreciating it.‾ For these experiences are perhaps the most significant of all those that we can know: the experience of the creator, because here man reveals himself as capable of escaping the realm of necessity and devoting himself to a gratuitous praxis; the experience of the spectator (and this would apply to the creator as well), because here man reveals himself capable of wonder. (This wonder, however, is not necessarily aroused by the artwork, for it can also be aroused by a sensuous unworked by man, the beautiful in Nature, as we used to say. It is in this sense that the experience of the subject as perceiver can claim primacy.) Wonder is the harmony between *perceptum* and *percipiens*. Everything begins with perception, as Merleau-Ponty has taught us, and aesthetic perception is perception *par excellence*, a perception that truly situates man in the world, and the inquiry of which opens the best way for philosophy.

For philosophy can neither deny nor forget the philosopher. Yet recently there have been numerous philosophies that have done so, and for very diverse reasons. These are philosophies that have become fashionable through the candid avowals of the disciples—even when they deserved better. If in *Pour l'homme* I have protested against these fashions—all the more readily since I cannot claim to be fashionable—it is primarily, let me say, for an ethical reason or, if one prefers, for a political one. If we carelessly play with the concept of man and announce its death, we risk accepting the lot assigned to human beings in countries where oppression, torture, and misery actually condemn them to an ignoble death. Must we accept the inhuman? I say absolutely not. And I can only say it in the name of an imperative—the only one required by ethics: do not harm your fellow man. This negative maxim postulates an affirmation: man is an end in himself—and if you feel like evoking Kant, you are welcome to do so! There is no shame in being a Kantian.

Neither is there any contradiction in subscribing to a Kantian ethic while claiming affinity with phenomenology. What draws me to phenomenology is precisely that it too can serve the cause of man. In opposition to reductive philosophies that posit both knowledge and desire as anonymous and so dismiss the individual in favor of structures that he has neither to think nor to live, phenomenology affirms the irreducibility of the subject. This subject is not necessarily a sovereign one whose self-sustained position would appeal to idealism. Phenomenology allows us to understand the subject as being-in-the-world: a radically finite being, destined to die, but whose birth we must also consider. This singular being is there, he exists in the world. As an individual, for "the individual alone exists"; and this venerable formula can be interpreted in the light of existentialism. Tearing away from the capacity and inertia of the in-itself (*en-soi*), this individual becomes capable of consciousness and choice. He is in the world because he is open to the world, because there is a world for him. But this being-in-the-world is born into the world; the registry records his birth and birthplace, within a social history where he lives his own history. Moreover, in the course of this singular history, he is continuously reborn: upon each awakening he is born again into the world, because he returns to consciousness. Does he return to the world empty-handed? No, and not only because he has stored memories and acquired habits; for even at the moment of his official birth the individual is endowed with an equipment that is not merely biological; we can say he carries some a priori that compose an existential a priori for him and individualize him. This allows certain thinkers to say that there is no first time, and we should therefore abstain from invoking an origin. They are right on two counts. On the one hand, it is true that the individual, far from being a *tabula rasa* passively offered to experience, is always in himself a singular power of reception. On the other hand, it is true that in objectively considering the time in which the experience is inscribed, we discover that there is no time of time: we cannot specify a point zero of this time, in which the causality of a first cause might be working without falling into antinomies, as Kant has so aptly demonstrated. But we must push this paradox a bit further. For if it is true that for an awakening consciousness the world is always already familiar, then it is also always new. As Alain has said, the instant is new. A transcendental is at work, but it allows the empirical to be revealed in the newness of a first moment. If when beginning one begins again, when beginning again, one begins; each reawakening is an awakening, each rebirth, a birth.

Thus we must indeed think over the birth. This event is an advent, an emergence. But an emergence from what? If we cannot think the origin, we can at least think the originary. This originary is everything that is, the massive and raw being, the ground from which all things taking form emerge, that is, man and the things of the world. It is not itself the world, for the world is always the correlate of a being-in-the-world. The originary becomes world at the same time the subject arises. Man and the world are simultaneously born from the ground that I call Nature. Ecology has given new life to the term Nature (for which we should be grateful) by opposing the natural to the artificial, the open countryside to the urban landscape, and the spontaneous natural balances to the imbalances created by industrialization. But we must think this ground in more profound terms, as precisely what is unthinkable, as what precedes all thought, before man is born in order to think of and live it as world. This is neither chaos nor cosmos, but rather, let us say along with Joyce, *chaosmos*. Yet we can at least think this unthinkable Nature as naturing. It gives birth to both the man and the world that the being-in-the-world lives. It is truly the mother, this mother, who, perhaps, in archaic societies was portrayed by certain effigies and celebrated by fertility cults. Nature is the mother that Goethe's Faust pluralizes when he becomes awed by her mystery, the mother of which every mother is the image. We can perhaps say about the relation between man and Nature what psychoanalysis says about the relation between mother and child. If, when the umbilical cord is cut, when the subject asserts himself, the lost object is the warmth of the breast, the happiness of the oceanic feeling, it is also the originary in which the coming consciousness is initially immersed, as long as it is still absent to itself since it blindly experiences the fullness of a presence that is not illuminated by any representation.

We have lost all memory of this prenatal state and can only think of birth as unthinkable, just as Nature giving birth is also unthinkable for us. But perhaps thinking can sometimes be replaced by certain other experiences. We must thus once again examine the experience of perception, as Merleau-Ponty did so relentlessly. Perceiving is both being in the world and being soon separated from a world that is kept at a distance and becomes a spectacle. But this distancing is not immediate, for perception presupposes a certain prior and native complicity between the world and man. The a priori can be evoked in this respect: if they allow the perceiving subject to articulate the world and discover within it places and moments, things and relations between things, it is on condition that the given lend itself to these determinations. I have tried to show that they are simultaneously constituent of subject and object. But we can also think of an a priori of the a priori, that is, of a fundamental co-naturality of perceiver and perceived; man and the world are linked by the same flesh and blood. I can feel this profound familiarity whenever, instead of attempting to master appearances and thereby form a perception that subsequently lends itself to intellectual analysis, I remain fully sensible to the sensuous; whenever I am sufficiently present in it to let it resound in me and lose myself in it. For example, when I am all ears, I no longer have ears, for the sonorous completely inhabits me; I then live the primitive distinction between subject and object, just as I live it between self and other in the ecstatic moments of love. At this juncture I am in contact with the ground: the sensuous offers me a face of Nature that is, of course, for me, but for "a me" that has barely been born, still immersed in Nature, still situated in the vicinity of the originary. Here I am close to experiencing what I am in principle forbidden to experience: the ground.

This philosophy of Nature has been suggested to me by aesthetics. In turn, it privileges aesthetics. For two reasons. First, because aesthetics summons perception, for the aesthetic object is such only for and through the perception that aesthetisizes it. And this perception is the one I have just invoked, which carries us closest to the originary. This idea, however, can be contested. The artwork today prompts a number of scholarly discourses by critics and often by the creators themselves. Could it be that it requires intelligence rather than feeling, and that it is more fully appreciated through speaking of it rather than feeling it? But we should not harden this opposition, for if the work becomes an object of knowledge, it is on condition that it be welcomed initially by the body, and perhaps in order to be more intensely savored by it. Thus the spectator's experience directs the philosopher's reflection toward the first manifesta-tions of this pact, which always is already sealed between man and the world.

The same is true of the creator's experience. The *poietics* evokes this same pact whenever it describes the amorous struggle between the creator and the material from which the work will issue. It may suggest the idea of an imaginary that is assuredly subjective insofar as it is nourished by a singular desire and expressed in a singular creation, but that is also objective insofar as it constitutes the aura of the real perceived whenever perception does not intend to reduce the sensuous to the intelligible in order to master it. If the creator's flesh becomes one with that of the world, it is Nature that imagines within him; his work is his own because it is not totally his own, because he has been receptive enough to allow the sensuous to be, because his concern for formal problems has not prevented him from being inspired, that is, summoned by the sensuous.

But there is still another reason for privileging aesthetics. The aesthetic object not only elicits a perception approaching the experience of a ground, but also suggests a certain face of the ground as a universal birthplace. For it shows us a genesis, and sometimes in two ways. On the one hand, this object may manifest its own genesis. Certain of Michelangelo's sculptures already show us the work in its emergence from the stone, which is here the image of the ground. Today works are considered unfinished where traces of their being worked still remain, whenever the creator, far from claiming a monopoly on creation, seem-ingly summons other individuals in order to render the creation continu-ous. On the other hand, what the work says insofar as it speaks, what painting renders visible, as Klee says, and music audible, is also another genesis—one of a world brought about by the genesis of the sensuous. We say *a* world and not *the* world because today art forgoes imitating appear-ances, and perhaps it always has, despite certain catchwords. What it produces is an apparition, thereby revealing the power of appearing. And what appears is what Klee calls the *Urbildliche*: the upheaval of the sensuous. The aesthetic object, returning perception to its beginning, leads the subject back to presence. But this sensuous is not meaningless—it is of little importance if the work represents the real or not, for it always opens a world to us and promotes its genesis. Aesthetic reflection is thus always elicited by the theme of Nature.

This theme never disavows a philosophy of the subject, with its ethical and political implications. And I adhere to this philosophy as much as to a philosophy of Nature. For it can easily pose the subject as an end without absolutizing him, by recognizing on the contrary that the "lover of forms" is also a "son of the earth," to use Platonic terminology; he is born from Nature and is never radically separated from it, and so, being-in-the-world, he is in harmony with it. This type of humanism can then advise us to be heedful of maintaining our roots, of establishing a friendship with the world, and, in the world, with our fellow man. Civilization's true "malaise" is violence; it is due to the Will to Power of a subject wishing to the sovereign, and who, attempting to establish his own empire upon things, ends by exercising power over others. Descartes established a new science "in order to render man possessor and master of nature." Today we feel uneasy about a science that tries to enrich uranium ore, toy with eugenics, dump on its citizens, and develop strategies of *Realpolitik*. Has there been a malifice of knowledge? Has reason become madness?

I will not delve into this debate: if you are interested, read the texts of the Frankfurt School. What I would like to observe is that here again the aesthetic experience justifies that philosopher's interest in aesthetics. For in this world that is sinking into barbarism, this experience preserves the image of what may be an innocent and free praxis. This is, of course, an ambiguous and vacillating image: commercialization denatures art; the honors heaped upon it prompt it to prostitute itself; artists remain jealous of their monopoly, as experts of their competence. No matter: there are always men who paint, carve, sing, and dance; men capable of playing and enjoying, men who have no desire for power. Art is still living, and sometimes in places where it is neither celebrated nor corrupted. In reflecting upon this type of life, the philosopher can still find some reasons to hope.

Acknowledgments

In the final analysis, this book is entirely the work of its author, Mikel Dufrenne. It consists of the thoughts, insights, and conclusions of a lifetime dedicated to furthering our understanding of art and human experience. But the actual piecing together of the finished volume required many more hands and a great deal of tiresome, often mundane effort. We would therefore like to acknowledge our gratitude to those who so graciously contributed their time and effort to the completion of this project.

First, we would like to thank Mikel Dufrenne himself, who at considerable expense of his own time guided us through many of the difficult problems encountered in organizing and rendering the essays. In this connection he has read all of the newly translated essays and made authoritative and valuable suggestions about each of them. Secondly, we would like to acknowledge the excellent and tireless efforts of our translators, who, oftentimes under our anxious scrutiny, completed their tasks with speed and acumen. We would further like to thank professors David B. Allison, Edward S. Casey, and Hugh J. Silverman of the Department of Philosophy and Professor Konrad Bieber of the Department of French and Italian at the State University of New York at Stony Brook for their valuable suggestions with regard to the manuscript, with special recognition of Professor Casey for his generosity in making available his vast store of knowledge in Dufrenne translation. Professor Joseph Margolis, a consummate authority in the field of aesthetics, also lent valuable assistance at various stages of the manuscript's completion. Recognition also goes to Ellyn Allison for her generous and expert help in editorial matters. I would like to thank *Philosophy Today* for generously granting permission to use material from various reprint articles.

Editors' Introduction

Like all too many artists, philosophers often suffer belated recognition, particularly outside of their own cultures. We have frequently seen the results: now-familiar names like Sartre and Merleau-Ponty were little more than curious foreign locutions to English speakers until their major works reached us in translation. The same holds true for the important French philosopher and aesthetician Mikel Dufrenne. He has met with a situation almost exactly paralleling that of his two eminent countrymen. As late as 1970 he was known in the United States only to a handful of philosophers and aestheticians, and this minor recognition was largely due to the translation of two rather specialized works, *Language and Philosophy* (1963) and *The Notion of the A Priori* (1966). But in 1973, following the pattern of Sartre and Merleau-Ponty, his reputation became greatly enhanced by the publication of a single important work. Directly subsequent to the English translation of the second edition of his *Phénoménologie de l'expérience esthétique* (*The Phenomenology of Aesthetic Experience*),[1] there appeared a remarkable upturn in interest in his work. This trend continues with the development of a serious English-language Dufrenne scholarship, which includes numerous articles and commentaries in the professional literature, the forthcoming translation of his important work *Le Poétique*, and several dissertations at American universities.[2]

This volume—the first major collection of Dufrenne's essays to appear in a language other than French—will add to this burgeoning interest in his thought. It articulates and expands upon numerous features of his work that are either unavailable or undeveloped in previously translated works, and three of these features should be of particular interest: 1) The essays realize, in a very succinct way, Dufrenne's concern with integrating aesthetic practice into his existentialist notion of the primacy and irreducibility of human experience in general, particularly, in terms of the artist's contribution. 2) They provide a clear indication of the development and subsequent refinement of his socio-political thought in its relation to aesthetic experience. 3) They signal an expanded dialogue with a number of postmodern philosophical and aesthetic perspectives, including those commonly associated with the poststructuralists and the philosophers of nonteleological desire (Lyotard, Deleuze, et al).

Our first-mentioned feature that is elaborated in the essays—the primacy of human or subjective experience—has been central to Dufrenne's thought ever since he first addressed it in 1946. The issue regularly punctuates the *Phenomenology*, and it continues to reverberate in virtually all subsequent works. The problem of the primacy of human experience, however, is not Dufrenne's invention, nor is it in any way limited to his own writings. Indeed, its historical roots can be traced back to Aristotle, who was far less prone to submit man's concrete existence to the exigencies of fate and to the cosmos than were his Ionian and Pythagorean predecessors. The place of human experience in its relation to the world and cosmos was then somewhat obscured during the theologically contentious Middle Ages, but reemerged as a result of the Classical scholarship of the Renaissance humanists. Modern-day configurations of the problem owe much to Nietzsche, Rilke, and Kierkegaard, who all made human subjectivity (or our misconception of it) central to their observations and interpretations of the human condition.

The species of subjectivity that most interests Dufrenne—man's existential condition—was not fully articulated until Sartre made it one of the principal focuses of his *Being and Nothingness*. Here Sartre was able to attribute radical constitutive and negating functions to human consciousness, and thus, in effect, remove it from the strictures of the traditional knower-known relation. This in turn served to remove it from its very limited role in conventional epistemologies and theories of cognition and place it in far more direct encounter with the world. For Sartre, then, consciousness becomes a way of encountering the being of the knower strictly in terms of his being conscious of his own consciousness and the world presented to it. Human subjectivity consequently stands as the indissoluble basis for revealing concrete events, in their fullest and most complete form. The event in turn becomes constitutive of that consciousness, thereby indicating that subjectivity alone is the true object of inquiry and is irreducible to supervenient laws, principles, and systems.[3]

Dufrenne readily subscribes to the spirit of this existential "law," but prefers to apply its letter in a different area of human experience. Whereas Sartre had been primarily concerned with the primacy of human experience with regard to intersubjective relations (*Being and Nothingness*) and the complex functions of groups and institutions (*The Critique of Dialectical Reason*), Dufrenne finds its main field of applicability in aesthetics. His most extensive account of this problem appears in the *Phenomenology*, where he set out to resolve and articulate the specific place of a subject in relation to an external object (the artwork) by suggesting that a sensuous element (i.e. a *tertium quid*), inherent in aesthetic experience or perception, mutually involves both the spectator and the aesthetic object. Or, in other words, the aesthetic object, serving as a kind of quasi-subject, enjoys the response of the spectator via the medium of the sensuous: "the sensuous is an act common to both the person who feels and to what is felt."[4] It is thus the sensuous that opens the two principal kinds of aesthetic depth—that of the spectator, and the expressed world of the aesthetic object. These two registers are in turn defined by their realization on an affective level, and feeling becomes the occasion whereby subject and object merge in the aesthetic experience. For the Dufrenne of the *Phenomenology* this testifies to a fundamental reciprocity between subject and object.

A priori elements—structures conditioning our receptivity—tend to deepen further this basic reciprocity between subject and object within the aesthetic experience. The a priori encountered here serve to order the expressed world, that is, become manifest insofar as the aesthetic object expresses a world of affinity. These a priori elements are likewise encountered by the spectator or experiencing subject, since he could not recognize the expressed world of the aesthetic object unless he had a virtual knowledge of its content in the particular, existential sense. But virtual knowledge also involves a knowledge of the a priori in its cosmological embodiment, that is, as the inner link between the subject and the content of his inner experience. This reconciliation of subject and object within the aesthetic experience effects an even greater unity—the unity of Being. The a priori, as determination of both subject and object, testifies to an all-encompassing being that makes this affinity possible in the first place.

Dufrenne's notion of aesthetic experience indicates that human being and participation is absolutely essential to this experience. Each stage of aesthetic revelation unfolds within the boundaries of *our* experience, and a full understanding of any artwork is impossible without our full participation in its expressed world. Nevertheless, it seems that one crucial participant in this aesthetic process is missing: the artist himself. For, with regard to the art object, there would be no experience possible unless there were someone to create it in the first place. Unfortunately, for a variety of reasons enumerated in the introduction to the *Phenomenology*,[5] Dufrenne had been quite reluctant to introduce in investigations the problem of the creator's experience. This reluctance continued for some time following the publication of the *Phenomenology*, but during the past decade or so he has focused on the problem, and has made several attempts to integrate the "other participant" into his overall conception of the human subject's primacy in the aesthetic experience. Some of the more recent essays exemplify this trend.

A particularly salient example of Dufrenne's attempt to understand the artist's role in the aesthetic process appears in his 1976 essay "Painting, Forever," which has as its main theme an explanation of easel painting's remarkable durability in an era in which firing a pistol at a departing jetliner is considered art. Like many of his previous attempts at describing aesthetic experience, this essay opens with an account of the spectator's response to the artwork (in this case, the painting). But the opening descriptive phase of the essay is not seriously sustained, and we eventually get the sense that it is intended more as Dufrenne's own response to Merleau-Ponty's conception of the visible than an in-depth analysis of spectatorial experience.[6] This seems confirmed when he shifts from what amounts to an "immanent" analysis of the eye to an explanation of how the painter goes about eliciting the spectator's vision. With this move, Dufrenne seems most concerned with questioning precisely how the act of painting complements the act of seeing, that is, what elements are common to both the producing and seeing of a painting.

Dufrenne proposes that the common ground uniting artist and spectator is nature, since it serves as the source of their mutual inspiration. The painter is moved by nature to the extent that it provides his subject matter and the motivation for his personal commitment, or, as Dufrenne puts it, it inspires his choice to "make his profession his craft." Such a commitment to the actual act of painting, to the gesture of placing a thick substance on canvas, also leads to another state of desire: the desire for making. And making is viewed by Dufrenne as an act that reveals a still higher desire in man. This higher desire is what has traditionally characterized us as *homo faber*, and thus it resounds deeply in both our personal and collective makeup; it motivates the body to interact with its environment and eventually to attempt to transform it. The subject matter of this tranformational act is the world; for the painter always views the world *as* subject matter, as an inescapable focus and repository of potential transformations. But, according to Dufrenne, the world cannot merely be copied or rendered in cold, systematic fashion, as in the color schematics and cast renderings so favored by the academies. Rather, the inspiration for this supreme transformational act must issue from nature itself, out of which the artist is able to express the gestation of a "possible," a world that is not merely a copy of the real world, but that truly shares the desires, aspirations, and feelings of all individuals.

The painter, like the spectator, thus shares an integral function in the full gestation of the aesthetic experience, and Dufrenne attributes this function to the artist's constant awareness of the world's transformational capacities. These transformations, moreover, do not simply result from an imitation of nature or from a reaction that is exclusively limited to the spectator's experience; they are rather expressions integral to the artist's commitment to and bodily experience of the world around him. In this connection, the artist, like the spectator and aesthetic object of the *Phenomenology*, takes on a central function in the circuit of aesthetic experience. His feelings, gestures, and desires are given a full and important place in the aesthetic process, and the long-missing "other participant"—the creator—begins to emerge as an essential factor in Dufrenne's conception of human completeness and its absolute primacy with regard to the aesthetic process.

The concern with man in general brings us to the second feature of Dufrenne's thought that is reintroduced and further developed in the essays: his politics or, more precisely, his political humanism. We say "reintroduced" because it would be misleading to state unequivocally that his interest in politics and social issues is entirely new, or that it is peculiar to this text alone. Dufrenne did, after all, begin his career, in the mid-forties, with a series of essays examining the integral relations between philosophy and sociology, an effort that eventually took the form of a book, *La Personnalité de base*, devoted to formulating a sociological concept of man. But these intensive early concerns with the spectrum of our social existence eventually gave way to more speculative ones following the publication of the *Phenomenology* in 1953. And it was not until the appearance of *Art et Politique* in 1974, following a twenty-year hiatus, that the social aspect of his thought began to reemerge in an extensive, systematic way.

Dufrenne nonetheless kept his socio-political insights acute during this period, which was mainly devoted to speculative philosophy, through the medium of the essay. From 1953 through 1974 he wrote a considerable number of essays and reviews directly related to this field, and one of the most comprehensive and interesting, "*Mal du siècle?* The Death of Art?" appears here. This work, ostensibly intended as a prescriptive antidote to the malaise affecting modern art, also incorporates a far-ranging analysis of the socio-political factors contributing to the modern predicament in general—the *mal du siècle*. Dufrenne begins the essay by focusing on the issue of art's relation to society, endeavoring to analyze this relation in terms of the basic distinction between informal and formal modes of creativity. The conclusion he reaches at these early stages of the essay is that these two modes of creativity, far from constituting the modern predicament, are symptomatic of a "fundamental inconsistency" in the status that Western civilization accords the individual. In principle, the individual still has the basic freedoms and rights inherited from the humanistic tradition, retaining the tools with which to forge his personal destiny. But in actual practice, in his relations with society in general, the individual demonstrates a tendency toward both self-exhaustion and alienation.

The most obvious manifestation of this "fundamental inconsistency" is a tendency to overformalize all aspects of social and intellectual existence.

This leads the individual to delegate his own initiative to institutions, to "savants" who do the thinking for him, and ultimately to a fruitless controversy over the content and status of freedom and the proper social conditions for its actualization. On the level of global politics, this frustrating situation manifests itself in highly formalized political systems that oscillate between chauvinistic nationalism and the affirmation of general solidarity. Formalization also affects philosophical thought, which, according to Dufrenne, reflects the political tenor of its environment; it forces this type of thought, subject to a pantheon of systems, to suspend its concern with historical erudition and the repudiation of all systems in favor of a formal analysis of science and language. Aesthetic thought, hardly exempt from these exigencies, likewise follows suit; it tends to divide itself between an overfactual art history and a morphology that views works from a purely formal standpoint, disregarding their lived, cultural meaning.

The symptoms of the modern predicament, however, do not end here. The process of formalization, born of a basic misunderstanding of the status and function of freedom, extends to art itself, taking the form of abstraction. Abstraction (and by this Dufrenne does not mean all nonobjective art, but rather a type of artistic process that is excessively mechanical and calculated) tends to polarize artistic production into distinct systems. On the one hand, we find an art that issues from purely formal intentions (e.g. de Stijl), an art that devalues content and personal expression in favor of form. In this instance, the artist's loss of a sense of grandeur, of scale and meaning, leads to the production of neutral and "bloodless" artworks; to paintings that treat line, color, and form as elements of a plastic calculus; to an architecture that plans urban monstrosities composed of "anonymous cells." But conversely, Dufrenne argues, there are artists who reject formalistic abstraction and turn to an art that is primordial, raw, and sensuous, that is, an art that is basically informal, involving the direct, unmediated expression of nature, desire, and feeling.

The opposition between the originary and the overcalculated, the informal and the formal, serves as Dufrenne's basic model for explicating the artist's relation to modern society. This binary set conditions the very choices the artist must make, and ultimately serves as the indicator of society's own direction: a direction that oscillates between restrictive systems and the freedom of the originary creative act. But for Dufrenne, freedom is a tenuous proposition. It slips into controversy and formalization, and the basic rights guaranteed by the Western tradition of humanism can become obscured in our actual societal relations. In the end, however the artist can overcome these difficulties. He can choose to express his freedom though an art that is motivated by a deep commitment to human needs and a "friendship with the world." In short, he can opt for an informal type of expression that opposes all attempts at reducing human experience to a set of abstract rules and principles, to the form of expression rather than its content.

The political conception fundamental to this essay is clear: politics, institutions, governments, and societies are not exclusively the result of ideologies or the play of conventional exchanges. They are also the expression of a very special reciprocity between the individual and his culture. Indeed, in Dufrenne's view, I am my society and it is me.[7] The limitations imposed by society on man and *vice versa* are the result of his living in society and its living in him. The concept of formalization, then, is far more than simply a device for implementing a certain creative option; it is also an insidious means of circumventing the relationship between man and society by replacing its fullness with a functional rationality, that is, with a pure thought devoid of any object. But Dufrenne's political humanism opposes this shortcut, for he has continually emphasized that the essential a priori relationship between man and world cannot be reduced to abstract terms; to metalanguages, to sets of relational calculi, or, in opposition to some Marxist thinkers, to a de jure alienation that is neither lived nor thought by its supposed victims. This relational bond is rather the result of the conscious operations of a subject who refuses to be wholly individualized by the social conditions of his actualization, who holds out the hope that beyond any particular set of socio-cultural norms there exists a detached, communal, but yet fully human subjectivity.

With his emphasis on subjectivity and humanism in general, Dufrenne might be expected to take a somewhat dim view of the abstractions of postmodern thought, and with regard to his earlier works, this is not far from the truth. His essays of the late fifties and sixties and his book *Pour l'homme* were quite candid in their attacks on what he termed "dehumanizing philosophies," particularly with regard to structuralism.[8] He has certainly not lost his ability to champion humanism (witness the Author's Preface) or his eye for spotting sheer philosophical formalities, but his work of the past decade has become more concerned with interpreting and analyzing the basic presuppositions of postmodern thought than with contrasting them unfavorably with existential phenomenoloy. This move forms the third important feature of Dufrenne's thought made evident in the essays.

There are numerous examples in the more recent essays (those dating from the mid- to late seventies) of Dufrenne's attempts to make sense of and, in certain cases, even to draw upon postmodern thought. Among these we can count "Painting, Forever," where, with certain qualifications, he goes so far as to borrow aspects of Jean-François Lyotard's notion of painting as desire, and "Why Go to the Movies?" where Barthes's, Metz's, and Althusser's conceptions of ideology play important roles. But none are quite so elaborate or telling as the 1976 essay, "The Imaginary." Ostensibly, the work is a reevaluation of recent think-ing on the subjects of the imagination, the imaginary, and the image. Dufrenne begins by running through some of the twentieth-century man-ifestations of this thinking, giving special attention to the contributions of Alain, Husserl, and Sartre. He is less critical of Alain and Husserl than of Sartre, whom he accuses of confusing the image-forming act, a mental configuration, with the *analogon* effecting this configuration. In short, he claims that Sartre views the *analogon* formed as a mental correlate of the thing, as something that exists apart from the "life of consciousness," and thus as something that stands outside the remarkable constitutive and epistemological capacities of human perception.

This fullness of the "life of consciousness" and its relation to nature and the world leads Dufrenne to a discussion of the Freudian and Post-Freudian approaches to the subject of the imaginary. He concludes that these approaches are basically incorrect, in that they posit a subject divided and decentered by an unconscious revealed by the imaginary. But, Defrenne concedes, the interesting aspect of the Freudian vision is that it encourages thought to return to the originary—to an "oceanic feeling" in which the subject is primordially submerged, and that consists in a kind of originary presence. This presence in turn constitutes a "within," a private, subjective space, and not an outside or absence. And it is this conception of presence that motivates him to explore the three concepts that presently enjoy the greatest popularity among contempor-ary thinkers: desire, language, and world.

Dufrenne pursues his investigation of these three terms by dividing them into several binary combinations, including one entitled "Language and World." His primary focus in this section is on the recent linguistic work of Barthes, Foucault, and, especially, Derrida. The point he wishes to make here is that this type of thinking tends to emphasize the opposi-tion between world and language, positioning language as the "other" of the world, in basically the same manner as the Freudians and Post-Freudians place desire in conflict with the world. According to Dufrenne, this conflictual opposition between language and the world is best demon-strated by Derrida's deconstruction of the linguistic sign. In this connec-tion, Derrida wants to claim that the signified is originally and essentially a trace which is always already in the position of a signifier.[9] But Dufrenne disagrees. He counters with: ". . . what can a signifier signify that, instead of designating an absent signified, is itself a type of absence?" This further prompts him to suggest that we should concentrate on the opening rather than the closure of the relation between language and world; on the post-Kantian notion that makes language an a priori of perception, a preexisting grid, imposed from the outside, through which the world appears. The connection between world and language, then, establishes an essential relation between what is named and its referential term or, more precisely, between signifier and referent. Every time we feel complicity, or even resemblance, between words and things, we are obliged to name this experience, and the world brings forth speech so as to be transported into and expressed by it. By formulating the relation between world and language in terms of the preconditions necessary for any utterance, Dufrenne can then claim that the essence of the linguistic sign is determined initially by presence—our presence in the world and to things; and subsequently, that the difference between signifier and signified—Derrida's conception of *différence*—is not necessarily required to be absolute and irreducible and thereby guaranteed by a creative logos. Indeed, quite simply he states that the guarantee issues from the fact that the world is immediately announced in the signifier, and this embedding of the signifier in the signified establishes language's power to designate.

Beyond his analysis of language's relation to us and our world, Dufrenne also deals with the binary combination "Image and Desire." In this section we find a rather marked use of some of Lyotard's analyses. His principal debt to Lyotard consists in the use of his notion of desire in art as a way of dispelling certain views that treat the image as a symptom of desire and as completely unconscious. In opposing this view, he claims, along with Lyotard, that even the most seemingly unconscious and informal art images create a structured domain where other, as yet unexpressed, images take hold. Thus the "genuine work" is not merely a symptom, a piece of dreamwork, but rather a place, a matrix of desire, in which desire organizes the space and time of the imaginary and images in general. Desire in effect commands the invisible ruling form, according to which the visible is organized. It is difficult to speak of it, it has no real place, but yet it is not unconscious; rather, it is an ordering principle that is not itself unconscious but that gives place to the deepest and most subliminal expressions of primal fantasy.

The above summary only indicates a few of the interesting and new facets of Dufrenne's thought available in this volume. There are many more, We could have spoken of Dufrenne's unique and poetic style as a writer of short philosophical pieces—of a stylistic virtuosity that ranges from humorous irony to precise scholarship. We could have also indicated texts that have never before appeared in print, such as "Valéry's Leonardo," or the important but previously unavailable translations of

Dufrenne's work in literary criticism. But in introducing Dufrenne's work it seems quite sufficient to indicate the basic contours of his contribution to the study of art, aesthetic experience, and philosophy in general. For these contours invariably surround us and our world. And this insistence of the primacy of our place within the world and our indisputable connection with nature, art, and society constitutes his great contribution to aesthetics. His work may not answer all the questions raised by aesthetic analysis, but it always poses these questions from the vantage point of human experience, and most significantly, it communicates the sense of wonder that we can all freely experience when we are making or enjoying an artwork.

Notes

1. This work will be referred to throughout as the *Phenomenology*.
2. For further details on secondary material, see our bibliography at the end of this volume.
   Professor Véronique M. Fóti of the New School for Social Research in presently working on the translation of Dufrenne's *Le Poetique*, which should appear sometime in the near future.
3. Although Sartre established the basic groundwork for this notion in his *Being and Nothingness*, its fullest realization appears in *The Critique of Dialectical Reason*, particularly with regard to his critique of Lévi-Strauss's sociology, which he saw as an attempt to reduce the concept of man to instrumental structures.
4. Mikel Dufrenne, *The Phenomenology of Aesthetic Experience*, trans. Edward S. Casey et al. (Evanston, Ill.: Northwestern University Press, 1973), p. 48.
5. Ibid., pp. xlv–xlvii.
6. For a detailed account of Dufrenne's response to Merleau-Ponty's conception of the visible, see "Eye and Mind" (p. 69–74) in this volume.
7. Paul Ricoeur, Preface in Mikel Dufrenne, *The Notion of the A Priori*, trans. Edward S. Casey (Evanston, Ill.: Northwestern University Press, 1966) p. x.
8. We should perhaps qualify this statement a bit, lest the reader get the impression that Dufrenne was simply butting existential phenomenology against postmodern thought in his earlier works. This of course was not the case. Naturally, he was concerned with critically evaluating the positions of postmodern conceptions (see "Structure and Meaning: Literary Criticism," p. 173–186, for example) in these earlier works. But his approach in later works differs in that he seems more concerned with operating a dialogue with postmodern thought, and in certain cases, even incorporating some of these modern conceptions into his own investigations.
9. See Jacques Derrida, *Speech and Phenomena: And Other Essays on Husserl's Theory of Signs*, trans. David B. Allison (Evanston, Ill.: Northwestern University Press, 1973), pp. 17–26 and passim.

A Note on the Translation

As editors and partial translators of this volume, our main concern was with keeping the various essays, with their differing terminologies, consistent throughout. This was not always easy, since Dufrenne's style often varies with his subject matter, and like many existentially oriented writers, he pushes language to its outer limits. But Dufrenne has read all of the newly translated essays and in many instances has clarified difficult points in translation.

We have also had the good fortune of being able to consult Edward S. Casey's definitive and comprehensive translations, *The Phenomenology of Aesthetic Experience* and *The Notion of the A Priori*. These works have helped immensely in circumventing problems in translating elusive terminology. We have, for example, continued to translate *le sensible* as "the sensuous"—a term that Casey treats in some detail in his translation of the *Phenomenology*. In most cases where there existed a number of possible translations we have deferred to Casey's renderings.

We have, however, developed our own renditions of certain terminology appearing in essays. Words such as *le possible* or *l'apparaître* have been translated by nominalizing the respective adjectival or verbal forms. Such a procedure is suggested by Dufrenne's own thinking, since he makes it quite clear that we can also speak of the real, the unreal, the imaginary, etc. A particularly difficult word to translate is *l'originaire*, which we have rendered as "originary being" or "the originary," depending on the context. We have, in any case, based our decisions on style and vocabulary on our attempt to render faithfully and present clearly the French texts.

PART ONE

PHILOSOPHICAL FOUNDATIONS OF AESTHETICS

1. *Intentionality and Aesthetics*

By reviving the traditional problem of the relationships between the subject and object through the notion of intentionality, Husserl has placed this idea at the center of philosophical reflection. On the one hand, the analysis of the *cogito* reveals that the subject is transcendence, that is, intends an object. On the other hand, intentional analysis reveals that the appearing of the object is linked with the intention directed toward it. The relation between subject and object thus appears prior to its two terms, and it is this relation, as a totality and in totality, with its noetic-noematic structures, that becomes the basic theme of the Husserlian phenomenology. Because of this relation, phenomenology erases all suspicion of reviving idealism and is correct in affirming the identity of "constituting" and "seeing." It seems to us that the aesthetic experience—the experience of the spectator and not that of the creator—can be evoked in order to clarify this difficult notion, or at least one of its interpretations.

Several interpretations of the idea of intentionality are possible. According to one of them, phenomenology turns toward ontology. The reduction appears as a step, analogous to the one by which Hegel promotes absolute knowledge,[1] that is necessary in order to pass from the empirical to the speculative: it forbids the subject, be it the "I" of the "I think," from taking itself for a radical origin as well as from taking the object for an absolute. Intentionality fundamentally signifies the intention of Being, which reveals itself—being nothing more than its revelation—and gives birth to the object and subject for the sake of this revelation. The object and subject, existing only within the confines of the mediation joining them, are thereby the conditions for the emergence of meaning, the instruments of a *Logos*. Heidegger, albeit without integrating dialectic into ontology, identifies this *Logos* with Being. From the side of the object, defined as being, and not as in the style of Kant's *Transcendental Analytic*, as the seat of objectivity, he emphasizes the reference to Being, because Being is the disclosure permitting the manifestation of beings. From the side of the subject, defined as *Dasein*, and no longer as consciousness, he emphasizes the power that the subject has for opening itself up to Being, but he assigns this transcendence to the very Being that calls upon the subject to serve as witness, that is, to make itself a place for a presence, so that the subject's project becomes a project of the Being concerning the subject. Object and subject are thus deprived of their prerogatives; it is Being as light that at once commands the look and the thing seen, and is thereby responsible for the relation between the subject and the object.

But if in that case phenomenological reduction culminates in the nomination of Being, one can also say that "the greatest lesson of the reduction is the impossibility of a complete reduction."[2] Intentionality is then no longer guaranteed in Being. It always expresses the solidarity of the object and subject, but without either of them being subordinated to a superior agency or absorbed into the relation uniting them. The externality of the object is irreducible, even though the object is only an object for a subject. The selfhood of the subject is also irreducible, that is, the selfhood of the *cogito,* which, even in transcendental philosophy, is denoted by the first person. Transcendence is nothing other than the movement through which the subject constitutes itself as a subject in directing itself toward an object. The only problem is to describe the alliance established between subject and world, prior to any reflection, as the very life of the subject. "Prior to any reflection" means that this union is on par with perception, which is already for Husserl, as Fink has noted, an "originary mode" of intentionality.[3] It is the analysis of the perception that throws the best light on the specific reciprocity of the subject and object involved in the notion of intentionality. Through such an analysis, which returns to the investigation of the concrete subject, phenomenology brings together, in order to integrate them rather than subordinate itself to them, the empirical studies of anthropology and the lessons of epistemology. One knows that this is the direction taken in the works of Merleau-Ponty, and already suggested by Husserl, if we follow the remarkable exposition of Tran-Duc-Thao.[4]

At this point the aesthetic experience can be illuminating. Aesthetic perception is, in effect, the most distinctive and uncluttered type of perception. It wants to be only perception, refusing to be seduced either by imagination, which invites one to muse about the actual object, or by understanding, which tempts one to reduce the object to conceptual determinations in order to master it. Ordinary perception, always tempted to become intellectualized as soon as it reaches the level of representation, seeks a truth *on* the object, which eventually provides a basis for praxis. It also seeks this truth *around* the object, in relation uniting it to other objects. Aesthetic perception, in contrast, seeks truth *of* the object, such as it is immediately given *in* the sensuous. The spectator, being completely responsive, gives himself over without reservation to the manifestation of the object. The perceptual intention culminates in a kind of alienation comparable to that of the creator who sacrifices himself to the demands of the creation. One might venture to say that, in its purest moment, aesthetic experience fulfills the phenomenological reduction. We suspend all belief in the world, as well as all practical or intellectual, interest. More precisely, the only world still present to the subject is not the world *around* the object or *behind* appearance, but—and we shall return to this—the world *of* the aesthetic object, which is immanent in its appearance to the extent that this appearance is expressive. This world is not the object of any "thesis," because aesthetic perception brings about the neutralization of the unreal as well as the real. For example, when I am at the theater, the real—that is, actors, scenery, auditorium—is no longer truly real for me, and the unreal—that is, the story performed in front of me—is not truly unreal, since I can completely participate in the play and allow myself to be lost in it without being duped. But what is real and "holds me" is exactly the "phenomenon" the phenomenological reduction wishes to obtain, for the aesthetic object is immediately given in presence and reduced to the sensuous, here to the sonority of language in harmony with the gestures of the actors and the glamour of the setting, whereas attention is completely directed toward preserving its purity and unity, without ever evoking the duality of the perceived and the real. Thus the aesthetic object is perceived as real without referring to the real, to a cause for its appearing, that is, to painting as canvas, music as the sound of instruments, the body of a dancer as an organism. The aesthetic object is nothing more than the sensuous in all its glory, whose form, ordering it, manifests plenitude and necessity, and which carries within itself and immediately reveals the meaning that animates it.[5]

This identification of the phenomenon with the aesthetic object perhaps allows us to clarify the bond intentionality forges between the subject and object. Indeed, one must examine the status of the aesthetic object. We define it in terms of the sensuous; does that mean it is produced by the consciousness that apprehends it? Yes and no. The sensuous is the common act of the sensing and the sensed. This initially signifies that the aesthetic object is realized only in a perception respecting its integrity. The artwork does not yet exist as an aesthetic object for the Boeotian who accords it only an indifferent glance. The spectator is not only the witness who confirms the work; he is, in his fashion, the agent who completes it. The aesthetic object cannot appear without him. Surely this is true of any perceived object, but ordinary perception does not dwell upon the phenomenon as such: to the very extent that it is oriented toward comprehension, it examines appearance as a sign which reveals other appearances and not the thing-in-itself, but which, in any case, invites one to distinguish a being-real from a being-perceived and seek the truth concerning the real outside of what is immediately given. It is the very object that appears, and not its semblance, but one must penetrate beyond the appearance in order to conceive intellectually of the object and grasp it in the relation to the exterior world that constitutes it as an object. Aesthetic perception, in contrast, has appearance blossom so that appearing is identical with being. Owing to the spectator, the being of the aesthetic object *is* its appearing. In contrast to an ordinary object, which calls for producing an act as well as a concept, the artwork elicits (*sollicite*)—imperiously, if it is good—only perception. Does this mean there is no being of the phenomenon, and that the painting ceases to exist when the museum door is closed behind the last visitor? Not at all—its *esse* is not *percipi*, and this is true also of any ordinary object. One must say only that it ceases to exist as an aesthetic object and now exists merely as a thing or, if one prefers, as a work, that is, as a simply possible aesthetic object.

Nevertheless, if in a sense this object exists only through-us and for-us, there is for it an in-itself at the moment it appears as the common act of the sensing and sensed. This is manifested in several ways. First, the aesthetic object incessantly exercises a demand on the one who performs or observes it; through this demand, it reveals a desire-to-be that somehow warrants its being. The spectator knows that he must be equal to this object, which is achieved only through the rigor and mastery of his perception, and sometimes at the cost of a long apprenticeship. Secondly, perception, if it does justice to the object, discovers in the sensuous an interior necessity that in some way grants it a natural mode of being. Finally, the form ordering the sensuous proves to be a meaning, immanent in it, that animates it; this meaning is altered or blurred as soon as reflection predominates and claims to translate this meaning into another language, but it is obvious and relevant for the feeling that gathers it in the very act of perception. It amounts to the singular world of the aesthetic object, to which the reading of expression gives us immediate access. This world is not a circumscribed totality populated with classifiable objects, but rather the possibility of these objects, that is, the a priori thanks to which the *a posteriori* can appear. That is why the nonrepresentational arts nonetheless open up a world, and why in the representational arts the represented serves to illustrate the world of the work rather than constituting it: the represented does not contain within itself the power to expand into the dimensions of a world; it can accomplish this only insofar as it is expressive, and expression appears to be proper only to the sensuous. This is why expression must appeal to the feeling in order to be read.

Moreover, the examination of aesthetic signification takes us still farther. But let us first maintain that in expressing this world, the aesthetic object transcends itself toward its meaning and affirms itself as autonomous. It is thus both for-us and in-itself, both constituted and seen in accordance with Husserlian terms. This sums up the paradox of intentionality: the ambiguous and nevertheless irrefutable being of the phenomenon attests that the subject as intending and object as phenomenon are both distinct and correlative,[6] since the object exists both *by means of* and *in front of* the subject. But if in one sense the objectivity of the object is as irreducible as the subjectivity of the subject, what is the ground upon which rests the bond that unites them and which the notion of intentionality expresses? Is it not a kind of consubstantiality at the heart of perception? Is it not true that the idea of intentionality leads us to the idea of an originary communication between the subject and object, in a fashion somewhat similar to the doctrine of the transcendental elaborated in the *Critique of Pure Reason*, and according to which "it is we who introduce order and regularity in the phenomena that we call Nature"? —leads to the teleological doctrine stated in the *Critique of Judgment*, according to which subsumption presupposes "an accord of nature with our faculty of knowledge"?

Here again, the aesthetic object constitutes a privileged case in that it is doubly tied to subjectivity. First, to the subjectivity of the spectator, from whom it requires the perception necessary for its manifestation. Second, to the subjectivity of the creator, from whom it has required the activity necessary for its creation, and who expresses himself through it, even— and especially—if he has not expressly desired it! So that the world of the aesthetic object is named after its creator, as when we speak of the world of Bach, Van Gogh, or Giraudoux in order to designate what the work expresses. This indicates an even more profound bond between the object and subjectivity, for if the object is capable of expression and contains within itself a world of its own that is completely different from the objective world in which it is situated, then one must say that it manifests the aspect of a for-itself, and is thus a quasi-subject. The meaning that it expresses is the form of its body, that is, a soul that responds to our own soul and elicits it, "which attaches itself to our soul and forces it to love." No doubt one can easily say it of the aesthetic object because it is the result of a making and can thus have infused in itself something of the subjectivity creating it, like the trademark a worker stamps on his product. But perhaps one must say this equally of any object to the extent that it is capable of beauty and susceptible to intelligibility, that is, not radically the *other* of the idea—although it is evidently only a question of affinity and not kinship between the subject and object.

But it is on the complementary aspect of this affinity that aesthetic experience can be the most instructive. To understand the language of the aesthetic object, to read the expression that lends it its form, is to enter into a more profound intimacy than one could through the knowledge given by understanding, where the subject stands at a distance in relation to an inert and neutral object reduced to something that can only be thought or manipulated.[7] To know (*connaître*) is in this case truly to occasion a mutual birth (*co-naître*). This proximity of the subject and object lived through in aesthetic experience demands that the idea of the subject be reshaped, for it can no longer be entirely identified with the transcendental subject. We are already invited to this reshaping by ordinary perception: my commerce with the perceived is possible only insofar as, when encountering the real, I am already equipped with an acquired knowledge that the imagination reanimates in contact with the object. But in order for this experience to constitute itself, I need an absolute anticipation, that is, a power to be in keeping with the object. Such is the role of our body: the senses are not so much apparatuses intended to collect an image of the world as they are the means by which the subject is sensitive to the object, that is, in attunement with it as two musical instruments are in attunement with one another. What the body understands, that is, experiences and takes charge of, is in some sense the very intention that is within the thing, its "unique mode of existing," as Merleau-Ponty says. The subject as body is not an event or a part of the world, a thing among other things. Instead, it is pregnant with the world just as the world is pregnant with it: it is aware of the world through the act by which it is a body, and the world becomes aware of itself in the subject. This pact of vital intentionality is only broken when the dialectic of perception leads to the representation wherein the subject becomes conscious of his relation to the object, questions appearance, and distinguishes between the perceived and the real.

But this pact is renewed in aesthetic experience. Certainly, this experience requires a stage of reflection and maturation, because the truth of the aesthetic object appears to us as a requirement, and we must learn to perceive well in order to obey it, just as the musician must learn the technique of his instrument. But on the one hand, the *habitus* that we thus acquire becomes bodily, and, on the other, we momentarily detach ourselves from the object only in order to join it more intimately. Then do our feelings enable us to penetrate the expression of the object and thereby comprehend this meaning, which is beyond language. On what conditions, however? The subject is capable of feeling only if he is a truly concrete and human subject. First, this indicates that the subject is corporally present to the object. Second, that it is totally present, with its entire past immanent in the present of contemplation, offering to the object its total substance[8] as a place for resounding; and finally, so to speak, present as sensitive to the sensuous, that is, with a virtual knowledge of the affective significations the aesthetic object proposes. For if the affective quality giving form to the object as if it were its soul is not in some sense already known by the spectator, then the spectator will be incapable of recognizing it and will remain indifferent or blind to the object. Indeed, some works are never understood by a particular public.

We would like to conclude by insisting on the following point: the affective qualities that are disclosed by the aesthetic experience constitute specific a priori. On the one hand, and most traditionally, they are virtually known, and without this knowledge, which is made explicit in experience, experience would be impossible. Those who are able to feel the tragedy of Racine, the pathos of Beethoven, or the serenity of Bach can do so because, prior to any feeling, they have some idea of the tragic, pathetic, and serene. But this implicit knowledge is not in them like an essence infused in their understanding; it is, rather, like an a priori taste, an aptitude, and finally, a certain existential style of their personality. How is the person recognized, if not by what he is able to feel?[9] On the other hand, this a priori also has a cosmological signification. The affective quality not only belongs to the spectator as the foreknowledge that experience actualizes, but it also belongs to the aesthetic object as what provides it with meaning and form and constitutes it as capable of producing a world. A certain serenity, for example, is the a priori constituent of the works of Bach just as spatiality is an a priori constituent of the objects of external experience as such, and at the same time a mode of being of the subject as capable of spatialization.

Thus the a priori—and particularly the affective a priori of aesthetic experience—qualify both the subject and the object. They are thus involved in the notion of intentionality: more specifically, the relation between subject and object that this notion designates presupposes not only that the subject is open to the object or transcends itself toward the object, but also that something of the object is present in the subject prior to all experience, and that, in turn, something of the subject pertains to the structure of the object prior to any project of the subject. The a priori is what is shared by the subject and object, and is thus the instrument of a communication: that is, what implies for it the theory of intentionality. But in turn this conception of the a priori clarifies intentionality. By explicating the affinity of the subject and object, it cautions against both the naturalism that conceives of the subject as a product of the world, since the subject is capable of anticipating the world, and against the idealism that conceives of the world as a product of the subject, since the object carries its meaning in itself. It thus clarifies the difficult idea of constitution, which in Husserl accompanies the theory of intentionality, and it prohibits conceiving of this idea as the latest avatar of idealism. Aesthetic experience shows that to constitute the object is to devote oneself to it, to reanimate the signification implicit in it, to know it as the man knows the woman, in the intimacy of a common act in which the frontiers of individuality are experienced.

Intentionality thus signifies that man and the world belong to the same race; it involves a form of communication based on community. It therefore has an ontological sense, but without authorizing, for all that, an ontology, for it does not necessarily imply the idea of Being as a transcendent agency, as a sense of which the subject and object would be the phenomena. Rather, intentionality suggests that because the subject and object remain distinct within, and in order to bring about, their relationship, they cannot be subordinated to a superior principle. The totality that they form by virtue of their affinity does not engender them; dualism, be it dialectical or not, cannot be reabsorbed into monism. Man is in the world as in his homeland, but not as an anonymous object among others. In the same way that the aesthetic object is both in-itself and for-us, the world is for man and man for the world. It is because man is in some sense equal to the world that he is also in truth, and that truth is defined fundamentally as adequation.

Notes

1. As indicated by M. Hyppolite in a striking summary statement (*Logique et Existence*, p. 177).
2. Maurice Merleau-Ponty, *Phénoménologie de la perception*, p. viii.
3. Eugen Fink, *Problèmes actuels de la Phénoménologie*, p. 83.
4. It remains to be determined, and we cannot debate it here, whether this anthropological interpretation of intentionality excludes or, on the contrary, clears the way for the ontological interpretation defended by Fink and practiced by Heidegger.
5. Undoubtedly this exegesis of the reduction will be impugned as "psychologistic" by those who slant phenomenology toward ontology. But is it not always necessary to understand the reduction as proceeding from subjectivity, even if one specifies that "it is not in the least a possibility of human *Dasein*" because it consists in "breaking with the natural attitude" as a means of engaging in philosophy (Fink, *Kantstüdien*, 1933, p. 346)? And is this rupture so different from that which is accomplished by aesthetic experience?
6. Once again, this runs counter to ontological interpretation, which makes the subject and the object into dialectical moments of a mediating movement, or the instruments of "the truth of Being." Such an interpretation is given by Heidegger, who discloses the presence of Being (one could say almost the act of Being) at the heart of subjectivity, whether under the heading of temporality in the ipseity (as in his *Kantbuch*), or of an absolute freedom in the freedom of *Dasein* (as in *Vom Wesen des Grundes*), or of an appeal in the destiny that lives an authentic existence (as in *Sein und Zeit*).
7. The scientific attitude is here understood in terms of the technological attitude, and precisely that of nonartistic industrial technology, that violates nature in order to impose upon it intellectually conceived forms and functions rather than the inherent forms suggested by the material itself and relying on the spontaneity of gesture.

8. For a theory of the subject, one can possibly find room here for returning to the Bergsonian distinction between the surface and the deep self, and the Bergsonian notion of a memory that, prior to being a representation of the past, is first the immanence of the past in the present, and to that extent has an ontological density. This density, which for Bergson gives the act of freedom its sense, can also lend its sense to the act of contemplation, and aesthetic contemplation in particular.

9. The a priori thus defined can be related to what Heidegger called the foreknowledge (*précompréhension*) of Being (*l'être*), and on the basis of which, in his view, man is defined fundamentally as the being (*l'étant*) called by Being (*l'être*) to reveal it. But according to Heidegger, this knowledge depends upon the Being of the being (*l'être de l'étant*) rather than upon its nature; that is, it manifests the relation of *Dasein* to *Sein* rather than the kinship of man and world.

2. The A Priori and the Philosophy of Nature

The reflections I am proposing here form the guidelines of a book I am working on, which undertakes to make an inventory of the a priori. The book will again take up the themes sketched in *The Notion of the A Priori*, but proceed further along the same line, harmonizing those themes with the idea of Nature that impressed me while I was writing *Le Poétique*. Hence the title of this communication.

Why speak of the a priori? The notion of the a priori can be used for quite different purposes. Kant used it to give a foundation to the Copernican revolution, to establish the prerogative and the function of the transcendental subject. Logical positivism calls on it to specify the nature of certain expressions. My purpose is again different. I should like to have this notion express a certain accord between man and the world, an accord whose agreement, which has long served, quite legitimately, to define truth, is a secondary and derived form. For this accord must not be limited to the phenomena of knowledge. And perhaps there is good reason to denounce the imperialism of knowledge, which is so patent today in positivism, structuralism, and the philosophies of the concept or system. Husserl also, while reviving a philosophy of consciousness, gave a place of privilege to "representative acts" as "objectifying"; but Merleau-Ponty questions whether that position is maintained in the unedited manuscripts where "for example the sexual instinct is considered from the transcendental point of view."[1] It seems to me that if we are to speak of knowledge here, it must be in the biblical sense of the word: the accord between man and the world is a carnal one, which attests to their co-naturality, their common belonging to Nature. We know how subtly Merleau-Ponty has shown how the flesh of man is joined to the flesh of the world.

How can we express this pact? There is no doubt that it is tacitly experienced by all men, at least at times. I would even see in it the surest criterion of good health, for if it is more common to define health by a predominant normality, it should not be forgotten that normality requires for its exercise a certain trust at the heart of "perceptive faith," the feeling that the young Parca regains after having traversed the hell of narcissism, of being at home in the world, in agreement with the situation and with the spirit of the times. Unhappiness (or sickness) weighs upon those who cannot experience this trust, either because the world withdraws from their gaze and offers them only an inhuman face, or because they make themselves responsible for their distress by closing themselves off from the beauty of the world by glorying in their importance, allowing themselves to be fascinated by the folly within which nihilism finds its realization. But how can we express that feeling? The arts—particularly song, architecture, and music—find in it the source of their inspiration. The archaic religions do likewise when they celebrate the cult of the Earth Mother. But philosophies have also recognized and approved it under different names: the love of fate, Spinozist joy, Nietzschean jubilation, *élan vital* . . .

Much more prosaically, and without immediately involving an ethic (or the counterethic found in Nietzsche), a theory of the a priori can also express the alliance of man and the world. In fact, such a theory teaches us, already under the form that Kant gave it, that man is capable of certain judgments whose content experience has not taught him and whose validity is not subject to the verdict of experience, that from the first he possesses certain kinds of knowledge that can very well be called innate. Now it turns out that these kinds of knowledge are true; or more exactly, they constitute the powers that place man in contact with the world, that open up and articulate his experience, by which man is a transcendental subject. Does that mean that experience lends itself to the a priori only because the subject, sovereignly constituting, orders experience to this a priori? On the contrary, it is possible to consider that the given is of itself informed by the form—that it responds of itself to the expectation—of the subject. This mutual preordination of man to the world and of the world to man can express itself by making correspond to the subjective a priori, which is a virtual knowledge of the world in man, an objective a priori, which is a virtually known structure in the world. This implies, of course, that the a priori be not only formal but also material: that it be constitutive of the object without being introduced there by a constituting consciousness. But this requires also that the a prior within the object must have something corresponding to it in the subject. Where the a priori is only objective, as when Canguilhem speaks of a morphogenetic a priori to designate a meaning inscribed in matter as a system of instructions for the development of the organism, it does not merit the name of a priori. In fact, it is not only in things but always stands in relation to knowledge. If it is defined as an "innate pattern of behavior," it is not only that which structures the living organism but also that which anticipates and structures the *Umwelt* for the living organism.

If it is defined at a higher level of generality as that which specifies the living organism, the incorruptible form in which the whole is present in the parts (or as that which specifies the thing, the technical object, or my fellow man), then there corresponds to it in man a virtual knowledge of the ontological realm. In the language of Canguilhem, even though he speaks only of the concept in living organisms, it could be said that there is an a priori when for the concept in the object there is at once a corresponding concept of the concept in man, again on condition that this concept of the concept be conceived, not on the model of scientific knowledge that conceptualizes empirical data, but rather on the model of the instinct, as a foreknowledge that prepares man to encounter the object, harmonizing man with the world.

Carried out in this way, reflection on the a priori preserves dualism. It defines a pact formed between two contracting parties. It supposes, therefore, a man who, while facing the world, already exists separately by himself, man presented as correlative to the world, who claims the autonomy of the *cogito* and the liberty of the for-itself at the same time as he affirms the reality of the "external" world, so that what is to be considered is not so much his rupture with the world as his reconciliation with it. Furthermore, this reflection introduces dualism into the a priori itself, since it distinguishes there the known and the knower, an objective aspect by which the a priori constitutes the object and a subjective aspect by which it constitutes the subject. Here the reflection remains encamped on the frontiers of a philosophy of knowledge. Without doubt, dualism is so insistent only because it yields to the aspiration of man: every birth is the rupture of the umbilical cord, and the vocation of man is to affirm his autonomy and to establish his sovereignty. But at the height of his glory can he ever deny his origins and forget the Mother? From whatever height he surveys his empire, can he bring it about that he is not present to the world? Then the problem arises that has haunted many philosophies: Can reflection return to this side of dualism? Within the perspective I have chosen this means: Can one not reascend to this side of the idea of an accord? To the idea of an alliance between man and the world, can we not add the idea of consanguinity, and perhaps of filiation? In other words, can we not clarify and ground the accord by a genesis that would show how duality arises from prior unity? Such an investigation requires a twofold procedure. On the one hand, we must proceed from the two distinct moments, man and the world, to a prior moment that engenders them, which can be called Nature. On the other hand, we must proceed from the two states of the a priori, the subjective and the objective, to a prior state, a primitive state of the a priori in nature, which would also engender them. The accord of man and the world, sanctioned by the correspondence of the two a priori, would then appear as a result, produced by Nature and metaphorically desired, if it is true that unity desires duality in order to know itself, at the risk of being misunderstood as unity.

It seems to me that this endeavor is close to that of Merleau-Ponty. His unswerving aim is to think man's being-in-the-world, to the point of extracting a new ontology from it, and he refuses to construct it in terms of accord or adequation. This refusal is not expressly motivated by the requirement of monism, but is rather the result of an anxiety to stay away from idealism and realism at the same time, as well as from intellectualism and empiricism.[2] Merleau-Ponty sustains the transcendental subject in its rights, but he inscribes the transcendental in the body (the living, speaking, cultivated body). Within the body is produced the chiasm, the interchange of consciousness and the world, so that the world is known in "that continual questioning" that we are. Thus if there is no adequation, it is because no one has the initiative or control over it, because it is always already realized, because man and the world are the same race and of the same flesh. This flesh, "this common tissue from which we are made,"[3] is Nature. And if Merleau-Ponty always returns to the beginning, to the beginnings of philosophy and the beginnings of man, to that perceptive faith in which is consummated to the point of identity the accord of the sentient and the sensed, of the seer and the visible, is it not because with all his might he puts himself into the originating unity, so resolutely that now his problem is rather one of engendering duality, of conceiving the advent of man as distinct and of vindicating the Sartrean *pour-soi*? We shall not be confronted with the opposite difficulty of resisting the fascination of dualism in order to think monism. Merleau-Ponty does not ignore this difficulty: the "description of savage Being" is an impossible ontology.

We see the difficulties that confront us. In the first place, are we able to think Nature? We think world precisely because it is our correlate, our *Umwelt* (the difference between the *Welt* and animal *Umwelte* is that the former embraces and "comprehends" the latter: man shifts far enough to put himself in the place of animals, while the converse is not true). This implies not that we constitute the world, but that we are equipped to communicate with it, to live in it and to live it. The world is Nature lived by man, naturalized by man, as its environment is naturalized by the animal; not that man is, we repeat, the naturalizing universal, but that he is "measuring" because he bears within him certain measures of Being and because through him Being arrives at consciousness. The world is then always a world for man. But then how can one think of a Nature that would be a world without man, before man, and consequently a world before the world, from which would proceed the world and man, but which would have to be conceived first without reference to the world and to man? How can one think with no thought there to think? Strictly speaking, it is impossible, and that is why philosophy sometimes has recourse to mythical or artistic expressions.

Of course one can pursue history, but that is altogether different. The prehuman universe is still the correlate of a consciousness, that of the scholar who reconstructs it. Yet if that consciousness cannot be forgotten, if it is consciousness of the world and not of Nature, perhaps through the image of the world it can have at least a presentiment of the dynamism of Nature: the force of the inexhaustible ground, the power of engendering man and the world that is for man. Surely every genesis that science describes is recounted by the scientist, and the scientist cannot recount his own genesis, for it is always a scientist who narrates it. These geneses are empirical; they appeal to a knowledge already constituted; they are never radically the genesis of the genesis, that is, of the transcendental. But they can suggest the idea of it. Science, true in its own order, is then at the same time the index of an ontology. An impossible ontology, however, because only a speaking subject, already distinct, who plays the game of dualism, who presupposes a dualism at least already set into motion, can speak of monism. At least this subject can try to situate itself at the origin of speech, where the thing and the word, the object and the consciousness of the object, still adhere to each other.

This leads us to a second difficulty. How can one think, even in Nature, of a first state of the a priori anterior to the rupture of the knower and the known? What must be conceived then is the identity of being knowing. Parmenides, Spinoza . . . A Philosophy of Nature invites us to think a being that aspires to knowing, as a god who creates in order to be mirrored in the adoring gaze of his creature, as a painter who desires to see himself in his canvas, and perhaps be seen by it. That may be, but what is required of us here is more difficult: to identify knowing and being, exclusive of any reference to a knowing subject or demiurgic action, is to place preknowledge in prethings. We cannot resort to the services of dialectic here. True, we can think, metaphorically, that Nature engenders man as consciousness, but we can hardly think that a preconsciousness would be gestating in the very heart of still invisible being, in the night of the depths of being. Undoubtedly, if we implicitly presuppose dualism, we can place knowledge in the thing, in this sense at least that the concept is in the object, since we have just said that a logos is inscribed in the living organism. This means that the object lends itself to knowledge, and that knowledge seizes the object, but in saying this we do not go much further than the idea of adequation; and we do not assert that knowledge as such, the act of knowing, is a thing or is in the thing: we retain as understood the difference between knowing and the known. Can we then soften this difference to the point of thinking of an original identity of being and knowing, or, modifying the formula of Aristotle, a state common to the sensing and the sensed? For that it is necessary to conceive another form of knowing and the known that preserves between them a fundamental proximity and whose description avoids the distinction of object and subject. Such is indeed the aim of Merleau-Ponty, who constantly returns to the analysis of perception. If he is not trying to capture the first state of the a priori, he is at least exploring the place where it can be found.

What is that place, then? What is there to say of Nature, of that *Grund* of which the very idea forbids all discourse, of that Night that not even the natural light of a gaze lights up, and that no language can name in order to contrast it with Day? To have a presentiment of it, it may be necessary to put oneself in the moment when speech is silent or the gaze extinct, at the hour of death. We have to die to the world for the reign of raw being to come again, for Nature to be restored to itself; and that is why every authentic word is haunted by death and every work of art contains a core illegibility. There a muted murmuring is heard, the tireless murmur of "there is," the inarticulate voice of the desert. The work of art speaks only to be given over to that silence. The exegesis of Blanchot is recognizable here. But there are all kinds of silence. Why mention only the silence of death? Why place oneself after death rather than before birth? For my part, calling on Nature, I prefer to speak of life, and science can serve as a guide here. According to Claude Bernard, science unites two formulas: life is death, and life is creation. Since we can speak only in images, I would oppose the desolate images of inertness and repetition with images of the stirring of life, of rustling and variegated reality, enlivened by the power of the possible. The mineral order itself may be movement, merely slowed down to the point of seeming to be fixed: think of the Sainte-Victoire of Cezanne. What is inexhaustible is this movement without return, this tireless force, the swelling up of a silence that will culminate in a voice, the deepening of the night when dawn is gathering.

What does the a priori signify here? Does it retain any meaning in the absence of a transcendental subject? Perhaps, if Nature itself is transcendental; if the transcendental designates not a condition for the possibility of experience but the power of the possible, which prepares within the real the advent of experience, when the inertia of the in-itself in the real is animated by a movement that prefigures the for itself.[4] The a priori here is that beginning organization that must be supposed in embryo within the ground: "the flesh is not contingency, chaos, but a texture that returns to itself and conforms to itself," writes Merleau-Ponty.[5] Or again it is that point of light that heralds the human gaze: "at the juncture of the body and the opaque world there is a ray of generality and of light.'"[6] However, if we wish a tighter grasp of this notion of an a priori that still mingles being and knowing, we must isolate and present one or the other of the terms in order to speak of it, without having to try to abolish its difference immediately. We can start with thought, but with thought that is not yet thinking, since it is not the thought of anyone, but rather the object of thought, an idea that is not yet *idea-ideae*. The a priori will then be conceived as a logos immanent in Nature, a formal framework, a lattice of logical possibles, a *mathesis universalis* at work within the ground, miming and calling for the thought that will explicate it. Here we come back to some ideas of Ladrière: not only that mathematical thought is less invention than discovery, but also that this objective mathematics is naturalizing, for from it sensible being proceeds by a Plotinian procession, as if blind thought, thought that is already a thing, were present within reality to produce and regulate it. At the same time, there is a guarantee here for the idea of a formal a priori that already constitutes the object inasmuch as it allows the experience of it. One can also start with that unthought, unnameable, in-itself, which is another name for nature. The a priori will then be identified as a structure of the thing that is already thought, or from which proceeds the thought that will explain it in turn.. Thus one would guarantee the idea of a material a priori, and rejoin the vocabulary of an epistemology that shows that things, or at least living things, are structured because certain information moves about inside them, and that "life has always been doing without writing, long before writing, and without reference to writing what humanity has tried to do by drawing, engraving, writing, and printing: namely, transmitting messages."[7] But we have said often enough that we must not confuse transmission and comprehension, execution and intelligence. We cannot bypass the distinction between the concept, and the concept of the concept.

This means that we cannot grasp a primitive state of the a priori any more than we can describe Nature. Every path that leads toward a radical indistinctness of subjective and objective soon fades out. The identity of being and knowing can only be thought of as unknowable. But this very recognition of failure vindicates the notion of the a priori. The a priori as subjective sticks to our skin, and we cannot think without it. It compels us to think of the world with a thought that can only be ours, but that is no less truly ours if an a priori in the object corresponds to the a priori in us, if Nature, so to speak, has willed that man and the world be solidary. This duality of the a priori, which installs us in the truth, prevents us from thinking of the truth of the a priori, the primordial truth of its primordial state. That is why the inventory of the a priori compels us to renounce an ontology of Nature and to take our hold at a point where dualism is already established to locate the a priori in the discourse or behavior of a subject. As soon as the subject arises, the original unity is lost. All that reflection can do to preserve the idea of an inconceivable origin, whose very memory is forbidden us, is explore the signs of the strict proximity, of the native familiarity, between man and the world. The a priori then appears as the means for man to be present to the world, to enter into communication with it and to reveal it to itself. It is—and man is by means of it—that natural light that unites the gaze to the thing seen, so closely that the theories of perspective from the Greeks to the Renaissance never stopped asking whether like a visual ray it came from the eye or from the thing seen. Forever incomplete is the analysis of that being present to the world about which every man, as soon as he becomes conscious of himself, never ceases to question, sometimes to the point of despair. "No more than facts are the necessities of essence the answer which philosophy calls for. The answer is higher than facts, lower than essences, in the savage Being where they were undivided, and where, behind or beneath the cleavages of our acquired culture, they continue to exist."[8] Merleau-Ponty adds, however, that reflection cannot return to the immediate, where all consciousness would annul itself in "an effective fusion with the existent." "The moment my perception is to become pure perception, thing, Being, it is extinguished; the moment it lights up, already I am no longer the thing."[9] The immediate can be only on the horizon, and it is never simply immediate: "the originating breaks up, and philosophy must accompany this breakup."[10] In other words, Nature, to be conceived at all, must be thought of as dynamism. It carries within it, at the heart of its inconceivable unity, the principle of openness, the germ of the mediation by which it will yield to daylight and to language. It is already articulating itself, preparing to be spoken. It allows a distance to be hollowed out within itself that will be that of a gaze. The a priori will be that mediation with which the immediate is pregnant. It will separate the subject and the object, but in order to bring them into accord with each other, since it will bring them into accord on condition of separating them. We cannot think without taking up our distance from the world, and the division of the a priori expresses that distance; but that distancing is still a means of being present to the world, and it is measured only on the ground of an inconceivable coincidence. Reflection on the a priori cannot avoid being lured by the inaccessible horizon of the origin and led to the threshold of that philosophy of Nature which thought spans only on the uncertain and lofty wings of poetry.

This turning of a theory of the a priori toward a theory of Nature has some consequences for a philosophy of man about which I should like to make some observations. But first, what man do we speak of, man in general, or the individual? Reflection on the a priori can enlighten us here. For the very idea of man is an a priori (which an inventory must be able to place). On the one hand, we are always capable of recognizing man, thanks to a virtual knowledge, and it matters little that in fact, as for so many other a priori, we are unable to make that knowledge explicit. The a priori within us can have both the sureness and the opaqueness of instinct. On the other hand, in man as an object this a priori is constitutive: in all men are found the essential traits of which we have the virtual knowledge. This means that we can handle very well the concept of man—and who dispenses with it?—even if that concept has not been hallowed by a rational interpretation. And perhaps the consciousness that we have of our ego derives from the primary comprehension of the alterego. This other is given to us as an ego, and when we say we, this "we" does not efface the characteristics of the "I." It belongs to the concept of man to teach us, at least implicitly, that each man is an ego, a singular being in a singular relationship with the world. In other words, man exists as an individual, irreplaceable and inalienable, consequently as a person. In this sense the concept of man is not a general idea: we can speak of man, even in the third person, only as a being who expresses himself in the first person. Every man is an *apax*, a one-time being, and every man is the correlate of the world. No man is ever a human being. To think so would be to do man a deep wrong, something violence can do but not discourse. Only violence can write on a railway car: forty men, eight horses.

That the thought of Nature is a limit-thought is due to the fact that the law of man is irreducible, his ipseity unimpeachable. There is no thought whatsoever, even that of the origin, that does not find its beginning in him. There is thought of man, of anything, or of Nature, only if there is a man to form it. Every genesis is a genesis that man narrates, he is already there to narrate. In this sense he is unengenderable. The a priori within him attests to this, and it can be said that he is all a priori. In fact the philosophies today that noisily proclaim the death of man are all written in the first person. It is always a man who says, "It is thought," or "that says," and that which can die is just a content of thought, a certain idea of man, not at all the man who forms that idea. Yet this man is mortal and he had to be born at some time in order to go on to death. Perhaps the species will disappear some day, as each individual disappears. This true death, just as unforeseeable on the horizon of the future as the memory of birth is shrouded on the horizon of the past, what is its significance for the species and for the individual? It is that man can exercise the powers of the cogito by which he is raised up to be the correlate of the world only on condition of coming into the world and of being in the world. By doing so he comes under the jurisdiction of science, with its patient investigation of the positivities, as Foucault calls them, that sustain and dominate him at the same time. And so he is an object of an empirical genesis. But as soon as reflection understands that this genesis is the work of an irreducible subjectivity and cannot be duplicated in a transcendental genesis (just as the formal, as Wittgenstein showed, cannot formulize itself), it is to a philosophy of Nature that it dreams of confiding that impossible task of engendering the unengenderable.

The philosophy of Nature can undertake this task only if it is conscious of its limits and limits to a phenomenology of lived experience, which in turn is nourished by the positive sciences. What does it say of man? It cannot describe his birth or prophesy his death. It begins with him as well as with the world whose correlate he is. But at least it seeks to clarify his most primitive relation with that world, and to describe the most natural face of that world. Let us say at once that this return of thought to nature—a nature always already naturalized—does not encourage the reactionary nostalgia for a return to the earth or to primitive life. Everyone knows, for that matter, that the *Natur-Völker* are cultured peoples and that simplicity and degeneracy should not be confused. The return to nature, in nature camps or in solitary ways, is still a cultural phenomenon initiated by a leisure civilization. This nature, even if not manipulated, is perceived by man, and that is enough to denaturalize it; that is, to turn it into a world. But conversely, in whatever thought or practice does to humanize the world, there still breathes the great unknown. If something of the power of the ground is revealed to us, *per speculum et in enigmate*, it is across the technological environment as much as the natural, through the city as well as the country, through culture as much as nature. In man even language and culture are as natural as nature; and the a priori that assign him a nature vary in their coverage according to history. If we prefer certain images because we believe that art and artifice are arbitrary and artificial, let us not be duped by our choice. There is no more innocence in the infant than in the old man, or in the artist than in the artisan, and if we try to go back to the source, we do not come any closer by seeking it in the heart of the forest than by maneuvering a derrick on industrial terrain. *Logos* and *techne* still bear witness to the *physis* that, carrying man along, moves and inspires them.

It is necessary then to understand being in culture and being in language according to the model of, and as an expression of, being present to the world. We should really take hold of this being present to the world at its coming, but we can only describe it after the fact, for there is no way for us to come up on the emergence of man by surprise—outside of animality, perhaps, but that adventure takes place in the world of science. More radically, from what night does man emerge? From what silence?

And why images of the void rather than of plenitude, of inertia rather than of the void? Why call on Chaos rather than Harmony? We can choose our myths. We have nothing to guide us except this warning: careful, this option expresses us and involves us. To be truthful, there is no option. For everyone the choice has already been made. Since we cannot examine the beginnings of man, we can at least describe a primal promiscuity. The prereflective cogito is the flesh, my body at grips with the world, not at all sovereign but rather participating; not at all a thing among things, if the thing is already a concept and if its idea supposes an already constituted knowledge. That is why Merleau-Ponty speaks of a flesh of the world, of which my body is a part. For if there is not yet an autonomous subject, neither is there an object. There is rather a "field," and it can be said indifferently that the world is that field as in the *Phenomenology of Perception*, or that the subject is that field, as in *The Visible and the Invisible*.[11] This field, where sensible and sensient are still indistinct, is the milieu of a reciprocal genesis that modern painters have helped us to grasp. The viewer is not in an abstract place where his eye, all by itself, ceases to be an eye and becomes a zero point around which the spectacle is arranged; the painting invites the spectator to put himself into it. To accomplish this the painter identifies himself with his body, which is everywhere, which is in turn identified with the landscape, so that the mountain Sainte-Victoire itself comes into the world under the brush of Cézanne. And the mountain looks back at him who turns his gaze upon it. The viewer is visible, and the visible is the viewer. This exchange takes place everywhere. The tool that man invents serves him at first not so much to master the world as to communicate with it. It is at once of the body and of the world. It is still the hand, and the motion of the hand is needed to make use of it. It gives rise to a new familiarity with the real. Since the domestication of animals requires that affectionate and tender knowledge of which Lévi-Strauss speaks so well, this complicity based on symbiosis makes man the most splendid conquest of the horse. It is the same with the elaboration of a cosmology. It can, of course, establish a taxonomy that will spawn logical games and a whole system, but first it is the expression of a certain intimacy with the images of the world. Again consider language. It is not surprising that Merleau-Ponty gives the same destiny to speech and to the flesh: both are the common denominator of man and the world. If language can be understood as a system, it is because it is nature, like an organic system or even a system of probabilities, but language must also be understood in terms of speech, which reactivates it at every moment, and speech itself is not the product of a sovereign thought already constituted; it is words that speak, that bear within themselves a referential meaning; and perhaps they only assume that function because things come to clothe themselves in them, because they name themselves to the one who names them, because they call out to the one who calls to them. Man speaks because language speaks, and language speaks because things speak. Just as the flesh does, speaking joins man to the world. Undoubtedly it also separates him from the world, since the sign is at the same time empty and full, formal and material, but the very distance that it places between things and us, and also between things and themselves, is already in Nature as the principle of a world and as articulated by the a priori: "this operative language . . . called forth by the voices of silence continues an effort of articulation which is the Being of every being."[12]

What then is the function of man thus considered at his beginning? In nature he is the mirror in which Nature is reflected and takes the form of world. Possibly he himself learns to know himself in a mirror, which later may be replaced by a psychoanalyst. But first he is the means by which something of the invisible is converted into the the visible, the non-sense into sense; he actualizes a potential of seeing that is prepared within the invisible, just as his freedom actualizes a spontaneity that is prepared within the movement of inertia. He can do it only by being himself naturalized as the mirror; philosophers will say: finite; and he has always known it. The whole burden of the world weighs upon his shoulders, and he may seek refuge in madness or in death. For from the ground of his finiteness he knows that he is responsible for the world, even though no one gave him that responsibility. Paradoxically he is both solitary and responsible. For that reason the will best defines man. We used to say: Nature wills man; we should rather say, Nature desires itself in man. It does not will that man should will; he wills by nature. So it is with everything. But it is in his being as man that he persists, in his being as echo or mirror, by which he has the dignity of being the correlate of the world.

This attempt implies an ethic. A philosophy of man based on a theory of the a priori brings an ethic with it. It is this requirement that leads the structuralist philosophers to reject the philosophy of man. Let us pacify them a little. To say that man is in some way the servant of Nature is not to place him under a transcendent law. To be present to the world is his condition, not a duty or a vocation assigned to him by some transcendent moment. He comes from Nature, he is Nature, and the nature in him is nothing external to him. In other words, he is not created, he is produced; he is a part of nature, that part where nature redoubles itself in some way, remembers and reflects itself. The a priori that he carries within him assigns nature to him through which he participates in the dynamism of Nature. But among the a priori there are values constitutive of certain objects, which call to him (as I hope to show in the inventory of the a priori). He can elude that call, he can turn values around, but only in the name of other values. This presence of values binds him to the ethical dimension. Finally among those objects of value there is man: the most formal law always has a content, which is the man open to the law, and the most material law, that which is expressed in mores, has the same content: the other as comrade, my fellow and my neighbor; social life is a moral life.

But the man who bears within himself a virtual knowledge of man, who wills man in himself and in the other, does not cease for all that to invent man, and ethics as well. Ethics is always open. The fact that man acquiesces to the values that he discovers and through them acquiesces to Nature, does not drive him up against the hard choice between consent or refusal. For to be docile to Nature is to be rebellious at the same time, since it is to affirm oneself as distinct. Reciprocally, to will power, or rather to will in order to be powerful, is not to deny Nature as the original power. To be actively the mirror of the world, what man must do is take up his distance and play; the will itself is play rather than obedience. In this respect the will is still in the image of Nature, which is not only ambiguous because it is always interpreted, but which is unpredictable in the development of its powers. And perhaps we come back here to an intuition that Granier finds to be central in Nietzsche: "the intuition of an essential ambiguity of Being which would exalt the conquering ambitions of the will to power even while demanding absolute submission to the 'text.'"[13] In a philosophy of Nature ethics is both necessary and impossible; necessary because human normativeness is invoked by values, and more profoundly because these a priori have their source in Nature; impossible because man can follow Nature only in turning his back upon it, as he can reveal it only by giving it form and thus dissimulating it.

But this paradox of being present to the world must not fill us with guilt. We have lost our innocence innocently, and innocently we have become responsible for the world. And if we are in Nature as distinct from it, we are in accord with the world and capable of happiness as well as unhappiness. The a priori tells us that. We cannot seize it at its source, since it prevents us from thinking nature at the same time that it proposes that we do so. Yet perhaps it is not fruitless to think that there is a source, and this thought can give direction to philosophy just as it can help us to be men.

Notes

1. *Le visible et l'invisible*, p. 291, note (Maurice Merleau-Ponty, *The Visible and the Invisible*, trans. Alphonso Lingis. Evanston: Northwestern University Press, 1968; p. 238, note).

2. "We do not have a consciousness constitutive of the things, as idealism believes, nor a preordination of the things to the consciousness, as realism believes . . . we have with our body, our senses, our look, our power to understand speech and to speak, measures of being for being dimensions to which we can refer it, but not a relation of adequation or of immanence." (Merleau-Ponty, *Le visible et l'invisible*, 140) (Ibid., p. 103).

3. Translator's note: The reference is to *The Visible and the Invisible*, but is missing from the text.

4. The theme is sketched out by Sartre in "Metaphysical Implications" at the end of *Being and Nothingness*. Jean-Paul Sartre, *Being and Nothingness*, trans. Hazel E. Barnes (New York: Philosophical Library, 1956).

5. Merleau-Ponty, *Le visible et l'invisible*, p. 192 (trans., p. 146).

6. Ibid., (trans., p. 146).

7. G. Canguilhem, *Le concept et le vie*, "Revue philosophique de Louvain", 64, May 1966.

8. *Op. cit.*, p. 162 (trans., p. 121).

9. Ibid., p. 163. (trans., p. 122).

10. Ibid., p. 165. (trans., p. 124).

11. Ibid., p. 212. (trans., p. 160).

12. Ibid., p. 168. (trans., pp. 126–127).

13. J. Granier, *Le problème de la vérité dans la philosophie de Nietzsche*, p. 532.

3. The A Priori of Imaginatiom

In undertaking an inventory of the a priori, we ask the reader to agree that they are locatable and can be categorized according to the discernable functions of consciousness, such as the imagination. But we must at least say how we conceive the a priori.[1] We can summarily define the a priori as testifying to a fundamental affinity, and permitting the communication between subject and object. It is both in the object what makes it a given object, well before the operations of knowledge, and in the subject a virtual knowledge immediately actualized in the presence of the given. In other words, for man, being in the world is being in harmony with the world; and if there is a world only for man, it is somehow with the agreement of Nature, which allows itself to become world for man: a world of which man is the correlate because he is a product of Nature.

Thus the a priori is not merely, as is the case in critical philosophy, a subjective condition of the objectivity of the object. It is also a constituent quality of the object, whose objectivity is acknowledged rather than elaborated by a subject. Reflection on the a priori of imagination, then, calls for a reevaluation of the theory of imagination. It becomes necessary to assume that the imagination, too often considered the subjective part of man, is actually capable of objectivity if it involves a priori. Imagination normally appears in conjunction with perception, thereby revealing some aspect of the world and, through the world, an aspect of Nature. Such is the consequence of attributing a priori to imagination: if the a priori is a principle of truth because it assures communication between man and the world, imagination must be true in its own way. The a priori of imagination undoubtedly mingle those of sensibility, insofar as their faculties cooperate, and with those of affectivity, because feeling and imagining are interdependent. But we think that we can differentiate these various a priori. albeit non rigorously. The study of imagination can throw some light on that.

What then is this power of imagining? To produce or to register images? Is the image fashioned, or is it, at first, also perceived? Indeed, we call image the inconsistent and impalpable product of dream or reverie as well as the object to be perceived, whether it has been created for perception (the popular designs from Epinal), whether it is evoked to illustrate an idea (an example is an image), or whether it actualizes an essence ("he was the very image of confusion"). The same word names both the nonsensical and the meaningful (yet through psychoanalysis we have learned to view the nonsensical *as* meaningful), and, above all, the unreal and the real. How do we choose between the two? We will privilege the unreal if, like Sartre, we are concerned with demonstrating the freedom of consciousness, its power of denying any receptivity, of negating the real and inventing the unreal. We, however, adopt an inverse position.[2] It seems to us that on the one hand imagination is in its own way "realizing." Certainly the imaginary is not to be taken for the perceived as far as it is the product of an image-forming subjectivity (*subjectivité imageante*), as, for example, in the dream in which the dreamer meets only himself. But imagination also cooperates with perception as far as it grasps another dimension of the object: the possible, irradiating from the real. Thus, on the other hand, imagination is signifying. It can add meaning capriciously or playfully to a barren given; but primarily it can gather a nonintelligible meaning. This is the function of the image: when it is given in the world or when it acceeds to reality in a poetic work, it is a symbol, it shows what cannot be said in words (unless, very simply, as the comic strips, it comments on what is said!). Whenever it remains unrealized, the image at least evokes what cannot be shown, the other side of the perceived, or it summons an absence: it is still turned toward the real, or, if one prefers, it turns away from it only in order to return to it. It may sometimes turn away from the real so as to delight in the unreal; then it gets carried away and endeavors more to realize the unreal than to grasp something surreal, and in doing so it perhaps betrays its mission.

We think, then, that the function of the imagination is not so much to create images as to experience their meaning, or to produce these images as things—as works of art, for example—in order to express a meaning. The most authentic image is not an imaginary presence that we conjure up despite the real; it is rather the real presence of the thing, man-made or not, that is offered as a spectacle. But what kind of thing? After all, all things are not images. An image is a thing that adds meaning to meaning; it is the thing that is given for what it is *and* for something else, which, in brief, appears as a symbol and so "gives rise to thinking."[3] But primarily to imagining: the true dreamer is not someone who, in the abyss of night, produces transitory images in response to internal bodily agitations or convulsive movements of the limbs, he is rather the dreamer of things. This dreamer of things may also be, like Bachelard, a "dreamer of words." For as soon as we are in the world, we remain in language.

Ricoeur, following Bachelard, also emphasizes that the three dimensions of symbolism—the oneirical, cosmical, and poetical—all originate in language:[4] the heavens do not tell of the glory of God, nor does the cosmos become hierophantic except by the lips of the prophet or poet, and every sleeper is already a poet whose dreams are private myths; imagination always calls for the mediation of speech. If, however, the imagination is a storytelling spontaneity, the stories it softly murmurs or loudly shouts make explicit the images offered to it. In this sense, cosmicity is a dimension common to all species of the imaginary: the dream, as well as poetic inspiration, binds man to the world. What haunts subjectivity at its most secret point is the images invested in it by Nature during its prehistory. Moreover—but we cannot stress this here—language itself has Nature as its source; man speaks only because Nature speaks to him, and the verb has semantic power only because the world is pervaded by an expressive force: it is because the cosmos is the promise of hierophany that the poet bursts forth and language is instated.[5]

Whether it is poetic or not, imagining is letting oneself be elicited and guided by the image, an image all the more provocative since it exists more fully in the form of verbal or physical material. It is the image that arouses imagination, because perception is not equal to the task, and because conceptualization is useless whenever the meaning is so deeply embedded within the object that it would be lost if abstracted. Imagining is to perceive a surreal, that is, a "sur-signifying" reality (not at all, as in the case of surrealism, signs addressed to us by chance in order to be deciphered, but entangled significations). Thus imagining is already a certain mode of thinking: thinking flush with the image, and letting oneself become enchanted. It can also be that thought tries to take charge of and articulate whatever confused meanings are given in the image. One might say, then, that the image "gives rise to thinking."

How do these images speak to us? Through what may be called their *ontological quality*, which the imagination must grasp. We have spoken elsewhere of the *affective quality* that calls for feeling. Between the two, between the luster of gold and the innocent charm of a face, what is the difference? Very little, if any: affectivity and imagination work in close proximity. Affectivity opens a world that imagination can inhabit, and imagination, in turn, excites feeling. The difference, however, lies in the way in which this meaning that reveals itself and expands into a world is able to engage us. Through the affective quality we are literally touched. If we give a name to the world it displays, we use an adjective—sometimes used as a noun: the tragic, the graceful, the noble—that primarily designates a certain impression made on us; so, in experiencing this quality, Kant is entitled to say that we as subjects are in question: we are not judging our pleasure, but rather the object recalls us to ourselves, since its constitutive quality is one that affects us. On the contrary, when imagination prevails, it is the very substance of the object that is indicated by the ontological quality, and that quality is not easily expressed by an adjective; the image is the object itself, whose proper name is a noun: abyss, heaven, gold, death. That object is undoubtedly not just any object; it has a quality that calls for imagination; but this quality expresses less in its being for me than its being in-itself: purity, splendor, force are qualities that affect me mostly insofar as they give rise to thought or to dream.

For these images provoke thought all the better as they disconcert it by the polyvalence of their meaning. And this polyvalence inherent in the symbol in which a first meaning always refers to a second ambivalence becomes mixed. The water that can both wash and absolve, refresh and regenerate is as well baptismal and polluted; the earth excites the will as well as inviting repose; blood is a principle of life as well as of death. We might also say that these images tend to be articulated in couples of opposite terms, which in turn motivate logical thought to play on these oppositions by combining them; so the child stands opposed to the old man, day to night, whiteness to blackness, and so on. But it does not appear that the polyvalence of the image may always be logically explicated, nor that the meaning of each term resides in its being opposed to or being joined with forms within some structure. Each image has a meaning by itself; a meaning that is not merely differential, that does not define it only by what it is not. Nevertheless, this meaning is not univocal; it is rather inherent in it, so that playing with opposition may be developing the meaning rather than constituting it. Moreover, this play is not always clear. It hardly entails an internal dialectic that would submit equivocalness to a logical movement. What appears, rather than a logical system, is often a chaos, a war, as Empedocles says: the elements begin to struggle without any regulation. If there is any order between the images, it results from their ontological qualities; their meaning proceeds from those qualities that constitute them.

It is on these qualities that we now focus our attention: 1) because they are the a priori of imagination; 2) because they give us a way to classify images. What we are seeking is what is a priori in imagination. We are tempted to answer: It is the images themselves, or at least certain among them, the most immediately and eloquently meaningful, that seem to be situated at the point of encounter between what the world itself offers to us and what proceeds from us, so that the poetic, oneiric, and cosmic dimensions of these images commingle. We immediately think of Jung's archetypes, of those images entombed in the collective unconscious. But as much as images, these archetypes are vectors of a psychic energy bound to the structure of the psyche: the image of the mandala appears only when a certain personalization of the self is achieved, which the mandala may symbolize. The archetype is both a principle of psychic energy and a symbol of psychic structure: hence its therapeutic function, which is more important than its psychic one. Moreover, its inherent psychic energy is put into action by different objects in different cultures: the dragon of modern dreams is often the concierge. This great variability of the objects invested with psychic value suggests that they themselves are not essential, and thus not a priori. For what is a priori is the essential, namely, the meaning pervading the object and which is immeditely recognizable to us.[6] Undoubtedly certain objects are so thoroughly imbued with this meaning that the a priori in them appears to be indistinguishable from the *a posteriori*: such are those privileged objects that one is tempted to call a priori in themselves: heaven, gold, blood, the grand images of the poets, and the archetypes. But these objects manifest the a priori, they do not constitute it. What *is* a priori is in ourselves the ability to seize these objects as, concerning their meaning, exemplary and, in them, this meaning by which they immediately speak to us before we speak about them, as they invite us to do: this is what we refer to as the ontological quality.

There are two reasons why we may consider this quality as a priori. First, there is the relation it has with the object. Just as in the case of the affective quality, the ontological quality so fully pervades and animates the object that it constitutes it; the constitution here is not the operation of a transcendental subject, but rather, occurring in front of the subject, the effect of this quality. And yet however narrowly it is linked to the object so as to constitute it and be apprehended in it as its singular essence, this quality retains the availability and independence of a general essence. For it can be invested upon different object as purity is on the transparency of water, whiteness of snow, or freshness of a face. Similarly, profundity, belonging to the subterranean depths, where the roots writhe, where desires teem, where the dead, our "profound fathers," sleep, can also hollow out the starry night. Conversely, one and the same object can be inhabited by different qualities, and from this proceeds the ambivalence of symbols. Thus the quality manifests its anteriority in that it is able to select a variety of objects in order to constitute them; but that does not prevent us from discerning or recognizing it on the object in which it is embodied, for we possess in ourselves the preconceiving of it.

The second reason favoring the a-priority of this quality appears to be brought forth by Nature itself. If, in effect, the a priori constitutes both the subject as knowing and the object as knowable, and thus assures the communication between the two, is it not prior to them, does it not proceed from Nature? Undoubtedly this invisible, which brings forth the visible and the seer, cannot be directly grasped; we cannot know Nature except in the form of the world. Yet Nature is in turn attested to metaphysically as a ground (*fond*) by the images that seem to proceed from this ground, and whose quality can thus claim a-priority (*l'a priorité*). Whereas affective quality belongs to things insofar as they have affinity with us and touch us, the ontological quality belongs to things inasmuch as they have affinity with a ground, as an elementary character, opaque or shining, distinguishes them from flat, superfluous, or artificial objects. If Bergson may find the true difference of the superficial and the profound in two modes of the self, it is perhaps through analogy with the one that opposes two families of objects, the object appearing to exist only on the surface and the object arising from the ground of being and sometimes from the ground of time, like the sea that is sung by the poet, "body of calm and visible reserve." As for us, we are always sensitive to this density or intensity, to this tranquil or terrible power, for we sometimes return to the innocence of the origin, and dwell in the elementary, very close to Nature itself. Such is the movement of imagination through which man consents to alienate himself, to benumb the consciousness that makes him separated—not in order to yield to the private unconscious and those forces haunting it, but rather to allow him to be approached and inspired by a secret plenitude. Man, then, is not the guardian of Being, but rather a part of Nature; and the images are themselves that indicisive and confused speech which, in the world, speaks to him of Nature.

We must now try to classify these images. How should we do so? We might undertake this according to the dispositions of the subject that they put into play, so that the principle of this classification would also be genetic. It is thus that Gilbert Durand has sought "in the psychological realm for the great axes of a satisfactory classification."[7] The "dominant reflexes, as defined by Betcherev's school, are these axes: here the "postural" and "nutritive" dominants command the two great regimes of what Bachelard called the "axiomatic metaphors."[8] That is, the "diurnal regime" of the emerging and the "nocturnal regime" of the swallowing, which are later on dramatized by the "sexual dominant." We have not to discuss this ontogenesis; let us only observe that to this reflexological tripartition Durand joins (by reference to Dumezil) a bipartition whose designation at least proceeds from the world: day and night; and he adds that everywhere, throughout the time of the genesis, we find the essential image of a space. These references to the world allow us to propose, without polemical opposition to that first classification of images, a second classification that, instead of subordinating them to the subject and thereby stressing their subjective aspect, takes account of their objectivity or, more precisely, of their roots in a primordial reality.

Is it not precisely this reality that substantiates the evocation of the elements? Bachelard, in evoking them, has demonstrated that the imagination is itself "material." The dreamer of words is is not compelled to the seduction of forms, to idealism (in the sense that Biran calls sight idealistic); he dreams of substances. Certain aspects of modern art also suggest it: informal painting invites the glance to question the matter. This is why the table of elements offers an excellent guiding thread to the phenomenologist of the imaginary. It is certain that the elements have been and remain for sensible consciousness "pregnant" materials. It is less certain, however, that they permit a classification of all of the objects—the great images of the poets—that elicit imagination: where would be situate the child, the blood, the tree, the night? We thus propose another way of classifying images, in which the guiding principle will be the ontological quality, that is, the a priori of imagination. But then we encounter another difficulty (one that we have stressed elsewhere), residing no longer in the diversity of objects but in the polyvalence and ambiguity of qualities. The a priori here is not a concept that can be "deduced" or examined objectively; evident as they may be to imagination or feeling in the object they inhabit, these constitutive qualities cannot be definitively discerned or categorized; even if they take some distance in regard to this object, they are not totally conceptualizable.[9] We can therefore only propose several themes that serve to guide our inquiry.

Since among the faces of the world, ontological qualities are approximative figures of the ground, we should perhaps choose the *elementary* as the first of these qualities. The elementary, in being fundamental and first, has the power both to found and to originate. That it has the ability to enter into combinations with other elementary givens does not necessarily imply that it is simple; this idea is introduced by evolutionism, which ascribes to nature a course similar to that of deductive reasoning, that is, a movement from the simple to the complex, from primitive concepts to theorems. The elementary is rather the natural as opposed to the cultural, the raw as opposed to the cooked. The artificial can, however, have or claim something of the elementary: we see this in certain forms of contemporary art, where the introduction of machine or chance represents the supreme artifice through which the artificial is renounced. For instance, *ta Eonta* of Xenakis sets, magnificently, the elementary to music. But among the natural, the elementary is specified by its inscrutable countenance, its mute obstination its immovable solidity of a foundation; it is like the rock or the root, like the earth that is always Earth Mother.

There are, however, other elements that are lighter, more mobile and ravenous, as or water, elementary because they are invincible, inexhaustible, always similar to themselves; if they are not solid foundations they do animate (fire can be an agent or artist), and they can also destroy, raze, and accelerate the process of entropy. The elementary is uncontrollable. Its images are ordered only by reflected thought. But perhaps, confronting each other or taken separately, they form the two great antithetical figures, chaos and cosmos, which are reflected in all cosmogenies.

The second ontological quality is *power*. To have power is the very fact of what is, the principal manifestation of the fundament. Power evokes the dynamics of Nature—what Spinoza, in the *Short Treatise on God and Man and His Well-Being*, calls Providence—the perpetual actualization of the possible and the upheaval of the unforeseeable. It is measured according to the contrasting figures of strength and weakness appearing as well in Nature (the mighty oak and the slender reed) as in culture (the master and the slave) and in what stands between the two (the masculine and feminine).

These figures are no doubt ambiguous, but their ambiguity is, as we have stressed, not due to an image-forming subjectivity. The figures of power are often associated with the schemata of spatiality, which in themselves constitute the objectivity of the object in general, but which also evoke Nature as soon as they lose their formal character. Thus the elementary, experienced under the sign of spatiality, already becomes boundless, the immeasurable: the two extremes of smallness and greatness, for these two infinites both call for imagination, and their solidarity may be experienced without man reflecting upon himself and proposing himself as a middle term. Power, on the other hand, is revealed by the polyvalent schema of the high and the low: the sky, in being above, is often thought of as infinite and majestic, and what is below is looked upon as weak and base, even if it compensates for this by trickery, as does the serpent. Power is also manifested through the image of permanence, which represents timelessness in time. The immense see is "always started anew," as the gestures of the mythical ancestors are constantly repeated. In a theology that is already rational the Almighty will be named as the Eternal, whom Heaven and Earth evoke, because they too are seemingly without beginning or end; although they do not have the divine privilege of inaugurating the beginning, that is, of creating time as well as the world, nor of fixing ends, that is, of presiding over eschatology. And when, according to Nietzsche, God is Dead, the Will to Power affirms the Eternal Return . . . So we can see that the images of power are bound to the modes of temporality, whether they be to temper the bite of them. When power is experienced as vitality, it is through two antithetical images that illustrate temporality: childhood and old age. Power then belongs to what begins, and the child becomes invested with it; Kerenyi observes that the mythical child, who has sometimes an aspect close to that of infantile divinity, sometimes that of "a juvenile hero," appears 'invincible.'"[10]

Depth (*la profondeur*) is akin to power. Depth is the characteristic of the ground when *Grund* is revealed as *Abgrund*. It too is related to the incommensurable: deep is what is remote in space and time, enhanced by the seduction of the inaccessible and hidden. Hence the fascination proper to those mysterious places such as the source, the heart of the forest, the abyss, and the summit, which is an inverted chasm; Simondon has shown that "they structure the magical universe after the most primitive and preganant organization; the articulation of the world through those privileged places and moments."[11] At these nodal points, the secret is joined with power. And also the virtue of the originary; depth carries the seal of the past, appearing to emanate from what the night recovers, the lost Paradise of childhood, the primordial abyss whose mythical memory haunts the genesis, or the tales of the ancestors, which survive in tradition. But the originary is also the authentic. And precisely what specifies depth is perhaps an allusion to a virtue stemming as much from man as from things. We have tried to demonstrate elsewhere how the depth of an object is doubly linked with that of the subject.[12] The latter conditions the grasp, and illustrates the notion of the former. The person is profound who is gathered and wholly engaged in his act, and whom this mobilization renders all the more receptive, open, and generous. The person then harmonizes with the depth of things, and intentionality becomes participation. What is "interiority" in him—richness, density, power of the "profound self" to receive—accords with the signs of interiority offered by the face of an object—the difficult, the obscure, the uncanny—that which signifies equivocally by dint of plenitude. An artwork can be profound, but so can a natural thing:[13] the abyss or the jungle of which we have spoken, those figures of the world that magic tries to master only when feeling and imagination have first ascertained their depth. In this way, the thing resembles man (which suggests animistic behavior to him): it is itself interiorized, and burdened with a necessity that is no longer entirely physical, but also existential; and, while enfolding upon itself as upon the secret of the origin, it seems to radiate some message from its hidden center.

Finally, alongside these themes, and often in counterpoint to them, is the theme of *purity*. The pair pure-impure dramatizes in an astonishing fashion certain objects that are in this regard exemplary, as, for instance, gold or blood. We should add to this pair another: the pair light-dark, whose resonance is both cosmic (day-night) and already ethical (blackness-whiteness, innocence-impurity). If these images evoke Nature, it is insofar as they concern that secret consciousness we have of them, and to the extent that they are truly elementary. But we cannot assign to Nature one of the terms of these pairs to the exclusion of the other. We know that the sacred can be both pure and impure, fascinating and terrifying. Nature, too, the hearth of all possibilities, can at times be Heaven and Hell, Good and Bad. Within these pairs, images can change roles: Audiberti evokes the blackness hidden in milk, Wagner lends the virtues of day to night, when love's death is consummated. Just as water can be clear or polluted, blood can be the image of life or death, and depth an image of plenitude or chaos.

This means that if structural thought wishes to apply itself to imaginary figures it must make itself sufficiently comprehensive to conceive "how pure gold has been changed into base lead." We would say that structural thought should become dialectical if there were to be an *Aufhebung* for these figures. But there is none. The a priori of imagination give rise to thinking without providing us with a means of methodical or exhaustive thought. They do not even allow themselves to be catalogued, except in a continuously provisory way. And we are conscious of having barely begun this task.

Notes

1. We have examined this in an earlier book, *La Notion d'a priori* (Paris: Presses Universitaires de France, 1963); English translation: *The Notion of the A Priori*, trans. Edward S. Casey (Evanston Ill.:, Northwestern University Press, 1966).
2. See Mikel Dufrenne, *Phénoménologie de l'expérience esthétique* (Paris: Presses Universitaires de France, 1953), vol. 2, p. 122; English translation: *The Phenomenology of Aesthetic Experience*, trans. Edward S. Casey et al. (Evanston, Ill.: Northwestern University Press, 1973), p. 357.
3. See Paul Ricoeur, *Finitude et culpabilité*, II (Paris: Aubier, 1960), p. 123.
4. Paul Ricoeur, "Le conflit de hermeneutiques," in *Cahiers internationaux du symbolisme*, 1: 158.
5. This is that primordial power to signify that words naturally evoke in response to Nature: a power that structuralism cannot adequately account for, since it presupposes it in demonstrating how meaning is organized, and instead relies on the artifice of grammar to support that demonstration.
6. If actualization of this meaning energizes, frees, or illuminates us, it is a secondary effect, but essential to a therapy and a pedagogy. Bachelard too places imagination in the service of a pedagogy. This secondary effect is also crucial to a theory of the a priori in that it shows how deeply the a priori cuts through to the nature of the subject; it invites one to think about the a priori in its function as a natural power, and finally, it invites us to psychologize the transcendental.
7. Gilbert Durand, *Les Structures anthropologiques de l'imaginaire* (Paris: Presses Universitaires de France, 1960), p. 38.

8. Gaston Bachelard, *L'Air et les Songes: Essai sur l'imagination du mouvement* (Paris: J. Corti, 1943), p. 18.

9. This adds another difficulty, which we can only briefly mention here—namely, that the a priori, as Scheler has seen, is affected by historicity. It constitutes in the subject something that makes it sensible to certain aspects of the real. Consequently, individuals, and especially cultures, do not all have the same equipment or transcendental natures. In this sense the field of the a priori is never totally available and totally locatable.

10. Karl Kerenyi, *Introduction á l'essence de la mythologie* (Paris: Payot, 1981), p. 109.

11. G. Simondon, *Du mode d'existence de l'objet technique* (Paris: Aubier, 1958), p. 164.

12. Dufrenne, *Phénoménologie*, vol. 2, chap. 4; English translation: pt. 4, chap. 18.

13. Monroe Beardsley, seeking a criterion of aesthetic judgment, chooses vividness or "magnitude" (a trait that is itself the function of three others: coherence, intensity, and complexity) (see *Aesthetics*, New York: Macmillan, 1966, p. 527). It appears to us that depth is a different criterion, and always an important one as well.

4. *The Imaginary*

In May 1968 the walls proclaimed, "All power to the imagination!" From the depths of the stagnation prevailing today, we can feel to what extent power has failed to heed this cry. Nevertheless, many philosophers nowadays reflect upon the imaginary. Is it to rehabilitate it? There is initially a greater inclination to denounce and dismiss the imaginary, opposing to it what is presently called the epistemological break and which could also be called the "rational break." Why? Because it is often identified with the unreal: the imaginary invalid is someone who imagines himself to be sick although he is not; in order to cure him of this illusion, he must be invited to submit to the reality principle: such is the procedure of all rational thought. But the unreal is an ambiguous notion, as is the real itself: what is real, this table on which I am writing or an atomic structure? The word *unreal* can in fact be used in several ways as a means of designating: 1) an object whose existence is impossible in consequence of a transcendental requirement (a body without surface) or a logical one (a square circle); 2) an object whose existence has never been observed and is presumed improbable in consequence of empirical laws (a unicorn); 3) an object whose existence was once observed but is no longer observable: in this last sense, the unreal is the absent object (that can be evoked by an image) or the lost object (the mother's breast). We know how popular these themes of absence and loss are today; they are heirs to the theme of negativity for a thought that rejects Hegelian dialectic. The doctrines can emphasize either one of these aspects of the unreal, but in any case they willingly link to it the fate of the imaginary, as the unreal is set in opposition to the real, and because the real is supposed to be already determined or at least determinable, for it can exclude the unreal only on this condition. And it can itself be determined (conceptualized, mastered) only as far as it is given. Thanks be to perception: it gives the real, and in the final analysis, the judgment of reality always refers to it. But perhaps we should cautiously control this perception so as to separate the wheat from the chaff in it, the perceived from the imaginary. For in defining the latter as unreal, it is also tempting to see it as illusory insofar as it claims to be the real. This represents a trap that consciousness must be aware of, and that a certain type of rationalism constantly denounces: the imaginary is its foremost enemy. This particular lot of the imaginary is, however, not inescapable: we know that Sartre rejected the idea that consciousness allows itself to be trapped—save by itself—and may posit the unreal as the real. For others, if the unreal may create an illusion, so much the better: the illusion is stimulating and may reveal to man something about himself. But can it also reveal something about the world? In this case, the relations between the real and the unreal must be more precisely articulated; or rather, if these relations can only be oppositions, unamenable to any dialectic, we must rethink the hasty identification of the unreal with the imaginary. This is precisely our goal in this essay.

In order to proceed with our task, we will have to untangle an extremely confusing semantic field, and primarily the paradigm image/imaginary/imagination, for it is difficult to examine one of these terms without having recourse to the other two. Let us note first that these three terms separately considered raise three different problems. The imagination, a critical or anthropological problem:[1] what is this power (this "faculty") to imagine, how does it proceed, and what does it signify for consciousness? The image, a gnoseological problem: according to the aspects it assumes, what is its function in knowledge? The imaginary, an ontological problem: can it be defined in relation to the real, and what is the implication of such a confrontation for both of the terms involved? We will try principally to examine the third problem. But such an inquiry compels us to set aside the other two by initially dissociating the three terms of the paradigm. In this regard, ordinary language is helpful in that it suggests the following:

1) The image is not necessarily an (imaginary) product of the imagination. Rather than referring to an imagination that in one way or another would break with perception, the image refers to perception itself, and in several ways. The word *image* can, in the first place, designate the very thing perceived: image from Epinal, portrait, postcard, inset in a book, and so on—these are the "image-things" that Sartre calls *analogons*, and that according to him "serve as material for the image." We tell the child to look at this pretty picture, and in this case the image is of the perceived or the to-be-perceived. But we cannot go so far as to say that every perceived object is an image. The term is in fact reserved for those things presented as representations of other things; the image is an image *of* in the same way as the portrait is *of* the model. Similarly, the schema—graph, tree, or map—belonging to the family of images, is also a schema *of*. These things are posited in order to be perceived, but for the sake of something else: whereas usually the perceived object only calls for being perceived, schemata summon another kind of intention. They invite us to understand, and the image itself can do similarly: the perceived becomes the image of a concept whenever the concept seems to dwell in it and be illustrated through it. Confonting a screaming and stomping man I say,

"He is the image of anger," because it seems as though an essence has become embedded in the particular behavior of this man; the perceived is understood as revealing this essence; the concept of anger may be looked for in this telling image that functions as a type of schema, and not as a symbol would. The anger in the image is the truth of anger. But the image-thing may also prompt us to imagine as well as to conceive: before the photo of someone who is absent, if "it's him"—himself and not an essence I would be looking for—I end up dreaming. So the image, far from being produced by the imagination, provokes the play of imagination because it gives itself first to perception.

We can evoke yet another use of the word image that binds it even more closely to perception while remaining completely separate from imagination. Here we must think of the Latin *species* and the Greek *eidolon:* those detachable and movable skin-like layers, conceived by a materialist doctrine of perception, that deliver the message of the thing to the eye, for the thing can never be present "in person." In this case the image is conceived in order to explain the workings of perception: what is perceived is not the thing itself, which always maintains its distance, but its representative, which alone is able to bridge the gap between subject and object, and thereby to arrive at the threshold of a separated consciousness. But let us conceive of a consciousness open to "the thing itself," that is, one that does not require representation to accede to presence: the image can then designate perception itself, a relation to the perceived that has no need of mediation. Thus we may indifferently say that from a particular viewpoint, we have a beautiful image or a beautiful view of a valley, bringing together in one and the same work both what is seen and the vision. Then the thing is presented without requiring representation. And the image is the best approach to the object without recourse to a concept. From this "viewpoint," this valley offers itself to the eye in its sensuous truth, in its singular essence, which is not the essence of *the* valley as the gesticulating man was of *the* anger. Such is the privilege of the image, capable of sometimes bringing forth the thing and sometimes its concept—without ever engaging the imagination.

2) But then what about imagination? It must now in turn be dissociated from the imaginary. When stating that the image is not necessarily the product of imagination, since it can elicit perception and sometimes measure its truth, we have presupposed that the imagination is, on the contrary, "master of error and falsity." Now, it must not be forgotten that philosophical reflection ascribes to imagination extremely diverse functions that are by no means limited to the production of a more or less delirious or deceiving imaginary. Even the most banal thinking is used to distinguish a creative and a reproductive imagination. The idea of a

creative imagination is undoubtedly extremely confused. Whenever certain works of man are so new and unforeseeable as to earn the prestigious name of creation, we attribute their production to a mysterious power entitled imagination, which may forgo further reflection upon the procedures of the labor and its social conditions. This is not to say that the imagination, even as a creative factor, creates the imaginary. What is imagined is not imaginary but real, and even in a heightened sense. The artwork has for a long time aimed at a type of perfection giving it a fuller and more imperious existence than that of the ordinary object.

But philosophy, whenever it conceives of the imagination as a faculty, has often assigned more precise functions to it, owing to which it cooperates with knowledge without always being subordinate to understanding. In Kant the imagination, viewed as the power to schematize, assures an indispensable mediation between sensibility and understanding. We know that Heidegger, in interpreting Kant, forces this theme of a mediating imagination to the point of situating imagination at the origin of the two faculties it conjoins. In this case the image must be emptied of any empirical or transcendental determination, and in the end must also be equated with temporal extasis, itself opening a place as a clearing in the full opacity of being in which appearing can emerge. Does the imagination lose its meaning here? In any case, it is here that we are furthest from the traditional meaning of imagination as re-presentation (*Vergenenwärtigung*) of an absent object or as presentation of an unreal (*Phantasie*). This pure power of opening does not produce anything; it is the condition of appearing before anything appears, the power to give form (*einbilden*) before anything takes on form. It is nevertheless important to keep sight of this meaning, for an unavoidable problem is created by it. In pushing the theory of the faculties to the extreme point where the question is of the emergence of consciousness—the advent of intentionality—we must ask: To whom does this power of appearing belong? Who is doing the imagining—man, whose imagination would institute the constitution of the world, Nature, which would constitute man? This idea of a transcendental imagination can be translated into another language, which already inscribes the *naturans* in the *naturatum*, that is, in what is equated to a transcendental field. But we are dealing with the imaginary, and the imaginary is not located in the domain of the archi-transcendental; it is the characteristic feature of the image—of certain images at least; it therefore implies that the image has taken form, and that it is not merely what gives form. So it invites us to go from the formal to the material.

Let us return then to the schematizing imagination. The empirical schema is analogous to the Sartrean *analogon*, with the exception that it is not a visible thing offered to perception but rather an invisible, thought to be at work in the functioning of perception: an agent of perception that itself is not perceived. If we find it difficult to posit an image of the schema in terms of Kantian critical philosophy, we can still interpret it in two ways that are more convincing and are not opposed to each other. On the one hand, the schema is a corporeal disposition allowing one to grasp and recognize the perceived object, for perception implies a familiarity between body and world. This familiarity is obviously acquired, at the price of an endless apprenticeship, but perhaps it presupposes a certain primordial complicity between the sensing and the sensed. In its own way, the distinction between the empirical and the transcendental as the condition of the possibility of the empirical expresses this priority. Following Heidegger, it could be said that the transcendental schema is the *Augenblick* that hollows out an empty space: it is what renders the body sensible to the sensuous in general, to the form of something in general (the problem, which we will only mention in this regard, being how temporalization can spatialize). The empirical schema is what puts the body in harmony with the form of the sensible entities that will eventually inhabit this space. On the other hand, schematism can be interpreted as the use of language. For the problem of subsumption examined by Kant is also the problem of nomination: to recognize a dog is to name it.

These two interpretations of the schema complete each other, for the schema as an involvement of the body only allows for the immediate apprehension of the object; in order to fulfill its mandate, the schema must bridge the gap between intuition and concept and permit the recognition of the object: this is precisely what denomination allows. The two interpretations are also interconnected, if we are willing to consider that language exists as a system only for and in speech; that it has the force of law only through the consent of the speaker who becomes one with it; and that it is from one and the same movement that this subject makes use of both his body and speech in order to open himself to the world. This is the reason why we would not say that the schema is the word, but rather the body's aptitude to respond to things by uttering the word. This aptitude is acquired, since one obviously has to learn his language. But perhaps it is learned, thanks to a certain primary disposition specifying man as *Homo loquens* which is in him as an a priori; perhaps also thanks to a certain complicity of the thing that would make language originate in nature and would thereby be an a priori of the a priori. In any case, we can see how imagination collaborates with perception: it does not produce the imaginary. In truth, imagination does not produce anything, for the schema is not an image that exists for itself; it has being only in its functioning. And perhaps imagination is nothing but the mechanisms assuring the body's capture of the world, and which, permitting recognition, lead, if not to a complete comprehension of the world, at least to a tacit understanding of it on condition that a certain invisible does not interfere and disturb the visible, a point that we shall address later.

The schema, however, can also be a fabricated one. In this case it is no longer a power assumed to be operating in the subject, but an object produced by dint of intelligence in order to promote the understanding of another object, as it is with all the maps, schemata, and tables amenable to a graphic semiology. We rediscover here the image-thing that by no means elicits the imagination, but rather a learned perception entirely regulated according to understanding: what we have to perceive is relations between elements, structures, mechanisms that yield a clear and distinct signification, delivered by an unambiguous signifier. If we insist upon mentioning the imagination in this case, it can only be of the creative type, as responsible for these images. But we have already stated that while examining this type of imagination, reflection scarcely progresses, and in any case does not explore the imaginary, to which we must now return.

In effect, we have only deferred our problem in loosening the knot linking the three terms of our paradigm: thus far we have isolated the imaginary; and now we must examine it for its own sake. For we actually have to deal with it: an imaginary that is not employed by understanding, eludes all grasp, and cannot be reduced to and fixed in images; besides, this imaginary can upset well-ordered plastic forms or beautiful stylistic figures, so that it can only be imputed to the imagination if imagination is understood as fantasy. Look around us: everywhere in the world people rave, either in a spectacular or discreet fashion; not only are there dreamers, poets, schizos, and utopians, but also the champions of rationality, academicians, defenders of order. The latter, however, cannot be placed in the same category as the former: if we can detect the imaginary in the refusal and repression of the imaginary—in the priest who burns the witch, in the conservative who denounces the leftist, in the philosopher who dooms presence to nonsense—we cannot say that it is the same type of imaginary: this imaginary blocks rather than opens, it is entangled and aggressive, like the imaginary of a miser. But whether it be right-wing or left-wing, how should we approach this imaginary? In stating that imagination does not forcibly produce the imaginary and that the image is not necessarily imaginary, we do not deny that the imaginary may qualify certain images and be imputed to imagination. So we could start once again with a discussion of the imagination (to which, in any case, we will have to return). But perhaps it is more valuable to begin from a certain attitude toward the imaginary, namely, a negative attitude inspired by submission to the reality principle. We could then immediately politicize our inquiry by stating that this negation is everywhere the practice of powers: there is nothing more dangerous to social or moral order than the unfettered imaginary. But our examination will first try to understand the discourse of rationality, that is, a discourse apparently reserved and initially hostile to the imaginary.

To begin with, Alain denounces in the imaginary the echo of corporeal uproar: irritations, convulsions, "such is the reality of the imagination." Besides concerning the image as a type of representation, the imagination is itself imaginary: "newly formed images flee into disorder; the strongest mind would be incapable of finding any link between them, and this pursuit is both inept and tedious."[2] The imaginary must rather be checked by a discipline of the body. Such is the function of art, which is at first gymnastics and training in civility, and which gives to perceive or think rather than to imagine. "There exists no work of art, in any genre, whose goal is to produce free revery within us." Certainly Bachelard would not willingly subscribe to this axiom, but let us not forget that he was the one who launched the idea of the epistemological break onto the philosophical market, and that, if he initially has recourse to psychoanalysis, it is in order to denounce in "the formation of the scientific mind" all those little insanities belonging to a cumbersome and stubborn verbal imagery from which this mind had to deliver itself; for it is at the cost of a long ascesis that man "comes to be a rationalist." Bachelard, however, did not go so far as to renounce poetry, or the revery it induced in him. Is he a divided man, who tries to find elsewhere some type of compensation for the demands of science, a man who tries to win on all counts? Nothing could be less certain, and it could be shown that he exalted the virtues of imagination within the very practice of science, and that the imaginary at work in the conquest of rationality is not totally different from that operating in poetry.[3] In Alain too, the last word on the imagination is not to assign it to the body. The imagination may be master of error, but it is not insignificant to be mistaken: error means that the subject keeps at a distance with respect to the object; it manifests itself as a for-itself, as Sartre says, it appears capable of conceiving the invisible, the gods. If the possibility of imagining attests to freedom, as Sartre emphasizes, the meaning of the imaginary attests to mind, and to that virtue of hope without which the mind would founder, but through which man asserts himself against the inhuman. Consequently, the poverty of the imaginary does not discount imagination. On the contrary, imagination must always be present to perception in order for it to be genuine, that is, not merely the passive recording of the given, but an act of mind. If perception is initially false, that signifies the servitude of thought as subject to the empire of the body, but it signifies also the freedom of judgment. The false is also the invisible that will never appear, that only art can form, and its introduction into the mainstream of the world is testimony to mind, that is, a mind revealed and experienced through the detours of error.

Thus man expresses himself in what he imagines, and sometimes, at least, he expresses what is most noble in him. But what we would like to show is that he initially expresses himself in his relation to the world according to what he perceives of it, what he expects, desires, and wants for it, as in utopian thinking. Consequently, the imaginary can also express the world, and the unreal can be offered or suggested to man by the real, so that in the end Nature imagines through man. Here we leave the path forged by Alain. In addition, the notion of the mind Alain refers to is rather outdated today, as well as the notion of the soul to which Bachelard refers. Contemporary vocabulary has changed, and not without consequence; it is as though a new light has been shed, outlining a new object whose contours are nevertheless not totally different. For one could find correspondences between what Bachelard calls soul and what psychoanalysis calls psyche, between what Alain calls hope and psychoanalysis desire, or what one calls order and the other interdiction. But our purpose is not to establish such a dangerous confrontation. What we would like to retain in Bachelard and Alain is the movement by which they come to justify and assume the idea of the imaginary. This movement is anarchistic at its core, for it contests the authority of what is recognized, that is, what is established and instituted; witness Alain's book *The Citizen Against the Powers*. Against all that determines and legislates, against what represses the development of dreams and utopias in the name of civic reason, or simply Reason. Should we then oppose the imaginary to the real? Not exactly, because it is rather against the reality principle that the imaginary poses a claim—if by reality principle we mean the positivist bias of determining what reality is and then relying upon this determination, of accepting necessity and condemning utopia as well as pleasure. A certain type of wisdom can readily posit this principle as primary, but reality is never primary: it is never something immediately given— instead, it is won over, as truth is won over error, whereas a primary truth is always a primary error, as Bachelard said. The path of this conquest is blazoned with lost objects, illusory ones of misconceptions (*méconnaissances*). The question is to discover whether these sacrifices are always legitimate, and if they do not simultaneously require what they sacrifice— namely, the energy of desire. To call for the imaginary, if it is not to renounce renunciations, is at least to refuse to concede that these renunciations are radical; it is also, while following the paths of wisdom via the reality principle, to return at certain moments to the origin, to this primary state in which we must question whether truth is only error. Let us turn now toward this initial state. Here what is given is neither the imaginary nor the real, but a mixture, a knot that will never entirely be undone. In other words, the imaginary is no more definitively imaginary—that is, separated from the real—than the real is immediately given. Everything is mixed at this moment.

And yet there have been attempts at breaking the Gordian knot: Sartre's effort cannot be ignored. With Sartre, Husserl's theory of intentionality, preserving reflection from "the illusion of immanence," is hardened to the point that it becomes a type of voluntarism through its alliance with a philosophy of freedom.[4] In the paradigm that we were examining, it is the verb that is significant and that could serve as the real title of Sartre's work: imagining is an act, the thetic act of an image-forming consciousness. And this verb is transitive: there is no imaginary save through imagining, as a product and not a given. This act must be attributed to a power of consciousness that may be called a function, to avoid the word "faculty." The imagination, says Sartre, is an "essential function of consciousness." On the other hand, because consciousness is consciousness (of) itself, as *Being and Nothingness* demonstrates, this act can neither be unaware of itself, nor allow itself to be taken for another. It is impossible to confuse imagining with perceiving, as they respond to two radically different intentions. We can readily see one of the consequences of this fundamental Sartrean theme: the imaginary is never illusory. But what is the nature of this act? It intends and posits an object that is specifically not offered to perception: an absent or nonexistent object. This point is essential: whenever Sartre writes image, we must read "object as image"; and since this object can only be given in an image, the intention cannot be fulfilled as fully as a perceptual intention. The flesh of the object is not the same in the image as it is in perception; it suffers from an inherent poverty that forbids the image ever to create a world; the imaginary is sustained only by artificial means. It is therefore an unreality that issues from an act of consciousness, since there is no way that it can be given; this act that Sartre calls unrealization is twofold: the image-forming consciousness both strays from the perceived and "posits its object as a nothingness."

Through this power to create the unreal, the imagination attests more than any other function to the freedom of consciousness, and this is precisely why it is so important to Sartre. But then Sartre must tackle two difficulties. The first is that this freedom to posit the unreal implies that the positional act of the image-forming consciousness is well aware (of) itself—in other words, the imaginary cannot create an illusion. As long as the image is voluntarily produced by a "willful spontaneity," there is no problem. But what about when the image is "involuntary," when the imaginary assumes intense forms, as in dreams or hallucinations? Sartre's analyses are in this case of an admirable subtlety in order to justify the idea that, in the hallucinated, the "intuition of spontaneity is not always abandoned." If this intuition is abandoned whenever the personality disintegrates and the "object and subject mutually disappear" in a twilight stage, then an impersonal spontaneity appears. The world of hallucinations is a world of "unreal lateral apparitions, the correlatives of an impersonal consciousness." There is still an awareness of the unreal, albeit nonthetic in nature, because it lacks a personal unity capable of producing the unreal. But what about the dream? I then believe all that is happening, although no object is actually present in it as in perception. But Sartre also says, "I do not believe in images as I believe in realities." I believe because I cannot not believe, because "consciousness cannot emerge from the image-forming attitude in which it has enclosed itself": it has lost the notion of reality, which it will rediscover only upon awakening; and this is why the image is "surrounded by an atmosphere of world," an intense world, albeit unreal, that fascinates consciousness. For dreams always imply a consciousness of forming images, but a consciousness in itself nonthetic and whose spontaneity is bewitched: it is compelled to imagine. Sartre even says that "the consciousness which is dreaming has resolved once and for all to produce only the imaginary"; but it gets caught somehow in its own trap and becomes entangled in itself. Such is the odyssey of a consciousness that dedicates itself, and in spite of itself, only to the constitution of an unreal world, and for which, as long as it dreams, the category of the real does not exist.

Whether this world may be deciphered from the outside like a symptom, and so can be seen as the representative of a drive in which desire is realized, does not concern Sartre, since he refuses any recourse to the unconscious. Besides, it is remarkable that his description of dreams does not evoke an *analogon*, probably because this effective *analogon* could be attributed to the unconscious. Sartre does not study the dreamwork but its lived experience, the adventure of a consciousness that remains intentional even when held captive. We will say more about this fascination; but what mattered to Sartre was to rest assured that even in the dream, and now more than ever, fiction cannot be taken for reality: the image is truly imaginary.

The second difficulty resides in the fact that consciousness can be induced to become image-forming, a point that forces us to examine the idea of the *analogon*. In truth, consciousness determines itself, but it can also be prompted to do so: it does so in the presence of an *analogon*, that is, of an analogical representative of an absent object. The unreal is in effect intended only through a real that the image-forming consciousness brings to life so as to make out of it the representative of an intended object. So Peter is intended through the photograph. In this case, "an exterior object functions as an image": it becomes an image-thing, a "substance" on which the image-forming consciousness apprehends the unreal object. Sartre describes an entire family of these *analogons*, from portraits to hypnogogic images (including the artwork: we know the famous, though highly contestable, hypothesis in which the *Seventh Symphony* is an unreality that consciousness attempts to seize through its various performances). But what about the situation in which the imagination does not have such a given substance at hand—when, for example, I conjure up the image of the Pantheon while sitting in my office? In this case there is a "psychic material which functions as an analogon": it is again a material for the image-forming consciousness. Sartre describes this given at length, though only conjecturally, as an affectivo-motor joined to a body of knowledge ("besides it is only in the abstract that we can distinguish movements, knowledge and effectivity"). In this moment the image is "mental." But in a certain sense it always is; for example, whenever an image-forming consciousness animates a photograph to create an image from it: Peter as image is no longer Peter in the photograph; he is given to me, as imaginary, only *mentally*, for he cannot be *given* otherwise. He is precisely the "imaginary object" correlative with this "consciousness of image which is strictly and inevitably directed" toward him. It makes no sense to say that the image exists as a kind of picture, analogous to the *analogon*, in consciousness, a fact that Sartre continually emphasizes. What is real is, on the one hand, the act or movement of a *consciousness*, its intention toward the object, that is its imagining; and on the other hand, the physical or psychical *analogon* that provokes this act and offers a type of substance to it. To image is to bring an analogon to life. But the imaginary object remains an unreal, although its (impoverished) existence is maintained through this substance.

We can now see Sartre's difficulty. How can we consider equally as *analogon* a thing, on the one hand, and a knowledge, an effect, and movements, on the other? At least we must understand that imagination organizes the entire subject, his body, and his "intellectual and affective experience." On the other hand, how do we conceive of this relation of matter to form that Sartre sees existing between *analogon* and image? What do phrases such as bringing the *analogon* to life, apprehending the imaginary through it, *on* it, mean? What Sartre is saying here is that the intention of the image-forming consciousness is specific and that it cannot be confused with the perceiving consciousness, or the consciousness that masters a type of knowledge, or one that experiences feeling, or one that registers a corporeal movement. Thus, in speaking of the material *analogon*, Sartre will say that the portrait cannot become an image, that is, it cannot encourage my intending it as imaginary, unless it ceases to function as an object and to be "perceived as a thing" for itself: in brief, imagining prohibits perceving. But even if the analysis is correct in positing the specificity of these diverse intentions, are they lived as specific in the life of consciousness?[5] It seems to me that lived experience lends itself rather poorly to these divisive distinctions. And moreover, perhaps the world eludes them, perhaps the real is not as foreign to the imaginary. In fact, it seems that even the imaginary forces Sartre's hand. Does not he say that the "imaginary represents at each moment the implicit meaning of the real," that this "apprehension of the real as a world implies a hidden transcendence toward the imaginary"? But taking this idea to its logical conclusion, we should not relate the meaning to a meaning-giving consciousness that "transcends the real," but rather to the world itself. Then, instead of thinking of the upsurge of the imaginary "against the background of the world," we should think of the world as ground, and as grounding for consciousness, so that the in-itself would not be radically separated from the for-itself, nor would consciousness be the complete sovereign of its acts. But the Sartrean analysis operates under the sign of dualism that is theorized in *Being and Nothingness*.

Here again, however, Sartre's hand is seemingly forced by his examination of the intense states of imagination. When dealing with hallucination he observes, as we have said, that "perception is obscured and blurred: the object and subject disappear together." This "together" is laden with meaning. Sartre is probably aware of the interdependence of subject and object in the "twilight stages," where the personality disintegrates, as psychologists would say. But can we not also uncover this solidarity in the auroral stages, in the simultaneous advent of subject and object, when the newly formed consciousness is captive not because it has been seized by itself, but because it has already been seized in and by the world? And is it not this state that consciousness can always experience?

If we forgo defining the imaginary in relation to a specific and spontaneous act of consciousness, and if we commit ourselves to discovering how it can issue from the real itself, we still cannot deny that it issues from the subject. Such is its essential duplicity: the image is the appearing of the object that is introduced through it, and it is also what a delirious consciousness produces, projects, and substitutes for the object.[6] We must again insist upon assigning the imaginary to the private imagination of a subject, but this time according to another perspective. It might be amusing to place Freud in Sartre's wake: both testify to the subjectivity of the imaginary, but certainly in radically different contexts. For Sartre, the subject is a consciousness that nothing can compromise. For Freud, the subject is divided, decentered, and dispossesed by an unconscious revealed by the imaginary; and little remains of what we can call a subject in modern versions of Freudianism that sing the song of an anonymous desire. But what is of interest here, at least in a negative way, is the fact that the Freudian imaginary does not issue from the world. This is why we can emphasize *Fantasia*, the producer of the fantastic. The fantastic summons the fantasy that must obviously be looked for in the whereabouts of the subject. We know from his letters to Fliess that Freud abandoned trying to find in fantasy the trace of an event that would have traumatized the child (e.g. primal scene, scene of seduction); and in fact, he goes so far as to accuse Dora of lying. Moreover, fantasy is linked to the subject by its contents as much as for its production: it is a scenario that, representing the fulfillment of desire, stages the subject himself. On the other hand, fantasies, though unconscious, are highly organized and constitute a type of system, a fantasmatics that bears heavily on the entire life of the subject. Here is a kind of imaginary *princeps* whose underlying presence must be unraveled not only in reverie but also in dreams and other productions of the unconscious. In fact, "an explication of the stability, efficacy and relatively coherent nature of the subject's fantasy life is precisely the goal to which Freud's efforts, and the whole of psychoanalytical thought is directed."[7] If this fantasy is imaginary, and if, moreover, it sustains and nourishes the imaginary, we have to say that the imaginary is subjective. Insofar as the fantasy is structured and structuring, there is in it an impersonal element that is "irreducible to the contingencies of the individual's lived experience."[8] This fantasy, which Freud calls primal, is like an affective a-priori schema, which he may have conceived as constituting a phylogenetically transmitted heritage for the individual. We must, however, situate this fantasy within the realm of the subject, not only because it directs his affective life, but also because it represents for him the enigma of his upsurge. Laplanche and Pontalis have aptly stated that the primal fantasy is a fantasy of the origin—it represents the moment of emergence. In this sense this originary is extremely different from the originary choice, by which the Sartrean for-itself posits itself without ever initially being posited.

But in the same instance Freud encourages thought to go back toward the originary: toward that presence where the subject is held captive, and which he experiences when emerging through what Freud calls the oceanic feeling. Should we even look for a more deep-seated originary, conceive of the imaginary of the fantasy as vestigial, an echo of prehistoric lived experience, and thereby summon myth to aid of thought? It might be preferable to rely on ontogenesis. What matters, in any case, is to situate the imaginary at the wakening of subjectivity, that is, at the first movements of the drives, and also at the beginnings of perception, as they are inseparable from them. Freud never forgot this point, and he allows us to think that the fantasmatic is not entirely cut off from the world, that the imaginary issues not only from a fantasizing imagination, but also from the real itself.

We have spoken of the duplicity of the imaginary. But must we, along with Blanchot, evoke "two versions of the imaginary"? Blanchot says that the image is perhaps the "attendant" (*suivante*) of the object or its double, and thereby manifests truth of this object. Thus when the tool, no longer obscured by its use, begins to appear; and it is the same for language, when poetry replaces prose. "The category of art is linked to this possibility for objects to appear, that is, to abandon themselves to a pure and simple resemblance behind which there is nothing but being."[9] What Blanchot discerns here, what gives another meaning to the veracity of representation, is the "corpse-like resemblance": the corpse resembles nothing, the image that it is is linked to the primordial strangeness of absence; representation is no longer the doubling of presence, but the sign of absence, of the "absolute neutrality of death." Here nonsense is opposed to sense, and not subject to object. But Blanchot also maintains (and this is his second version of the imaginary) that the image "speaks to us about ourselves." "Thus it speaks to us, apropos of every thing, about less than the thing, but about us, and apropos of us, about less than us about this nothing that remains when there is nothing."[10] Without becoming engaged in this ontology of nothingness, we can in effect say that even if the image issues from us, it also issues from elsewhere: consciousness fascinated by the image does not produce freely. It is not a spectator at this "spectacle," as is the case when appearing arises, but neither is it a stage manager, for it has not the power to dispose of things as in fictional creation; instead, it feels itself to be staged, as in Freud's analysis of the fantasy. And if, in Blanchot's terms, nothing is what there is, the unconscious is this nothing of consciousness—this murmuring and inaccessible elsewhere from which consciousness issues. But does this elsewhere escape being, and is it not still linked to the experience of appearing? Is what issues from the subject not still issuing from the world? The imaginary always returns to this unassignable region of an original mixture, where the subject and object are still not distinguishable. It is not an outside, an empty space, but a within, a presence.

Let us venture into this region. Philosophical reflection is nevertheless forced to use concepts that already presuppose the distinction between subject and object, but it may at least use them without emphasizing this distinction. We will employ three such concepts, which presently enjoy the greatest popularity: desire, language, and world. They will help in loosening the knot of presence, but they will also restitute it if we can show how the three terms articulate with each other *and* with the imaginary to the point of their eventual fusion. But before undertaking this examination, let us make two comments about these terms.

In the first place, we are going to speak of world, and not of being: the world that the being-in-the-world comes to know when it is born into it, that is, what opens itself to him and what himself is open to once he begins to see. This world is the totality of beings (*étants*) that is initially experienced in a confused way by perception, before it is systematized as a universe by rational thought. Perception is an oceanic feeling of a presence to which I adhere without distancing myself, being ordered to it much more than ordering it to myself. Here there is no anthropocentrism whatsoever (geocentrism will be the first conquest of science, the first questioning of perceptual faith): the center of this circumference is not myself, it is everywhere and nowhere . . . The world is not present to me, I am present within the world, within presence itself. But for all that, presence is not being (*l'être*), but rather it belongs to the being (*l'étant*) that is, and that is present. There is not being, but *a* being, which is the real subject of the *there is*. I am part of that being; in other words, I am in it, and this *in it* summons neither an empty space nor a preceding light. It designates a place only for the beings (*étants*) that perception gathers and confronts, or rather which themselves confront each other in perception. Are we committing ourselves to an heretical position by effacing the famous Heideggerian "difference"? Let us agree that we remain captive to a metaphysics of presence, and thus are confronted with a double question. First, why is there something rather than nothing? This nothing is still a thing, and be it a *nihil*, it is thought of only in its opposition to an aliquid, without any reciprocity, so that the opposition is ontological, not logical: absence is only experienced on a background of presence, as Bergson has expressed in a different manner. Our second question stems from this: How is it that someone utters this nothing? How is it that a certain being-in-the-world distances itself from the world? By means of language, undoubtedly, but it is language used by a subject. Returning to Sartre's examination of the for-itself implies examining the advent of the subject, and perhaps thinking of the world as Nature in which the subject is born. In any case, we are speaking about world rather than being because the imaginary can only be described and situated in relation to a being in the world, in the field of presence. Being in the world can be concerned with Being (*L'Etre*), but it is not belonging to Being. In fact, the concern that it has—its primal fantasy—is perhaps a concern for Nature, for the originary where it is both founded and lost.

It may perhaps be surprising, on the other hand, that we have not provided room in our discussion for the other as alter ego. Whether it is capitalized or not, we know what place this term holds in current philosophical literature. It is quite true that the experience of the other is specific—it dominates a regional ontology, as Husserl showed—and decisive—it controls the relation of ontology with ethics; but what we want to emphasize here is that this experience of the other as our other half, even if he is invested with the father's strength or the foreigner's strangeness, is inscribed in the experience of the world and is subordinated to it. If one is emphasizing alterity, it is not necessary to hypostatize it in the figure of an All Other, as monotheism is prone to do; it is enough to situate it in the world, in this ground from which beings, both things and men, emerge. These beings themselves participate in this otherness: one thing is the other of another thing, as the individual is of another individual, but they are also others in the absolute sense for the being in the world that meets and confronts them. Materialism, so willingly evoked by certain philosophers, could be seen as the thought of the world as other, a thought that would inscribe the famous Oedipal situation in the world without unduly privileging it, and search for the source of desire in a more general relation to the world. The other is the world—before being an alter ego in the form of an other like me, or the Other in the form of the analyst or the god.

Imagining is perhaps simultaneously *being to himself*, that is, to its desire; *being in the world*, that is, grasping the image in the perceived; and *being in language*, that is, grasping the image in signs that arouse or fix it. In bringing these three threads together we would see our initial three problematics intertwine, which deal with the anthropological, the gnoseological, and the ontological approaches to the imaginary. But let us first observe, in order to justify our choice of these three terms, that they are interdependent among themselves, apart from the relations linking them with the imaginary.

DESIRE AND WORLD

Psychological theory places desire under the aegis of *Penia* rather than *Poros*, and defines it by means of the notions of secretiveness and nonrealization. Returning to Freud for a moment, we see that first is the libido, the energy of drives, the force exerting a thrust. Desire is born out of the encounter of the libido and the prohibition forbidding it to be satisfied as the need may be: its object is always unexpressed or lost; it aims at this object only through fantasy, at least insofar as this is a fantasy for an object. Its realization is achieved only through the hallucinatory reproductions of the indestructible infantile signs of a previous satisfaction. Desire has no future, only a past, by means of which it flees a reality that is hostile to it. Besides, there are two explanations for this unfortunate lot, and contemporary thought hesitates between them. Either desire encounters the law—the father, the language—but in this case we must not forget that the father can be appeased and the law bent, as long as they remain in the world and are not totally interiorized. Or the conflict can also be within desire, when it itself refused to be realized, finding in itself the movement that drives it further, as in Don Juan: perhaps this is a death wish—a death by exhaustion, which apears as the only possible accomplishment. In every case desire becomes unconscious and its destiny is cast in the margins of the world, at a distance that is by no means that of representation but of absence—cast into the silent darkness of wandering, near the edges of a secretly desired death: sole future of a subject whom this secret and blind force traverses and carries away without ever constituting him, and threatening to destroy him if he is constituted elsewhere and otherwise. There is no more a subject than there is an object of desire.

But must desire be cut off from the world? No, because in the first place desire is born in a certain experience of the world, even if this world is reduced to the mother's breast. The oceanic feeling that is experienced at the awakening of a still immersed consciousness for whom plenitude becomes totality, soon extends those limits. Whether the mother's breast disappears or is prohibited, it is always on the ground of presence that absence is experienced *and* by this presence that it is signified. (This is true for the Freudian child as well as for the Sartrean man.) To be sure, the world does not arouse desire, for only the subject, or a presubject, an individual living entity, can be desiring (and this is easily forgotten if desire is too quickly cut from need, or the sexual drive from that of self-preservation). But the world orients the subject's desire by offering him his first objects, just as it confronts him with his first obstacles, absences, and prohibitions. This is precisely why both the natural and human environment have such an impact on the development of the psyche. Second, the world itself is the object of desire. For if desire remains unsatiated, it is not necessarily owing to masochism, because it pursues its own death—the total discharge of tension: is *jouissance* not an appeal to intensity, even if it terminates in the relaxation afforded by orgasm (*la petite mort*)? And how are we to affirm that Thanatos prevails in every fantasy? This desire beyond grasp can be interpreted also as a desire for another life in another world. What is negative in it is not a nostalgia for nothingness, but a refusal of this world. If it wants the impossible, it is because it wants everything, all of the possible.[11] It is precisely the world that it wants, but as another: another world for another life. If it indefinitely defers its realization, it is not to allow it to be fascinated by the difference or by the absence in which difference is formed, it is by excess and not by lack. This other world is not the other of the world, it is the same world, but lived otherwise; in the light of high noon, without this "morbid half of the shadow" that is its counterpart. Midday sometimes shines. Sometimes "presence is splendid," as Rilke says, and not to make the death enthusiasts uncomfortable—desire can sometimes be realized, without ever being fully satiated.[12]

DESIRE AND LANGUAGE

That desire wants to be realized means that it does not want to be spoken. Its relation to language can even be antagonistic: it has been said that language, like the father, embodies the law. In truth, this is said too quickly, for if discourse is repressive, as our civilization can testify, we cannot hold language responsible for this repression, but rather the power using it for its own end. The rules governing language constitute it as a useful instrument, they do not manifest a frustrating or castrating authority. Moreover, desire, at least whenever it is conscious, can also employ this instrument to express itself. But the deepest desire, which gives patent desires their meaning, is always dissimulated. If, however, it reveals itself, it does so unconsciously by disrupting behavior and disturbing the relation with the real—for example, when speech becomes a cry or poetic utterance. Does this violence inflicted upon language imply that the relation of desire to language is unavoidable? Yes, but it is the same relation as with the world, and with every reality: language is captured in a kind of "global refusal," and desiring speech becomes another speech.

LANGUAGE AND WORLD

Precisely what relation is to be found between language and world? Contemporary thought emphasizes their opposition—language is· the other of the world, just as it was a moment ago the other of desire. It is a closed, faultless system that is self-sufficient and instituted from the outside. We find here several themes intermingling so as to assure language both its autonomy and transcendence. In the first place, the methodological bias of linguistics that views language as a system. Then, a certain type of semantics, which defines the sign by the internal relation of the signifier to the signified, and therefore only considers signification through the exclusion of the referent, that is, of the designation. Hence a certain approach to the works of language according to which discourses and texts must be understood only by their reciprocal exchanges within a synchronic and diachronic context (Foucault's network, Derrida's assemblage, Barthes' constellation): the only intent of the signifying praxis that constitutes writing is this perpetual relay from text to text by which the power of the writer is measured. This power soon contests even itself when the practice of writing (with some form of bad faith?) declares itself to be anonymous, summoned by a certain state of language and by the internal logic of the text. Here the voluntary prisoners of language connect a type of sociologism to a theory of inspiration. Thus a universe of discourse is constituted in the image of the world, but it is asserted outside of the world and tends to substitute itself for it. Such is the new avatar of idealism, which suprisingly at times gives materialism as its point of reference. Sometimes not only is the referent banished, but the signified itself is in some way volatilized. In Derrida's deconstruction of the sign, "the signified is originally and essentially a trace, it is always already in the position of a signifier."[13] But what can a signifier signify that, instead of designating an absent signified, is itself a type of absence? Here we are not dealing with idealism, but rather with nihilism. If we nevertheless maintain that language has some relation to the world, we must return to the post-Kantian idea that makes language an a priori of perception and conceives of it as a preexisting grid, imposed from the outside, through which the world appears and is thereby structured. But that does not mean that language, since it actualizes possible imaginaries, "inaugurates being," as Bachelard says, and thereby attests to an affinity and fundamental complicity with the world. And it is precisely on this opening of language that our attention must be fixed. A dual opening, in the first place, owing to its function, since it is primarily used to designate and name. We cannot insist enough upon some signs belonging to language that subordinate signification to reference: the deictic elements that prompt the association between gesture and speech, the shifters that introduce the speaking subject and the circumstances of *parole* into discourse, thereby situating discourse in the world. So language itself invites to speak in order to say something.

Secondly, the opening of language may be due to its own origin. To be sure, this origin escapes any investigation of it in a historical past, but is it not possible to look for its trace in the present, no matter how dissimulated such a trace may be? Thus we can feel what Ponge calls the original onomatopoeia whenever we experience a kind of complicity, even of resemblance, between thing and word. Then it seems that the arbitrariness of the sign is weakened, that the thing proposes its name to the speaker, just as in presenting ourselves we state our name. For the individual who speaks as the poet—and it has been said often enough since Vico's time that poetry is the first language—the model of metaphor is perhaps given there: the world brings forth speech in order to be transported into and expressed by it. Nature invents *homo loquens* as the means for this transfer. Then, and if the essence of the sign is determined initially in relation to presence, the difference between signifier and signified is not required "to be somewhere absolute and irreducible" and thereby guaranteed, as Derrida believes, by a creative logos.[14] The signified—Derrida says "meaning or thing," let us say world—is announced in the signifier, and the institution organizing and promoting the system is perhaps founded upon nature, on the embedding of the signifier in the signified that guarantees language its power to designate.

Although our examination has been much too hasty, we must now return to the imaginary so as to try to see how it is articulated with these three terms: desire, world, language, which are themselves linked together. Their solidarity is knotted in presence; for the subject who is born into the world as a being of need, does not stop being in the world when desire takes hold of him, or when he responds to the world by using speech or addresses himself to another human being (at least when his discourse is not solely perlocutionary). To be sure, this fullness of presence, which is the origin, never fails to be undermined as the subject, in order to constitute himself, breaks away from it and institutes representation. Then it is that the subject separates himself from the object, alterity becomes objectivity, the real is won over. But the imaginary—and here we can understand Sartre's lesson—introduces a new dimension of absence into the world: How is the unreal joined to the real? In the field of presence, is it against the imaginary that the real is progressively determined, at the same time that the imaginary is determined as unreal?

IMAGE AND DESIRE

There is no doubt that the imaginary penetrates into presence if we initially consider the narrow relation it has with desire. We must, let us repeat, think of the image as imaginary, and therefore different from the image that is simply available, or even voluntary and tamed, or image-forming knowledge, which comes second and must be considered as secondary: it re-presents because it reproduces, and its role is found in the secondary processes. This is the case whenever I form an image of the Pantheon or, according to Sartre's example, of the proletariat. But the imaginary is what intrudes in an unforeseen way, under the impulse of a boundless energy. It is therefore what upsets "normal" images, that is, those images of the world that are verifiable, unanimously accepted, and comforting, such as the representation given to tranquil perception as well as the representation offered by a painting or a film, which imitates the perceived. The characteristic of the imaginary is transgression, so its spring can only be the anarchistic energy of desire. Hence the idea of a symptomatic reading of the imaginary: Tell me what you imagine, and I will tell you what your desire is. This is not to say that desire can be totally contained by discourse, for it remains undeterminable, insatiable, a signified that no signifier possesses or brings forth. But one can at least say which next object it chooses in order to rebound, or which immediate goals it assigns itself in its indefinite movements. Nevertheless, when treating the image as a symptom of desire, one has to be cautious, for the operation of desire is not necessarily entirely unconscious. For instance (I am here following one of Lyotard's analyses), in the images produced by art, even when it has recourse to automatism or chance, or when it invokes inspiration, then a certain control may come into play, or rather a labor on the canvas or in language by means of which, instead of merely expressing the fantasmatic, a particular domain is created where other, unexpressed images can find a place. The genuine work is not merely a symptom, nor is its production a work analogous to the dreamwork; the secondary processes must engage in a struggle with what binds it to rules, norms, traditions, so that figures other than symptomatic, more profound and perhaps unimaginable, appear or may appear. In fact, desire sustains the imaginary in diverse ways: in order to be staged as it is in the dream, it makes itself the stage manager, it organizes the space and time in which the imaginary is cast, the narrative or the drama. In the artwork, desire commands the ruling form, which is not always seen, according to which the elements of the visible are ordered. This form may be absent, as in informal art; then desire abolishes all staging, and what it produces is an invisible matrix, a veritable non-existent place, transgressing all spatiality and figuration. If either plastic or poetic figures are born into it, they arise from the deepest part of the unconscious, expressions of the primal fantasy.

It is therefore not to be doubted that the imaginary has its source in desire. Sartre in an entirely different context requires also an affective *analogon* for the production of images. Then the question is: Does this libidinal origin cut the imaginary from the world and assign it to the unreal? This cannot be the case, for we must remember what we have said about the relation between desire and world. This relation leads us at least to emphasize an often neglected product of the imaginary—the utopia. Whenever (if) desire is, in the world, a desire for another world, why should we not give it the name of hope, as Alain did? Certainly, for Alain, hope was the awakening of the mind, but the mind is not an established metaphysical agency, its reign is always in the future. And the demand constituting it can easily be thought of as unconscious. The unconscious is not fated to be only the place of the unavowed or the repressed, for we can think of other forms of an invisible or an inexpressible that do not issue from representation. Even sexual drives can signal and bring about another destiny for the psyche than that of a mourning, the lost paradise, or the infantile regression. Eros can thus be conceived as being in quest of justice as much as of happiness. And agressivity can be directed toward injustice and hatred as much as toward the "bad" objects of a haunting childhood. It can be understood then that the imaginary can express in the subject both the refusal to abdicate and to rely upon necessity and power, in other words, to submit to the reality principle, and the ever-renewed and insatiable demand of transcendence and novelty: in brief, it can be manifested in utopian thought and practice. This utopia is flush with the ground: it causes the perceived to vibrate, it discovers its own demand in what the perceived denies as well as promises. This utopia therefore differs from the one that is expressed in programs where reason—that is, reasoning—develops the image of a world in which man would be the end, and to be so, would accomplish his ends. This imaginary of the second degree is still perhaps animated by desire, but it is revised and corrected—emasculated—by rational thought. But the utopian imaginary, which under the immediate impulse of desire, conjures (and sometimes already outlines) another world, remains in contact with this world.[15]

IMAGE AND WORLD

Let us say it in other terms. If man, through the utopian imagination, expresses himself as transcendence, that is, as capable of desire and thus a second dimension, as Marcuse would say, the perceived world also expresses itself through it: the imaginary is anchored in perception, as is desire. This can be understood in two complementary ways. First, if, leaving utopia aside, we return to a certain use of the word *image*, we realize that the imaginary, at least when it is imaginable, characterizes the image, and that the image is always image *of*, offered by something in the world. But this intentionality must not be conceived as if the image were reduced to the intention of an image-forming consciousness, and the intended object were necessarily a nongiven, as in the dream; for the image-forming consciousness can also be a receptive one. The object can in fact be given through the image in an exemplary fashion. But how is this so? What differentiates the image from ordinary perception—without conceiving of it as a "false" perception—and what also prevents us from conceiving of it as a copy or simulacrum is that what is given in it, as much as the object, is its very appearing—appearing as the irrepressible upheaval, the sensuous evidence, the epiphany that emphasizes the object. In this case the image is not the schema, the general rule explicated by the concept that leads perception to knowledge, as Kant would say. It lets the sensuous be, such as it reveals itself, surprises, ravishes, and sometimes mobilizes the affect, inviting the sensing to be in the greatest proximity with the sensed. The image is the plenitude of the sensuous, and it by no means requires absence or the emptiness of "difference" that conceptualizing thought introduces through notions of spacing, divergence, and "determination which is negation."

But, on the other hand, this very image, which is the perceived in the savage state, in its nondiscursive expressivity, can become transfigured by a touch of imaginary (by which the real becomes surreal). Tropes are testimony in discourse to what appears well before discourse, issuing directly from perception: the mountain is perceived as Titan, the spring as Nymph, the father as *Pater omnipotens*, the earth as Mother, and the mother as Earth. This implies a second relation of the imaginary to the world, which again links perception to imagination. But, as Sartre warns us, we must not go so far as to equate the imaginary with what is not perceived. Imagination does not assure us that there is always the other side of the coin, other sides to the cube, or that the table legs exist under the rug covering them; it is rather knowledge that has no need to become image-forming so as to convince us. The imaginary as invisible is not the always hidden portion of the visible, it is its very thickness, and it tells its meaning, a meaning not intended for knowledge, since the Titan teaches us nothing about the mountain, but speaks only of the density of the sensuous, of its force rather than its form: Titan is the being-here of the mountain, imperiously imposing itself on my view and barring my way; it is a surreal by way of which the real maintains that it is affirming itself, that it is persevering in its being and is impregnable and inexhaustible. But this forceful presence can only be experienced by a subject who is himself intensely present, that is to say, still mingled with the object. What allows for that is perhaps desire, which makes him sensible to the world, even if it aims at another world, for it awakens in contact with the world. In any case, this intimacy of the sensing and the sensed invites us to evoke a perception other than the visual one, which maintains a certain theatrical distance, and an imaginary other than the invisible, if we relate the invisible to the visible. Here we are thinking of what Bachelard calls "material imagination," linked to both savage and active perception by which we are truly in contact with things: hands molding clay, faces whipped by the wind, body becoming liquid in water. Such is presence without distance, lived in another space than the space of vision, which is soon ruled by geometry; here we experience the force of things, their weight, violence, and intensity. The mountain becomes Titan whenever we are intimately in contact with it, even if mountaineering is a "positivistic" praxis. The imaginary expresses this original proximity with the world and the depth at which it resounds in us.

But what about the duplicity of the imaginary, which we mentioned earlier? To ask, upon returning to the originary, if the imaginary is objective or subjective, and therefore real or unreal, is perhaps meaningless at this point. Surely, objectifying thought will end up by denouncing the imaginary as subjective when it castrates perception in the name of the epistemological break, so that we may understand that "we have art in order not to die of the truth." To focus our attention, however, on the imaginary immanent in the perceived, surreal rather than unreal, is not to deny that imagination can produce images of its own, elicited perhaps by an *analogon*, but remaining foreign to the real. Either the imagination voluntarily intends these images, as in the examples prompting Sartre's analysis, or, folded back upon itself, caught at its own game and renouncing all hold upon the world, it invents in a more or less delirious fashion. We have insisted on the ambiguity of the imaginary and the polysemy of the language that names it. But in the case in which an entirely subjective imaginary proliferates from the fantasmatic, we would have to speak of a perverted imaginary, just as we would also have to speak of perverted desire if we looked everywhere for the operations or the expression of desire. Today we have an abundance of theories about subversion, but a theory of perversion remains to be developed. For the imaginary, this perversion does not consist in submitting to the pleasure principle, but in radically separating pleasure principle from reality principle, and primary processes from secondary ones.

On the contrary, the imaginary that we want to privilege depends on us, but not on us alone. To imagine is to be inspired both by the world and by desire. But how is this possible? It is not enough to say that desire is awakened in experiencing the world, nor that the imaginary haunts the perceived; it would still be necessary to consider the fantasmatic and the images of the world as identical, or at least in harmony; otherwise we would not be able to transcend the distinction between two imaginaries, one subjective and the other objective. This distinction, let us repeat, is probably inevitable as soon as we consider an already constituted subjectivity, capable sometimes of folding back on itself, nocturnal *cogito* of the dream, exiled *cogito* of the neurosis freely worked by desire and whose images are symptoms; sometimes of opening itself to the world and accepting images that we have seen to be hardly imaginary, sometimes of fixing images and thereby creating utopias. But we would see this distinction weaken and in the end disappear if we could return to a more originary state of a subjectivity still captive of Nature. We can at least surmise this status of a deep-seated imaginary where desire, instead of staging itself, abolishes all stage, as in a painting by Pollock, a text by Joyce, or music by Cage. By transgressing all figuration and structuration, in this matrix figure where fantasies are rooted, desire manifests itself for the impossible. But this figure also manifests the world as it is experienced from within by the subject completely penetrated by it, its power, and opacity, "pythic consciousness." Here in the feeling of presence the three agencies of modality intermingle: being in the world, open to the real, is to experience necessity as the mother of the possible, as power; and this power, this *conatus*, is indistinctly sensed as both the power of things and the power of this self that has not yet taken its place as an equal in the world, but which confusedly desires all the possible, that is, the impossible, and through this wants itself. Thus the young Parca is awakened in the ever-renascent springtime.

It is here that we can look, as Alain did, for the "truth of imagination"; but this truth resides not only in the fact that the imaginary announces and prefigures the future of the mind in a subject capable of equaling the world, of challenging and transforming it; it resides primarily in that origin where man is born, in that realm of primary truth revealed to a savage perception. At the same time that there is hope and desire, there is also faith, what Merleau-Ponty calls perceptual faith, which puts us into this world and into truth. For truth is only propriety of judgment or adequation on condition of being evidence; but this evidence is not a particular grace that being would grant us by revealing itself in its very dissimulation, it is rather the invincible feeling of this presence to which we are born. The imaginary itself is anchored in this experience: if gods are true, it is not only because they are desired and express the desire of mortals who construct temples and "images" to them, but also because they are captured in this first text of the world where what will be discerned as real has not yet been distilled, but where truth is nevertheless experienced.

This is to say, in another type of language, that the pleasure principle and the reality principle are, at least at the origin, not radically distinguishable from one another. That means at first we must emphasize a point often omitted by those nostalgic for nostalgia or for the return of the mother's breast, namely, the drive for self-preservation that requires the reality principle. For one can assume that the "sexual drive" stems from this drive in a double relation of "anaclisis and separation," as Laplanche and Pontalis say.[16] These authors specify that, for Freud, "there exists from the time of the origin, at least in certain instances, notably that of perception, an access to the real." They also emphasize elsewhere that Freud has always tried to found the primal fantasy upon "the bedrock of the event."[17] This can also mean that emerging sexuality, whenever it produces fantasy and the hallucinatory realization of desire, thereby seeming to settle in the unreal, nevertheless, insofar as it is grounded in ego instincts, has still perhaps not broken every link with reality. The approach to this reality is in turn linked to the progressive constitution of the libidinal object that is always disputed and unclaimed, but the face of which is not always masked by familial histories. It is thus correct to state, along with Laplanche and Pontalis, that "what psychoanalysis understands by access to reality cannot be reduced to either the idea of a capacity to discriminate between the unreal and real, or the notion of fantasies and unconscious desires being put to the test on contact with an outside world which would, in that case, indeed be the sole authority."[18] But it is precisely because, in the most primitive experience of desire and perception, the real and the unreal are not discriminated: because the imaginary is as true as the real—both belong to the primary truth.

IMAGE AND LANGUAGE

Language is also rooted in this experience. To be sure, the subject encounters language as an institution and must learn how to use it. But he is already capable of language, and things prompt him to name them: appearing wants to be spoken. This is true for the imaginary, as Bachelard well understood. The relationship of image to language is in fact twofold: language calls for the image and the image calls for language. Poetry, being the springtime of speech, shows us how language calls forth images; it causes language to return to its source, before the institution. Certainly linguistic images can also be institutionalized; it is the function of rhetoric to see how they are codified and systematized, how speech produces language. But Bachelard admirably demonstrated that an institutionalized image is worn out and that its image-forming virtue has become exhausted. The image that is pregnant with imaginary, really only exists in the germinal state, in the movement by which it unforeseeably transgresses the lexical and grammatical constraints of language. This lively and singular speech can undoubtedly be degraded: the language of the schizophrenic represents its caricature, just as pathological hallucination is the caricature of an image-forming perception, or as Bachelard would perhaps say, the nocturnal dream is the caricature of diurnal revery. But how do we discover authentic language, how do we distinguish the language of Artaud from that of a schizophrenic or an infant?[19] This is an immense problem. All that we can say here is that the linguistic image is really an image insofar as the second relation that we mentioned is at work—where the image calls for language, forcing and arousing it; we might say, inventing it, for it invents language at least as different. The image does not have recourse to language as an already available and indifferent instrument; it takes the instrument up again in its native freshness, in this state in which it is itself nature, in which words have a visible and consummable flesh. For the *phonè* can be *jouissance*—"muscular pleasure," as has been said—and writing is not a trace only when the letter is illuminated or when it takes place in a painting by Klee. But why does the image flow into language? It is in order to become fixed and communicated, just as when it has recourse to other mediums such as stone or pencil, and we rediscover here Alain's aesthetic, and even that of Hegel. The images call for language not only in order to becomes metamorphosed, but also to become realized. For if the imaginary within the thing is this surplus of being or meaning that makes it boundless, always other, inexhaustible, beyond the objectivity assigned to it by knowledge or praxis, language is capable of expressing this addition as long as it remains poetic. It can say more than the thing or speak of the thing as more; it can speak of the world as invested with the imaginary. Robbe-Grillet prohibits writing about the village "nestled" in the valley; he is undoubtedly correct to the degree that the metaphor is well worn, but he is wrong to rely on the language of objectivity, to put language solely in the service of positivity. For language can speak of the designated as expressive, irreducible to the objectivity of an essence. It does so if, as we have tried to show, it is no more exterior to the world than the world is "exterior" to the subject. Its complicity with the imaginary is due to their common origin in Nature, where subjectivity itself originates, whose imagination and speech are not principally subjective.

Nevertheless, the subject's vocation seems to be—and today especially—to depart from this obscure place of the origin and to assert himself by controlling objectivity through knowledge and technology, by sacrificing the imaginary to the benefit of a "purified" and manipulable reality. Look at those who govern us: never has imagination been so removed from power, never has a civilization so resembled a termite colony. Perhaps praxis demands this sinister type of ascesis for its content. But what about its motivations? Perhaps praxis, and more specifically political praxis, would be more efficient, and less morbid in any case, if it were animated by dreams or hope. What still privileges the scientists in this ant-like population is perhaps that they invent, and in order to do so, they must still imagine. Certainly the origin is always here, but it is masked by thick sedimentations, as is Husserl's *Lebenswelt*. A single glance, however, would be sufficient to scatter these sedimentations, as Cézanne did with Mt. Sainte-Victoire, or a word, such as those written on the walls in May 1968: "Under the pavement lies the beach." This is why we can still ask the question: How can the imaginary be revived today? How can we reconcile the pleasure principle with the reality principle, which civilization has so carefully dissociated? How can we lift the prohibitions governing the fantasmatic and of which the theory of the unconscious is perhaps a part? But perhaps there are many types of imaginary, leading us yet again to another question: How can we avoid perverting the imaginary? How can we renounce power without sinking into impotence? How can we return to Nature without abandoning ourselves to barbarism? How can we become crazy without falling into madness? Rather than meditating on being, we should reflect upon, if not permit, this return to the imaginary.

Notes

1. A parallel problem can be raised at the empirical level: Who imagines, the individual or humanity? Should we conceive of archetypal images that would have the same relation to humanity as the fantasm does to the individual?
2. *Système des Beaux Arts*, p. 328.
3. We can find indices of this relation, if not in natural sciences, at least in human sciences, where not only the springboard of knowledge draws its energy from the "synmogenic virtue" of the imaginary, but also the conceptual apparatus itself may be looked for in the realm of the imaginary. The Freudian Oedipus, according to Lévi-Strauss, is a version of the myth; myths also are the primal scene or the killing of the father; and why not the logical interpretation of myths, as was the innocence of the noble savage in the past? Are we discrediting rational thought by according it the power of myth? Moreover, the myth is not necessarily a fable. And no matter how positive and verifiable rational thought would like to be, is it not mythical insofar as, in order to enlighten, it has recourse to analogy? That has well been shown by Canguilhem for the cellular theory, and perhaps might be shown for the theory of the genetic code. Is this anthropomorphism? No, for the human and the vital are just as much understood in terms of nature as nature is in terms of the human. But as soon as one domain is understood in terms of another, as soon as there is a transfer of one scientific discourse to another, there is metaphor. Does not this discourse become a mythical one? Undoubtedly it does not keep being mythical; if it is taken over by rational thought, which later may contest it, it recuperates its scientificity. But it has been myth for as long as its still unjustified eruption in a particular field of knowledge introduced into it a new atmosphere and energy. Undoubtedly analogy is a weaker form of the imaginary: it summons only secondary processes. But a more intense form of the imaginary could still be found in the scientific process when uncovering in it a *concupiscentia sciendi*, a will to power where primary processes are played out.

4. Although Sartre refrains from equating "intention, in the sense in which we take it, with will" (*L'Imaginaire*, p. 32), there can be an image without will—whenever the spontaneity of consciousness is without will; but there cannot be an image without intention, an image not posited as such.

5. The same question can be addressed to psychoanalysis with respect to drives or the imagery of the topics: What is the relation of the model to "psychic reality"?

6. We are not thinking here of the process of what is called creative imagination, for this process, which, in order to give body to the invisible, yields to the reality principle, only realizes the imaginary in a refusal to imagine. This occurs at least to a certain extent, for consciousness can play at annihilating itself by abandoning itself to automatism and inspiration. This is why in the creative act itself a certain duplicity could be discerned, but which should be assigned to the imagination rather than the imaginary. What we are thinking of here is a production that is not a creation, one in which consciousness is possessed and alienated by what it produces, and even if, as Alain suggests, this delirium is already a witness for the mind: it is another form of ambiguity characteristic of the imaginary

7. Laplanche and Pontalis, *Vocabulaire de la psychanalyse* (Paris: Presses Universitaires de France, 1981, 7th ed.), p. 153.

8. Ibid., p. 129.

9. Maurice Blanchot, *L'espace littéraire* (Paris: Gallinard, 1982), p. 271.

10. Ibid., p. 266.

11. I have tried to develop this point in my article, "L'imaginaire et le jeu."

12. Even religion does not imagine a world totally other than this one: bodies will be revived, as Peguy says.

13. Jacques Derrida, *De la grammatologie* (Paris: Minuit, 1967), p. 107.

14. Ibid., p. 175.

15. I have attempted to develop this idea of the utopia in *Art et politique*.

16. *Vocabulaire de la psychanalyse*, p. 337.

17. Even if this event were itself mythical; but precisely, for a science that wants to follow a primal experience, how else would one not have recourse to myth in order to explain a becoming where myth and reality are initially indistinguishable? It is to the very extent that psychoanalysis is true that it is a mythology.

18. *Vocabulaire de la psychanalyse*, p. 338.

19. See *La logique du sens*, in which Gilles Deleuze opposes the language of Artaud to that of Lewis Carroll (Paris: Minuit, 1969).

5. Eye and Mind

Eye and Mind is one of the last texts of Merleau-Ponty, and perhaps one of his finest. Sartre wrote of it, "*Eye and Mind* says all provided one knows how to decipher it."[1] But can this be done? Rather than risk such an undertaking, I would like principally to comment on the title itself.

One notices immediately in *Eye and Mind* that the two words are treated unequally in the text, for "eye" appears repeatedly in the writing of Merleau-Ponty, while "mind" is rarely mentioned. No doubt this is due to a certain danger in denominating it in the manner that delighted "philosophers of mind." For the mind is not an organ like the eye, nor is it a substance that can be designated by a substantive. If it is called by name, it is for the purpose of designating certain acts characteristic of what *The Structure of Behavior* called the human order. These acts demonstrate a *cogito* that seeks to be transparent to itself. In them is consummated (*se consomme*) the separation of the subject and the object that has already taken shape but that is not yet completed in vision: in brief, thinking as opposed to seeing. My first point of questioning bears precisely upon the *and*. What is the meaning of this conjunction? It cannot signify a dialectical relation, since there are only two terms; unless we adhere, as does Adorno, to a negative dialectic, in which case *and* would designate a relation of opposition as in being and nonbeing. But it can also mean a relation of priority as in cause and effect, or even a relation of complementarity as in form and content. Obviously, only a reading of the text will permit an answer to this question, and if the text stresses one of these meanings of *and*—namely, opposition—it persuades us perhaps not to exclude the others.

To begin with, the eye is foremost: it is first in the title because it is first in the becoming (*le devenir*) of man. Man sees before he thinks, and no doubt he arrives at thought because it is aroused by vision, although Merleau-Ponty does not describe this advent. In any case, seeing is opposed to thinking, and it is precisely toward this theme that analyses are directed. For example, if these analyses invoke painting at great length, it is in order to show that "we cannot see how a mind would be able to paint." All the difficulty lies here: by hardening the opposition between eye and mind, can we still account for the emergence of thinking, for the movement leading existence to a reflexive life? Between seeing and thinking, contemporary philosophy is given a mediation: *speaking*, which is the contemporary of seeing. Merleau-Ponty, however, does not invoke this mediation, and it is here that Lyotard, for example, raises his principal objection. According to Lyotard, Merleau-Ponty forgets that nothing happens before "entry into language," save the still blind vicissitudes of drives. It is true that Merleau-Ponty does not situate speaking in seeing, for his analysis of painting excludes discourse—and not only that of the expert or semiotician but also that of the painting itself. Poussin wrote to Chanteloup: "Read the story and the painting." Merleau-Ponty does not seem interested in paintings that tell a story, unless it is the fundamental story, that is, the very genesis of appearing. Thus speaking neither kindles nor illuminates seeing. On the contrary, speaking itself might be understood as a type of seeing: the speaking subject (*l'homme parlant*) is in language as he is in the world, he harmonizes with its thickness (*l'épaisseur*) as he does with the flesh of the sensuous, he lives it by inhabiting it. Moreover, speaking can perhaps be equated to seeing for the purpose of disclosing it. This would be the language of "hyperreflection" of which *The Visible and the Invisible* speaks. This language "becomes philosophy itself," endeavoring to "express beyond significations our mute contact with things when they are not yet things said."[2] This is indeed the admirable language with which Merleau-Ponty approaches brute being (*l'être brut*), leaving it to speak within himself as the dream allows desire to speak.

If philosophy requires this effort, it is because seeing, to repeat, is irreducible to thinking and cannot be comprehended by it. But what about the reverse? Can we not comprehend thinking through seeing? Is there not a type of seeing that, far from opposing thinking, would be its auxiliary? When, confronted with a proposition, we respond "I see," are we not in our response equating thought with a type of vision? *Wesenschau* is still *Schau*. Besides, thought has willing recourse to a visible of which it avails itself: one has only to think of geometrical figures, linguistic "trees," or the diagrams of graphic semiology. For Descartes, space without hiding places in which these signs are drawn is precisely the in-itself that knowledge masters. We can then ask the following question: Are there not two regimes of vision of which at least one, since it is regulated according to thought, presupposes it while the other precedes it? Merleau-Ponty does not state this explicitly, but it is what Descartes suggests to him. Indeed, if we follow Descartes: "There is no vision without thought. But *it is not enough* to think in order to see. Vision . . . is born 'as occasioned' by what happens in the body."[3] So "the enigma of vision is not eliminated by Descartes; it is relegated from the thought of seeing to vision in act." But Descartes is unwilling to "sound out this abyss." What is important for him is the edification of knowledge; and today science does not even trouble calling for metaphysics.

It can be said that Merleau-Ponty, facing this renunciation of reflection, directs all his attention to the savage regime of vision, and perhaps all the more so because this regime is never obliterated: even when the mind inspects signs of convenience, or, as Alain said, when perception brings judgment into play, the eye remains present and open, to the point of sometimes leading the rational vision astray in the same manner that discourse is distorted once tropes (*figures*) are introduced into it. Perhaps what one calls "totalizing thought" (*la pensée de survol*) is the vocation of thinking, whenever the subject stands at a distance with respect to the object in order to become its "master and possessor." This is precisely the purpose of language whenever it allows for the passage from presence to representation. This thought is, however, never fully realized, as it is always sustained by perceptual faith that anchors us in the truth of the sensuous. The eye, said Breton, exists in a savage state, and it may be that it is never completely tamed, even when it is employed by understanding; no more than when vision, instructed by language, becomes the utilitarian and assuring (*sécurisante*) vision of a prosaic reality.

Merleau-Ponty thinks of the savage in vision according to the Husserlian model of passive synthesis. This vision does not organize the visible, nor does it bestow a meaning upon it or constitute it as readable and expressible in words. It receives the visible, rising from an invisible that still clings to it; one can say at the very most that vision opens itself to the visible which is given to it. This act of giving is an event in the visual field. Lyotard says of this event that "it can only be situated in the vacant space opened by desire."[4] He also states that "it belongs to this giving which releases us." But what about this *us*? To think *id*, one must still think *ego*. And why say release us rather than seize us? We are only released when and because we are seized. If there is an event, something happens to someone. In this case we have an act of giving. It is no doubt correct that the subject does not exist prior to the event, for he is born with and from it. Is this a transcendental subject in a transcendental field? Why not? But for Merleau-Ponty, this transcendental field is not the place of desire, the ephemeral film traversed by anonymous fluxes. Rather, it is brute being, this originary being (*l'originaire*) that the philosopher calls flesh: the "last notion," he says, because it is the first. This event, forever starting anew, which takes place as well as inaugurating place, is the bursting forth of originary being. Consequently we have the upheaval of appearing, for this bursting forth produces a chiasm and institutes a distance between man and things, born simultaneously and continuing to exist for themselves without ever radically separating from each other. In addition, the reversibility of the visible and the seer, this double dehiscence of the visible in the seer and the seer in the visible attests that "things are the secret folds of my flesh."[5] We therefore cannot evade the question of origin. It is not the body that gives access to originary being, it is originary being that gives access to the body. And in the end, such is indeed the enigma of vision: far from the eye explaining vision, as a reductive science would want, vision explains the eye. Bergson has already claimed this, but for Merleau-Ponty this resilience (*le ressort*) of vision is not creative evolution, but rather the bursting forth of originary being.

Merleau-Ponty examines painting in order to think the unthinkable, and in particular he examines the kind of painting instituted by Cézanne. Classical painting can lead us astray, for one is inclined to believe that it originates from and appeals to the mind. On the one hand, in fact, the painters of the Renaissance claim that their art has attained the status of the liberal arts by their use of mathematics in order to substitute an artificial perspective for a natural one. In this manner their drawings are based on a fundamental law. On the other hand, these artists appeal to a spectator who is more concerned with the intelligible than with the sensuous. This can be seen in the perceptual studies of Alberti: in order to entertain a painting constructed through this perspective, the spectator must see with a single eye (monocular perspective), situated at the required distance and which is neither spherical nor mobile. But everything changes once painters abandon this exacting truth in their painting and look for another one that is primary and has no need of justification according to the standards of knowledge.

Truth is an unveiling; once again it is the bursting forth of originary being, the "deflagration of being," or the apparition of what Klee calls the *Urbildliche*. This being is not a different agency, even less a transcendental one. It is born in tearing itself from the invisible at the same moment that vision is awakened. Painting accomplishes what hyperreflection tries to say. What the painter, through sheer patience, wants to see as well as to present for our seeing, is the very birth of seeing in contact with its newly formed image. He wants to take this moment when "things become things and . . . world becomes world" by surprise.[6] He is not interested in what follows, after language or culture, or in what Adorno calls the administered world, in which fruit bowls are machine-turned and mountains explored by geographers. The painter returns to a pre-real, which is also a sur-real in the sense meant by the surrealists, as their objective chance is but another name for the inaugural event in which man is still very much mingled with things. The painter leads the noumenon back to what is properly the phenomenon, that is, to the manifestation of appearing.

We speak of appearing, and not appearance. Cézanne is not an impressionist, even when he invokes his "little sensation." For him it is not a question of restoring a truth of the seen that would dismiss line while making color vibrate; nor is it a question of the production of a playing field for fantasies brought about by the deconstruction of a system of representation. Cézanne does not deconstruct, he pre-constructs. He does not shatter the fruit bowl, he shows us its genesis, that is, not its production but its coming into the visible. And this space that the fruit bowl comes to inhabit is not a predetermined one in which it is able to take form, it is rather a space that springs from it, a dimension of its flesh. And it is definitely a question of the flesh: it is this texture of the sensuous ordered in this case according to the visible. The mathematical Logos by which the mind informs reality is unable to account for it, and thus this flesh appeals to another Logos, "a system of equivalences, a Logos of lines, of lighting, of colors, of reliefs, of masses,"[7] according to which a face of the world accedes to visibility.

Thus the eye deserves to be mentioned first in the title. It is not, however, for the purpose of designating a determined organ assigned to a precise function, but rather for designating this strange power of opening of the flesh. This flesh, which is not yet a body, is itself reflected once a chiasm is brought about in it. The eye, putting us into the world by opening a world to us, precedes the mind. But was it still necessary then to mention mind? We know that Merleau-Ponty challenges "totalizing thought" and the philosophies of consciousness that consider it as both possible and praiseworthy, and that he also does his best to render thought enigmatic by showing its roots in perception. The philosopher's thinking, forever beginning, as Husserl said, is a thinking about the beginning. It tells us that no thought can be absolutely liberated from this beginning, for mind is grounded in eye. What remains afterward is for the *cogito* to declare itself and proclaim its rights as well as a science to be developed and a human order instituted. Man forgets that he was born and that he belongs to what gives birth to him. One must therefore mention the mind even if it is only carnal and savage, even if, in order to think, it is necessary to be, and this being is always a being in the world, a seer-visible (*un voyant-visible*).

In the end, there is still a final question concerning the title: eye, of course, but why not ear or hand, for that matter? We have found in Merleau-Ponty the idea of a primitive Logos, a system of equivalences between elements of the visible. But this system of equivalences is also constituted between diverse sensorial registers, as the *Phenomenology of Perception* has already indicated. Synesthesias are the lot of all perception. The flesh is polymorphous and polyvalent. The sensuous must also allow itself pluralization, for no matter how subtle the discourse of hyperreflection may be, it can only divulge originary being as having already burst forth. For the language it organizes already designates a constituted world where the body *has* organs and where the perceived is reduced to distinct objects. In order to remain close to this savage Logos, should Merleau-Ponty have written "the sensuous and mind"? In any case, what *Eye and Mind* says about the visible can also be said of the sonorous and the tactile, since it is linked to them. But it seems that Merleau-Ponty wanted to bestow a radical privilege upon the visible. If he evokes music, it is in order to cast it aside. "It does not depict anything but certain outlines of being."[8] As for the tactile, he excludes it from painting: "When, apropos of Italian painting, the young Berenson spoke of an evocation of tactile values, and he wasn't the only one, he could hardly have been more mistaken; painting evokes nothing, least of all the tactile."[9] But in the absence of evocations there are equivalences attesting to the fact that the whole body is invoked. It is on this condition that the tactile makes itself visible. Vision is not devouring, it is mobilizing.

In the end the eye is still the most important organ for what Descartes called the practice of life. Here there is no need to invoke the symbolism with which psychoanalysis burdens it! I would willingly say that if Merleau-Ponty chose to write *Eye and Mind*, it is simply because he loved painting. Others will say that his desire was invested (*s'investissait*) in paintings rather than in music; and after all, that is not such a bad investment!

Notes

1.   See *Les Temps Modernes*, 184–85: 372.
2.   Maurice Merleau-Ponty, *The Visible and the Invisible*, trans. Alphonso Lingis (Evanston, Ill.: Northwestern University Press, 1968), p. 38.
3.   Maurice Merleau-Ponty, "Eye and Mind," in the *The Primacy of Perception*, ed. James M. Edie (Evanston, Ill.: Northwestern University Press, 1964), p. 175.
4.   Jean-François Lyotard, *Discours Figure* (Paris: Klincksieck, 1971), p. 22.
5.   Merleau-Ponty, *The Visible and the Invisible*, p. 46.
6.   Merleau-Ponty, "Eye and Mind," p. 181.
7.   Ibid., p. 182.
8.   Ibid., p. 161.
9.   Ibid., p. 166.

6.   *The Beautiful*

How do we speak of the Beautiful? This word, functioning adjectivally in ordinary language, becomes substantive in the technical language of philosophy and aesthetics. As logicians would say, the predicate becomes the subject and can in turn be predicated. Thus we say, "the Beautiful is a concept," or "the Beautiful is the common denominator of all beautiful things." But what does this dual use signify?

Let us first consider a judgment in which beauty is an attribute: "This sculpture is beautiful." It states a value and establishes the quality of a particular object when that object is grasped according to a certain attitude, which is aesthetic contemplation. If the mode of intentionality or the attitude were different, other values would be invoked: if it were a question of acting, one might say, "This object is useful"; if a question of knowing, "This object is true"; or of loving, "This object is desirable." Moreover, the judgment of aesthetic value could be made in regard to objects that would not appear to elicit the aesthetic attitude. It could be said, for example, that an heroic act, a logical argument, or even a fortunate turn of events are beautiful. This might suggest that the notion of beauty is quite elastic; but this flexibility also signifies that, in certain respects, many things can lend themselves to the aesthetic attitude. Conversely, our judgment may also be expressed hesitantly in a less categorical vocabulary, and instead of saying that an object is beautiful, we might say that it is good, valuable, authentic, interesting, and so on.

What specifies the judgment of aesthetic value, however, is its claim to universality. Kant observed this, and it is in fact the point of departure for his reflection. When I express an aesthetic judgment I cannot help claiming objectivity for it and thinking everyone must subscribe to it. To be sure, I can also express subjective judgments in the first person, as when I say I like that work, or I prefer this to that. But in such a case I am only aware of expressing my own tastes, and on the whole, of judging myself rather than the object. I thus discriminate objective and subjective judgments: and perhaps one must be in bad faith or naive by sheer subtlety to maintain a total relativism and affirm that all aesthetic judgment is irreducibly subjective.

Yet this relativism, which history and sociology willingly encourage, is perhaps at first a righteous reaction against a long-standing dogmatism, encouraged by the substantification of the adjective "beautiful." Indeed, if aesthetic judgment claims universality, it is tempted to justify this claim by appealing to a universal concept: the beautiful object is what realizes and manifests the beautiful itself. Here we recognize the strategy of Platonic thought that classical rationalism seeks to revive while perhaps distorting it in the process.

For Plato, knowledge and wisdom require that man break away from the sensory world and transcend perceptual experience in order to gain access to the Ideas, from which he subsequently returns to the sensory world wherein the destiny of his fellow man is played out. It is only for myth that these Ideas are realities in an intelligible world. For in themselves they are nothing more than a source of light illuminating the given or inspiring action. They constitute elements of a logical discourse that have no being whatsoever apart from the dialectical fabric they compose, just as words, unless regarded abstractly (as in dictionaries), lack meaningful being outside the sentence and the totality of language. But among those ideas whose being is necessarily unassignable (because their being consists in disappearing into the meaning they engender), there is one exception: Beauty. For only beauty shines; "it alone," says the *Phaedrus*, "has been allotted the power to be most manifest and to be that whose charm is most appealing";[1] whereas other ideas, such as "justice or wisdom possess no luminosity in the images of this world."[2] To be sure, this only signifies that the beautiful object captures and moves us more immediately than any other object, because it is both sensuous and significant. In this incomparable experience, the sensuous reveals rather than dissimulates. But it is tempting to suppose that what enraptures us transports us beyond the here and now to an ulterior world, and that its power comes from imitating Beauty itself.

It is thus with Plato's recommendation that classicism can conceive a normative aesthetic, founded upon the presupposition that there is an idea or essence of the Beautiful. This idea then justifies a two-fold normativity. On the one hand, it authorizes the critical judgments exercised by the "academies" and on the other, it establishes a didactic conception of art, which is expressed in the *ars poetica*. For the idea of the Beautiful does not preserve its transcendence: it is concretized and elaborated in determinate models, the most celebrated of which are the architectural canons and the rule of the three dramatic unities. These models weigh heavily upon both the critic who judges works by reference to them and the artist who must create in accordance with them, as the demiurge of the *Timaeus* creates the world by contemplating the Ideas. To find an excellent example of the spontaneous dogmatism practiced in criticism and pedagogy, we might read the judgments rendered by the Royal Academy in the seventeenth century: look only at the following passage from de Champaigne's discourse "against the treatise by Blanchard on the merit of color":

> I do not know, gentlemen, if one can believe that the painter ought to propose an object other than the imitation of beautiful and perfect nature. Ought he propose something chimerical and invisible? It is, however, certain that the most admirable quality of the painter lies in being the imitator of perfect nature, it being impossible for man to go any farther.[3]

This dogmatism is basically the expression of the tastes and aesthetic practices of an age, but it is not aware of it, and so promotes to the absolute an idea of the beautiful which is relative. It justifies this promotion by claiming that such an idea is imposed by nature and not proposed by culture. The idea is supposedly first imposed by the nature of things, and it is thus that one invokes certain forms such as the perfection of the circle (the golden section) as absolutely beautiful and already inherent in the nature that art must imitate even if it has to set aside what is ugly. This promotion of the idea is also said to be imposed by the nature of man, for aesthetic pleasure remains the sole judge of the beautiful, but it is thought that this pleasure is determined by an immutable structure of sensorality and reason, so that consonances, homophonies, good forms, and clear expressions will universally merit being called beautiful; whereas dissonances, hiatuses, equivocal forms, or confused expressions will be ugly because they displease. Here it is forgotten that what seems to be a natural fact is in reality a cultural one, that certain harmonies please the ear or certain plastic forms the eye because these organs have been preconditioned by an artistic environment. Thus the artist has a right to abuse tastes that are frequently nothing more than habitual, and thereby to provoke us to new experiences. The price of this forgetfulness is the uncritical maintenance of tradition, resulting in the conveyance of a certain number of recipes that are supposed to guarantee the beauty of the artwork.

This idea is surely not a foolish one. What history questions is whether a tradition can monopolize the secret of the Beautiful, as if the idea of the Beautiful were reducible to a prescribed system of models, and artistic practice to a prescribed system of rules. But it is true that (premodern) art defers improvisation and always requires apprenticeship and contact with a tradition. However, this apprenticeship, which provides the artist with a technique and means of expression, ought to free and not enslave him. In fact, every true artist, once aware of his real vocation, exercises his creative freedom and becomes a revolutionary figure in the eyes of the public or the academies. There are certainly great anonymous works associated with a school rather than an individual, but they have undoubtedly been possible only because the artist(s) has quite profoundly identified himself with and become truly inspired by the spirit of his time, rather than mechanically applying canonistic procedures.

It is at this point that inspiration might well be invoked, joining the image of artist as craftsman to that of artist as creator. The idea of this inspired madness that possesses the artist and draws him outside of himself is already in Plato. As interpreted by a rationalism that mistrusts it, this idea mainly signifies that the creation of a beautiful work is unpredictable and that craft has to be allied with chance. But a serious examination of this idea requires that we ask what inspires creation. The idea of the Beautiful cannot inspire creation insofar as it is reduced to a system of precepts or recipes, for the rule constrains and by no means inspires. Yet can an idea be said to be inspiring? Yes, for men live and die for ideas such as freedom or justice, but providing that the idea itself is beautiful, that is, irresistible in that it proceeds from nature. It is therefore necessary that the idea of the Beautiful cease being an idea; that it not move or speak to us as an abstract notion, but that it rather be already incarnated in beautiful objects.

By this detour Plato leads us to Kant. Kant in fact initially proposes a theory of aesthetic judgment. By what right can I judge a thing to be beautiful? The criterion is precisely the pleasure it arouses in me: a disinterested pleasure linked only to the form of the object and not, as is attractiveness (*l'agrément*), to its content. The beautiful is thus what pleases, but pleases, as Kant adds, universally without concept. "Without concept" means that there is no idea of the beautiful, no model that is able to guide my judgment and serve as its standard. The beautiful is only encountered in sensible objects, and sensibility (*Sinnlichkeit*) is therefore the sole determinant: "To seek for a principle of taste which shall furnish, by means of definite concepts, a universal criterion of the beautiful is fruitless trouble, because what is sought is impossible and self-contradictory."[4] It is contradictory because it is the feeling of the subject and not the concept of an object that constitutes the principle of aesthetic judgment. In this regard the beautiful object is only the occasion of pleasure, for the cause of pleasure lies within me, in the harmony of imagination and understanding, that is, in the harmony of the two faculties that every encounter with the object puts into play. However, whereas in cognitive judgment understanding governs imagination, in aesthetic experience the imagination is free, and what is experienced is the free play of these faculties and their harmony, rather than their hierarchy.

The paradox remains that the judgment of taste claims universality: without this we could not speak of beauty, but only attractiveness. For when we judge a thing to be attractive, we neither expect nor demand that others concur. Universality here has its principle in the subject and not in the object—it is a subjective universality. But how then is this claim to be justified? It is enough to assume that "the subjective conditions of the judgment . . . are the same in all men. This must be true, because otherwise men would not be able to communicate their representations or even their knowledge."[5]

We see that this analysis, conforming to the spirit of transcendental idealism, inclines Kant toward the negation of all objectivity in the beautiful. The beautiful is not an idea in itself, an idea in the object, an objectively definable concept, or an objective property of the object; it is a quality that we attribute to the object in order to express the experience of a certain state of our subjectivity attested to by pleasure: "As if, when we call a thing beautiful, it is to be regarded as a characteristic of the object which is determined in it according to concepts, beauty, without reference to the feeling subject, is nothing in itself."[6]

But is that Kant's last word? And given his claim that the beautiful is without concept, must he conclude that it is devoid of all objectivity? For, in the final analysis, aesthetic pleasure is given to us, and it is precisely the object that arouses it. If, far from being dictated by the object, "a judgment of taste consists in calling a thing beautiful just because of that characteristic in respect of which is accommodates itself to our mode of apprehension,"[7] it is nevertheless the thing that manifests this quality. The aesthetic judgment that registers this quality is objective, even though it refers ultimately to subjectivity. That the beautiful could not be experienced outside of this reference does not mean that it is not given in an unimpeachable experience. There is a fact of beauty, even if this fact is always a fact for us.

It is precisely this fact that interests Kant and inspires his project. What principally interests him is undoubtedly the way aesthetic experience supports moral experience. Ordinary language attests to the affinity between these two experiences, since "we often describe beautiful objects of nature or art by names that seem to put a moral appreciation at their basis."[8] We speak of a majestic edifice, a pleasant landscape, or an innocent or modest color. It is thus that the aesthetic ideas inspired by poetry—each of which is "a representation of the imagination belonging to its presentation, but which occasions in itself more thought than can ever be comprehended in a definite concept"[9] and which is untranslatable in prose—have some relationship to the rational ideas aroused by moral practice. The beautiful is the symbol of the god; it does not teach the good, but merely suggests it, for the good as an absolute can only be accomplished, and not conceived. And above all the beautiful suggests that we are capable of accomplishing the good; since the disinterestedness proper to aesthetic pleasure is a sign of our moral vocation, aesthetic feeling announces and prepares moral feeling:

> Now I admit at once that the interest in the *beautiful of art* . . . furnishes no proof whatever of a disposition attached to the morally good or even inclined thereto. But on the other hand, I maintain that to take an *immediate interest* in the beauty of nature . . . is always the mark of a good soul . . . [10]

One will have observed that Kant here privileges the beautiful in nature. And since this is constant in his philosophical reflection, we are brought back to the objectivity of the beautiful: we encounter in nature objects that elicit aesthetic experience. This experience does not interest transcendental philosophy except insofar as it instructs us about the subject, about the play of his faculties and, indirectly, about his aptitude for morality, but also in that it instructs us about nature, about what Kant calls "the external possibility of a harmonizing nature," that is, a nature that lends itself to the intellectual activity of the subject. Between the manifold of the intuition and the unity of the concept, the agreement required by consciousness is possible; the experience of the beautiful forewarns us that the world is thought because it is thinkable.

Therefore transcendental philosophy can be completed through a philosophy of nature, or at least through a line of thought initiating such a philosophy. The privilege accorded to nature resounds both in the theory of art ("beautiful art must *look* like nature, although we are conscious of it as art")[11] and, most of all, in the theory of the artist. If the artwork must have the apparent freedom of a natural product, it is because the rule governing its production is given by nature. This nature is manifested in man as genius because genius is that blind spontaneity "which is regulated by nature," which is sometimes called a force of nature. Thus, with works of genius, it is still nature that gives evidence as to its availability (*disponibilité*).

There is then no more an idea of the beautiful than there are definitive rules for producing the beautiful object. What is beautiful is the natural object or the work of genius, models that are both exemplary and inimitable. Can Hegel help us to go further? Actually, we have already touched upon his thought, for it is Hegel who makes explicit the idea of a reconciliation between nature and mind that is merely adumbrated in

Kant. To be sure, Hegel is primarily interested in art; he does not elaborate, as does Kant, a theory of aesthetic judgment, but rather a theory of art and its becoming (*le devenir*). He emphasizes this becoming because with his thought a new idea, "the idea of history," has gained full status in philosophy. Hereafter we know that the aspects of the beautiful are multiple, and their diversity irreducible through time. But this should not lead us to a superficial relativism or skepticism, for becoming is dialectically conceived by Hegel. It obeys a logical necessity that orients and rationalizes it. (Indeed, this dialectical becoming is hardly a becoming. But this is not the place to pursue the immense problem of knowing to what extent the dialectic is able to recover history and whether the logical does not in some way risk overwhelming the chronological it calls for and which illustrates it.)

But if this becoming is of a logical sort, is it a becoming of the idea? No; in Hegel we no longer find an idea of the Beautiful, but the beautiful is rather the idea itself as incarnated. Whereas in Kant the beautiful was at once the symbol of morality and the promise of truth, here it is truth itself in a sensible form. What, in effect, is the idea for Hegel? It is "an absolute object of consciousness," that is, the supreme truth in which all contradictions are transcended. This truth is not the truth of any particular object, it is the identity of truth and the object, of the idea and nature: the movement of truth reveals itself as ultimate reality. Now, this truth, which philosophy can only conquer with much effort, is in some way immediately given in aesthetic experience inasmuch as the idea presented in it assumes a sensuous form. It is thus that "among the Greeks . . . Art was the highest medium under which the community conceived its gods, and became conscious truth."[12] The entire history of art demonstrates the development of the idea under its sensuous veil, until the "far-seeing mind turns away from this objective form, rejects it, so as to return into itself."

Thus the beautiful is the manifestation of the "ideal." The ideal is not abstract, it is the idea present and transparent in the idealized object, whether it be the humble everyday objects of a Dutch still life or the face of a Raphael madonna. Art does not imitate, it idealizes. It expresses the universal in the particular:

> . . . the excellence of works of art is so much the greater in the degree that their content and thought is ideal and profound . . . The Chinese, Hindus and Egyptians, for example, in their artistic images, sculptured deities and idols never passed beyond a formless condition . . . and were unable to master true beauty. And this was so for the reason that their mythological conception, the content and thought of their works of art, were still essentially indeterminate, or

only determinate in a false sense, did not, in fact, attain to a content
which was absolute in itself.[13]

For Hegel, such is the consequence of introducing an historical perspective: there are degrees of the Beautiful insofar as the idea can be more or
less rich or successfully incarnated. At least Hegel does not yield to the
temptation of dogmatism, which approves or condemns absolutely in the
name of a certain atemporal model. He admits to a becoming of the
beautiful, though only as contingent upon the becoming of the idea: we
would say today that art draws its inspiration less from itself, from some
intrinsic exigency, than from the culture and world view it expresses.

Is the Beautiful judged differently in our age? Our thinking certainly
abstains more vigilantly than ever from all dogmatism; it strives to
accommodate all of the styles gathered together in the "Imaginary Museum,"it acquiesces in the extraordinary renewal of plastic and musical
forms that are aroused in artists both by the compulsion to invent and by
contact with primitive art. Should our age therefore refrain from rendering judgments? Certain people think so. Under the pretext of appearing
objective they endeavor to receive all works equally without ever choosing
between them. The word "beautiful" has disappeared from their vocabulary. This is a hypocritical or lazy attitude. First, because art does not
renounce beauty. The more disconcerting explorations—those that sometimes offend tastes ossified by habits or prejudices—are indeed aimed at
beauty. We can only appreciate these explorations if we understand that
they obey the creative logic of the search for the Beautiful, and the
perpetual exigency of renewal that this search entails insofar as the
beautiful is invented and not imitated. Secondly, because everywhere
values are discriminated more rigorously than ever: there is a veritable
Stock Exchange of plastic and literary works governing the art market.
We could dismiss these values as purely economic and entirely provisional, but such quotations weigh heavily on the destiny of artists and art
today as the taste of the courtly patrons did in the past, and it expresses in
its way the taste of a certain public. Is it therefore necessary to allow this
practical judgment to replace a theoretical one?

I would say no; but at least the theoretical judgment, if it still claims
universality, avoids all dogmatism. It does not confront the object with a
preestablished canon, but rather allows the object to complete and judge
itself. What is required of the spectator is that he have sufficiently
cultivated taste, compliant attention, and an open mind in order to do
justice to the object that proposes itself to his perception. Of course, he
will never be discrete enough in his judgment, for, if he is in good faith, he
is never assured of being sufficiently cultivated and unbiased. It is always

possible that we are literally blind or deaf to certain objects because of a lack of sophistication or an excess of biases—in which case it would be prudent to suspend our judgment, since it would be without an object inasmuch as the object does not as yet exist for us. But if we are not disconcerted, prejudiced, or impatient, then beauty manifests itself and at the same time the misfits, the inauthentic objects betray themselves.

What then is the Beautiful? It is neither an idea nor a model, but rather a quality present in certain perceptually given objects that are always singular. It is the plenitude of the perceived, immediately experienced in perception (even if this perception requires a lengthy apprenticeship and familiarity with the object). The beautiful is first of all the perfection of the sensuous, which imposes itself with a kind of necessity and immediately discourages any thought of improving upon it. But it is also the total immanence of a meaning in the sensuous, without which the object would be insignificant or, at most, attractive, decorative, or amusing. The beautiful object speaks to me, and it is beautiful only on condition that it is true. But what does it tell me? It does not address itself to the intellect as a conceptual object (a logical algorithm or argument), or to the practical will as an ordinary object (a sign or tool), or to affectivity as a likable or desirable object. Instead, the Beautiful above all elicits sensibility in order to enrapture it. Therefore, the meaning that the beautiful object proposes cannot be subjected to either logical or practical verification; it is sufficient that it be affectively experienced as present and compelling. This meaning is the suggestion of a world that can be defined neither in thing-like terms nor in terms of the state of the soul, but is rather the promise of the unity of both. This world can only be given the name of its creator—the world of Mozart, of Cézanne.

And nevertheless this singular world is not subjective, for authenticity is the criterion of aesthetic truth. Through the creator, if he is inspired, the world as *Natura naturans* seems to signal us and offer one of its faces to be deciphered. Each singular world is a possibility of the real world, the world lived by men. In the catalogue for an exhibition of paintings by Lapoujade on torture and riots, Sartre wrote that "art summons the artist to place on his canvas a true portrait of the human kingdom, and the truth about this kindgom, today, is that the human species includes torturers, their accomplices and martyrs."[14] Today, on the ethical and political plane, this truth is the most urgent, and it is fitting that art too bear witness to it. But there are other truths—Cézanne's fruit bowl and Lapique's horses—that can be expressed by art and expand to the dimensions of a world. For, as Carnap says of logic, there is no morality in art, no compulsory subject matter. The sole task of art, as Sartre also indicated, is "to restore the world." And the world is inexhaustible, always exceeding the principal human concerns and tasks of a particular age. One cannot do justice to the beautiful without acknowledging its right to actualize the nonactual, to express the lived or livable possibilities with which the world is pregnant, for nature is never given its share—not even within the artist.

Moreover, it is positivism more than existentialism that can question the creative freedom of art. Positivism is free to challenge the possibilities of art, to reject poetry for prose, painting for photography, music for noise, and thus free to posit a one-dimensional world. But conversely, if we say that a thing is beautiful, we confirm the presence of a sign whose signification is not reducible to the concept and yet is one that summons and engages us by communicating a Nature that speaks to us. Taste heeds this voice, and we need only be receptive to it, whatever its message, to judge the aesthetic object beautiful: beautiful because it truly *is*, according to the mode of being suitable to a sensuous and signifying object, because it realizes its destiny. And then my judgment rightly claims universality, for universality indicates objectivity, an objectivity assured by the fact that it is the object itself that judges itself in me as soon as it imposes itself upon me with all the force of its radiant presence.

Notes

1. Plato, *Phaedrus*, 250d.
2. Ibid., 250b.
3. Cited by André Lhote, *De la pallette à l'écritoire* (Paris: Editions Correa, 1946), p. 78.
4. Immanuel Kant, *Critique of Judgement*, trans. J. H. Bernard (New York: Hafner Press, 1951), p. 68.
5. Ibid., p. 132.
6. Ibid., p. 53.
7. Ibid., p. 123.
8. Ibid., p. 200.
9. Ibid., p. 158.
10. Ibid., p. 141.
11. Ibid., p. 149.
12. G. W. F. Hegel, *Philosophy of Art*, vol. 1 (London: G. Bell & Sons, 1920), p. 140.
13. Ibid., p. 123.
14. Jean-Paul Sartre, *Essays in Aesthetics* (New York: Washington Square Press, 1966), p. 120 (modified).

PART TWO

THE ARTS

7. *Mal du Siècle?* The Death of Art?

In this essay I would like to focus on how certain forms of contemporary art express certain characteristics of our time. Although a great deal has been said about modernity, the environment I will evoke is not exactly representable, nor is it even perceived as such by those who live it. It is, rather, a question of an atmosphere that envelops, directs, and inspires us as soon as we *breathe* it. The relation of the individual to such an environment is therefore one of expression in the sense meant by Leibniz when he asserts that each monad expresses the entire system of monads—but without requiring that this harmony be necessarily preestablished. In this way a type of isomorphism obtains between the individual and culture. Nothing prevents us from looking for its genesis in causal language, providing this language becomes flexible and dialectical. We can, however, simply describe this isomorphism as it is manifest without attempting to discover how this environment is already the result of individual acts or the mechanisms by which it exerts an influence upon the individual. We merely assume that what is expressed in the individual's behavior besets him unconsciously. This "soul" of the environment, the invisible reflection of the spirit of the times, is what is most present, most persistent, and also what is most indeterminable because of its sheer proximity. Yet it is absolutely necessary that we try to comprehend it.

This "soul" is all the more difficult to understand because it is stirred by conflicting movements. Our culture is neither homogeneous nor ordered upon a coherent and structured system of values, concepts, or attitudes. This is to such a degree characteristic of our culture that certain anthropologists have attributed many modern neuroses to the antagonism between culturally imposed imperatives. Of course, some of these contradictions belong to all time, especially those that oppose social norms to actual practices. These are most often carefully hidden by a type of social hypocrisy, as when one nation prides itself on being a free country while globally encouraging regimes of oppression, or in another that struggles for human rights while closing its eyes to torture.

In fact, a fundamental inconsistency appears to affect the status Western civilization accords the individual. In theory, we still live under the sign of humanism. Man is an end in himself, and increasingly more substantial means are put at his disposal in order to realize his goals and free him from the urgency of needs and the tyranny of compulsions. But in practice, man both exhausts and alienates himself. After the mercenary, the thug tends to become our model for behavior, and his Will to Power attests to both mental indigence and moral impotence. At times this loss of substance cuts man to the core: he can no longer invoke the *cogito*, for he now lacks a language to do so (Ionesco's theatre and the dialogue of the *Mépris* are testimony to this). Man no longer knows how to speak because he no longer knows how to think. He is assailed from all sides by images that leave no time for thought, by printed matter that substitutes for it, by myths that discourage it. He relies on others—the scientists and the politicians whom he gladly makes his masterminds—to do his thinking for him. And the vested parties willingly enter into this game! Thus, as Eric Weil would say, violence rather than discourse tends to predominate. It comes in all forms, from the most brutal to the most insidious, from magic to torture, from advertising to nuclear armament.

Let us not, however, paint too gloomy a picture. The very causes of this deterioration of the human suggest that it is temporary and embodies its own antidote. To what should we attribute this deterioration? To individualism? But in fact the ties surrounding the Greek hero and integrating him with the *polis* have been distended for a long time. Should it be attributed to the rise and prestige of technology? Not directly, in any case, for we would have to discover what gave rise to this development, and moreover it is not true that technology compels man to violence because it itself abuses nature. Simondon has admirably shown that technology rather conspires with nature, revealing it in its own way, as does art; and that it leads thinking to new cultural directions. To a latent materialism? No more, for the endeavors at demystification led by certain philosophers are fundamentally sound. Moreover, the churches retain their faithful and the various spiritual movements their devotees. But philosophers feel their powerlessness—sometimes they retreat to their own Aventine in order to cast oracles, sometimes they abandon their project entirely. Ideological conflicts no longer mobilize poets like Rimbaud, and instead of philosophizing, those who persevere allow themselves to be obsessed by the question of how philosophy is possible.

Current thought has not ceased to function, but rather has become caught in its own trap. Perhaps we must look for the underlying cause of the present confusion in the very movement of thought, in the conceptual apparatus that it develops. Today, in fact, modern thought confronts in every domain an object more difficult than all the rest: totality. Reflection upon this object was introduced simultaneously by field physics, the philosophy of form, biology, and history. One aspect of this totality that we should consider is the gathering of arts and styles from every location and period in what Malraux calls the "Imaginary Museum." And surely the ultimate degree of totality is the very world in which we live; today the world is round. Hegel's concrete universal is now offered to us. Hippolyte recently referred to it as a phenomenon whose meaning must be elucidated.[1] Living up to the universal is an awesome burden, and especially when we have to totalize an ever more detailed and abundant body of knowledge (thus the urgency for educational reforms). We are called upon to be world citizens. But it is less easy to do so now than it was in the time of the Stoics, for the world has expanded and the human demiurge has replaced divine fire, thereby rendering our world more precarious and historically unintelligible.

This unification of human environments is only realized by an ever-accelerated change in concepts, technology, and certain institutions. Progress relegates order to a subordinate position. But where is progress going, and where should it be directed? History is no longer easily manipulated; and in the confusion created by the inertia of some institutions and the mobility of others, action loses purpose. When this action is not inspired by some type of Messianism, it is quickly thwarted and deterred. Our time is surely in full gestation, but what will the mountain give birth to? People who do not have to direct what is to become, willingly take refuge in indifference or conformism. Others, according to the words that parody Heidegger, are resolved at being resolved. Undoubtedly, with Sartrean existentialism freedom is given a content that is not only freedom itself but also the social conditions of its actualization. But because no one agrees upon the nature of this content, human passivity is often opposed only by a directionless activity that is sometimes also characteristic of artistic creation.

In the backwaters of history, man sometimes loses his foothold, as does thought. This moving and variegated universal is difficult to master: the one is constantly absorbed into the many, the same into the other. Either thought returns to particularities and becomes embedded in them, or— and this sets the tone of our time—it answers to the problem of totality by giving rise to formal thought. Thought responds to the concrete universal by raising itself to an abstract universal, as if it could grasp the whole only by arresting its movement and emptying its contents—by privileging synchrony and formal structure. Thus political thought oscillates between a nationalism concerned with independence and greatness and the formal affirmation of global solidarity. Philosophical thought, in the face of the pantheon of systems, similarly hesitates between historical erudition intent on each individual system and the repudiation of all systems in favor of a formal analysis of language and science. Aesthetic thought, confronting the Imaginary Museum, also tends to divide itself between an overly factual art history and a morphology that, viewing works from a purely formal stance, ignores their period and their historically lived meaning.

We have just played with various meanings of the word *formal*, but perhaps they overlap. In any case, the most distinctive feature of modern thought is perhaps the ever greater importance gained by formalization, and in the precise sense meant by logicians. This tendency has a dual relation with the universal. On one hand, the formalization of thought has led to its universalization and has thus become more effective in promoting a universalizing technology. On the other hand, thought has been formalized in order to think in terms of the universal. For if we want to go beyond a perception that defines the whole simply as form, the whole must be thought of as a system of relations prevailing over the terms that it structures (this is also true on the molecular level). The techniques stemming from this formalization allow us to pursue the enterprise of universalization, and, for example, surmount the confusion of language, economies, or strategies.

Now the process of formalization that will initially weigh on the destiny of art is abstraction. In order simultaneously to disclose and posit structure, abstraction will eliminate intuitive content and, in dealing with the structure, it will subordinate the structured to the structuring, the term to the relation, matter to form. Certainly, formalization is a detour by way of which we return to the real. This return, however, is not readily apparent and, moreover, the real that it rejoins is in itself abstract, recreated by both thought and machine. The phenomenon, as Bachelard has said, is the product of a phenomenotechnics. Modern science has seemingly dissolved the object in this way. We spoke of a loss of substance—it is rather all substance that has been lost. In microphysics the real is the field where the object eludes the observer. Matter is a system of forces that Bachelard called "shadows of numbers." The mathematization of physics seems to break the necessary relation that, according to Canguilhem, science has with perception. Surely bees are still making Virgilian honey and men still see the Ptolemaic sun rising and setting, but they are remotely aware of the illusory quality of such experiences. It is rare to find those who, like Bachelard, know how to live on two registers; and besides, it is rather the lyrical world of the imaginary that Bachelard joins to the universe of science. Those not specifically concerned with the search for wisdom still live in the perceived world, but with certain reservations, as they feel that the real is no longer within their bounds and that it has lost some of its richness and savor. Nature hardly ever speaks to man nowadays, and he needs to go on vacation at least to rediscover it. Technology does not yet speak to him—the layman is too unaware of it, and others still see it as an excessive representation of improvisation and capitalist violence.

Thus the sense that is spontaneously lived slips away, and on another level the epistemology of meaning encourages such a desertion. We know what position structuralism holds in this regard, for it also tends to absorb the object into the system, depriving it of the sense that guaranteed its autonomy. In linguistics, the phonological object is only defined by its differences, and the entire system of signs constituting language is characterized by this play of differences. This system is governed by laws that assure its permanence throughout history and to which individual speakers unconsciously conform. The mind is acknowledged in linguistics, but relegated to the unconscious; and far from language being the tool of the mind, the mind is in the service of language. In the same instance, speech is no longer considered in its manifestation as intending to communicate a meaning. The form of the exchange receives more attention than its contents, and semantics is reabsorbed into syntax. Certainly, on the level of logical language, content is often reduced to syntactical arrangement. "The object or the operation is allowed to be expressed integrally by syntactic rules governing their signs."[2] The object is the product of an operation, and its meaning is the meaning of an operation regulated by syntactical rules. But what about the concrete object? Its meaning undergoes a similar transformation when structuralism, deciding that language is "the prototype of all organization,"applies the same abstract method to the exchange of wives in social groups or to symbolic exchange in mythical discourse. "The condition for this generalization of the linguistic model is the emptying of its contents and the elimination of meaning in order to account only for its arrangement."[3]

We are not trying to impugn the structural approach, but rather indicate its limits. To what extent can we treat a wife, a mytheme, even a word ("I say . . . a flower!") as a sign signifying nothing in itself? In order to account for the object, is it not necessary to join to the structural approach of its functioning within a system, a phenomenological approach to the meaning it has in itself?

At the same time and in the same way, both the conceived object and the lived object become blurred by dint of subtlety. The same holds true for the metaphysical object of philosophy as well as for the formal object of logic.

Philosophers have lost their naiveté—they can no longer believe in the tenets of their predecessors that referred to a now outdated science. Logicians are seemingly carried off into an increasingly rarified ether on the wings of a thought overcome by its own power. This type of thought, whose surprising development animates our *Weltanschauung*, seems simultaneously to abolish the object and the subject itself. Thought is impersonal, and because it develops a formal calculus that avoids the obstacle of the real, it is able to rely on machines. The myth of the thinking machine symbolizes the *mal du siècle*, that is, the difficulty that man meets with when reflecting on both his thinking and desiring in a world beyond his grasp and where he no longer feels his roots.

In fact, modern thought institutes a relation, analogous to that of object and field, between the living entity and its environment as well as between man and world and man and history. An authentically dialectical relation should give equal weight to both terms that it unites. The salutary teaching of Sartre is, however, rarely heeded, and our age seems to engage in the dialectic only by privileging one term at the expense of the other: by dissolving the subject in the same way as we have spoken of the object. For Moreno, the social unit is not the individual, but a bundle of relations; for the psychoanalyst, this unit is the locus of opposing agencies. Saving man means adapting him to his environment (Freud would not have wanted such a salvation!) at the risk of enervating his power of both assertion and invention. The dialectic of the one and the many is played out to the advantage of the many: salvation is found in conformism. Meanwhile science and technology undoubtedly continue to invent in order to adapt the world to man. But it seems that man does not comply, for he adapts to progress by allowing himself to be led by its promoters. In truth, progress appears to be realized without him, as though it were centered in and guided by an anonymous elite, so that it may be foreseen as a natural event. In any case, the great men allow the little ones to forgo being men: they do the thinking for them.

Philosophers are sometimes unwillingly made accomplices to this passivity whenever they relinquish man at the cost of capitalized entities: when they assign the artist to be in the service of Art, the thinker of Thought, and being of Being. It is in this manner that Blanchot, relying on a few prestigious and superbly analyzed examples, maintains that the artist abolishes himself in his work, that he desires it to be a failure, and that all inspiration proceeds from an experience of and a nostalgia for nothingness.[4] But must we believe that the sense which is aimed at and revealed by the speaking and the doing, gets its profundity from its own opacity—that it is only realized in nonsense? Silence is not the aim of speech, nor dissimulation the springboard of truth, nor death the crowning moment of life . . .

It is true, however, that man can be surpassed by his work and, in his activity, be inspired to the point of alienation. There are numerous ways for man to lose himself and his objective. By situating formal thought at the center of our world vision, we seem to attribute a certain type of dehumanization to it. And perhaps in effect it is necessary to balance it with poetry, which returns to the immediate. But it would be absurd not to see the promises that formal thought harbors and continues to hold, and which, authorizing numerous hopes, forbids us to play the role of Cassandra. For if this thought disorients man by disintegrating the object and dehumanizing the world, it is only in the initial moment that it does so. Perhaps it never completely shatters the original union between man and nature. In any case, formal thought stumbles against objects that, although ideal, become no less opaque and resistant as soon as the operations constructing them can no longer be executed in a finite number of steps. Semantic content then again transcends syntax. Moreover, in the final analysis, every formal system is directed toward the real; and that is why it itself calls for an interpretation. As Ladrière reminds us: "the question of the relation between the formal and the sensuous (*le sensible*) can never be evaded,"[5] neither can the contact with the sensuous be lost, neither art be disclaimed.

Contemporary art appears to me, however, to express the situation given to man by the advent of formal thought and to be marked by the same contradiction as his culture. In it we find simultaneously enrichment and impoverishment, exaltation and repudiation of the individual, conquest of the formal and loss of the real (sometimes to the point of refusing the world and calling for the self-destruction of the artwork). In effect, contemporary art is produced under the mark of reflection. Never before have artists written so much, attained such a keen self-awareness, or had such a lively impression of being devoted to an exemplary spiritual adventure![6] Today art is reflected upon to the point of becoming reflexive. Since Mallarmé, poets form poetry from poetry. Genet, following the Pirandello of *Henry IV* or the Sartre of *The Flies*, brings the theatricalization of human relations to the theatre. Whenever the plastic arts are no longer figurative, it is to represent themselves: action painting paints the act of painting, the sculptor his own gesture.

Artists nowadays are in the position of philosophers, haunted by the same question: How is art possible? In any period this question is probably roused in them by the phenomenon of inspiration. But today it is more directly provoked by the sudden awareness of the historical and the universal. Artists can no longer believe in Raphael or Racine, just as philosophers can no longer believe in Descartes or Hegel. We can admire them, but not repeat them. Besides, it is not easy to integrate oneself into the universal without getting lost in it, or to become involved in a continuity while remaining separate from it. It is easier to affirm one's singularity through anarchy. This is the reason why the incessant search for innovation is the reaction to the question posed by the unfathomable presence of the artworks in the Imaginary Museum. There is something frenetic in this compulsive drive to invent, endlessly hastening both the usury and the displacement of styles. Whenever the artist, lost in the labyrinth of history, decides to act, he seemingly is more intent on the act than on its product. The hasty and sometimes barbarous character of his creation arises from his attachment, as though the work were never anything but an attempt,[7] a superficial trace of making, a provisional stage in an endless enterprise. The evidence that it leaves behind is of little importance if the adventure is singular and passionate. For certain artists this adventure ends in silence or in repudiation because they aspire, as Mallarmé did, to an impossible purity or a suffocating depth: Crevel, for example, committed suicide. But even in others the feverishness of this search reveals a death wish, as if contemporary art wants to admit that Hegel was right. Toward what does this art feel compelled to overcome itself, if not toward the impossible metamorphosis where man and work are annihilated in order to be realized?

This is all the more the case since the artist, so heedful of the experience that he is living, no longer finds his attention attracted by the natural or human environment. People around him wander in a daily stupor and there are no directives given him save an occasional one, which by its tone of authority incapacitates or revolts him. The object that could say the poetry of Nature has dissolved; the world is now only prose. Of what use is it to construct a spectacular and meaningful object in this desolate solitude, and what meaning could be given to it? The real no longer calls for representation: contemporary art is largely nonfigurative, and to the very language it seems at times to deny its semantic value and challenge its syntactical rules. Besides, the merit of this art has been to teach us to distinguish the aesthetic object from the represented object. But it remains to be seen if representation should not at least be replaced by expression, because meaning, in one form or another, must exert a constituting function with respect to the aesthetic object.

But the artist often seemingly refuses to claim for the aesthetic object the elementary virtues of the perceived object—permanence, unity, grandeur. There are few monuments today that claim to be *aere perennius*. Architecture has some difficulty in finding new formulas for monumentality, as does poetry for the ode and the elegy (P. Emmanuel and La Tour du Pin are the old school). Oftentimes, as in the United States, things are built to last only twenty years. In the same way, the writer writes only for his contemporaries (see *What is Literature?*). Mobiles exist only for the moment by virtue of a perpetual movement that is not the doing of the sculptor.

Collages and assemblages will not stand the test of time as will the oils of the Van Eycks. (And the poems obtained by assembling titles cut from newspapers, of which Breton gives examples in *Le Poisson soluble*, are in fact easily dissolved.) When it is precarious, the aesthetic object can also appear bungled—we need only think of pop art. The layman poorly discerns in it this rigorous necessity that structures the sensuous in the works of other times, and even in front of well-planned works he involuntarily feels an impression of arbitrariness. Why is the circle placed here rather than there in a painting of Mondrian? In a serial composition, why is there a particular dissonance that does not prepare for a modulation? Why in a particular novel is there a temporal upheaval that is not inscribed within an interior monologue? At the same time that the sensuous loses its rigor, it also loses its grandeur. Many sculptors despise high-quality materials, and in painting "misérabilism" is contagious. There is a wide gap between the *chiaroscuro* of Rembrandt and the blacks of Soulages, between the impastos of Van Gogh and the "pâtes" of Dubuffet. The painter, in his rush toward painting, has seemingly gone beyond it. But toward what has he moved? The works on which the sensuous is still exalted, but in a savage way, beyond all proportion, make one think of what Hegel said of the Dutch still life, in which mind abandoned to objectivity a world from which it had withdrawn. Works such as those of the Cobra group serve as examples that could easily be called expressionistic, in contrast to works that are voluntarily stripped bare, neutral, and sometimes lifeless.

But our picture has been too rapidly and somberly drawn. The death wish operating within art is somewhat like an hypertelia: the extreme and aberrant form of a vitality from which a new meaning and splendor may be gained for the aesthetic object. But we must also distinguish these gains from those created by reflection or impassioned quests. For if we look more carefully, we shall see, still summarily, two faces of contemporary art that are apparently very different, one savage and the other well controlled: Pollock is opposed to Mondrian, Beckett to Robbe-Grillet, Lipschitz to Barbara Hepworth, Frank Lloyd Wright to Mies van der Rohe. The informal and the formal are two axes along which life and death constantly struggle.

Perhaps this duality is ordered according to the artist's mode of reflection, which itself can be directed more precisely toward him or his work. If reflection is directed toward the artist, there is a chance that his art will be informal, given over to apparently uncontrollable powers of delirium, for the artist can then feel himself lost or tempted to become lost in his work. This perhaps occurs in any period, as we have said. Questioning himself about his action, the artist feels moved in the work by some unknown force. Michelis accurately states that every quest for a new style has a divinatory characteristic: it is the trance of Pythia possessed by God.[8] But the classical artist, even when he is subject to this visitation, does not entirely lose himself, from our point of view or his own. From our standpoint his work speaks for him by offering his world to us. For the artist, Dionysus collaborates with Apollo in the endeavor, as he remains the lucid and wilful creator of his work. But the modern artist is apt to lose himself more profoundly. First, from our standpoint, if what he offers us is only an unidentifiable world. Is his work the savage world of genesis, the shapeless and the unnameable? Yes, but this world of creation is not really creative if it remains in a nondescript state. The contemporary artist especially becomes lost in himself and feels more alienated than inspired, for nothing in our world summons him to take on his compelling enterprise. What god possesses Pythia today? Apollo is dead, and the artist rarely thinks of invoking a *Natura naturans* that *Natura naturata* hides from him. Oftentimes his god is chance—Breton's "inexhaustible murmur," Casdou's "procession of steps."

If reflection does not drive creation to hopelessness, it leads us, at least in appearance, to rely on the uncertain. Hence automatic writing, or rapid gestures in action painting, or the multiple expressions of a spontaneity left to itself. Undoubtedly it is still hoped that chance will be laden with meaning, a detector of interior eddies of hidden forces. Art claims to be situated at the point where man, delivered from artifice, is joined to nature and allows it to speak through him. But what nature? The interior world only interests psychoanalysts, the perceived world no longer has an expressive voice, and the scientific universe only summons an abstract language. Other artists rely on machines rather than chance, which then becomes formalized, as in the calculus of probabilities: mechanization is the natural consequence of formalization. In this manner, the laws of a formalized nature reduced to probability become manifest in the production of images and sounds. Is this the music of the spheres? Yes, but the spheres are elaborated according to technology. This logical harmony does not always ring clearly in the sensuous; aesthetically the results of the uncertain are also uncertain.

But must we say that the artist registering these results has vanished? He is cheating if he makes such a claim, for he never ceases to control these results, and his final judgment can always hold in abeyance those results unworthy of being elevated to the ranks of the artwork. Moreover, he is most often always involved in the production of these results. In music, which we will discuss later, the technical equipment serves primarily in the production and stockpiling of sounds whose syntactical organization the composer reserves the right to direct according to the programs he feeds into the machines. The spontaneity of the gesture of the painter or writer is that of a nature slowly informed by culture, and is always restrained. The success he meets with is preconceived and prepared, for this learned gesture maintains a certain formalism in the informal, and thus saves him from self-destruction during his moments of rapture.

In fact, in exemplary cases the informal is not only controlled by taste, it also summons a new strategy of consciousness. This "crafty" consciousness, playing with the unconscious, feigns losing itself only in order to prevail, to rediscover a type of lucid virginity. Sometimes it gets caught at its own game, or even its manoeuvering becomes a deception. But for the true artist this trick—a new quest for inspiration—is a way of discovering a primary meaning usually covered by the cloak of ideas that rational consciousness throws over the world. It cannot be said then that the informal always tends to destroy itself because it rejects meaning. Does the nonfigurative reject it? Sometimes yes, whenever the work desires only to be the expression of an incommunicable subjectivity or the product of a meaningless and anonymous gesture. Perhaps with certain formalists, abstraction more often than not signifies that the artist, refusing an entire world in which he feels uncomfortable, intends the work to be self-sufficient, and even at the risk of its saying nothing and being annihilated in silence. But as Barrilli admirably states, all art, including abstraction, can still be figurative. First, it is figurative insofar as the aesthetic object asserts itself and is self-formed, "insuring its own salvation"; and secondly, insofar as it is "endowed with an intentionality, an opposing centrifugal force inducing it to become an image of an exterior reality."[9] These two forces can still be at play in informal art.

If art is nonfigurative, that is perhaps because it is attached to the perceived and desires to represent it. The distortions of the object effected by Impressionism, and perhaps by early Cubism before its systematic geometrization, were based on the intention that it was necessary to restore to perception both its impetuosity and its freshness. Cèzanne spoke of "my little sensation." Whenever art is expressionistic (or at least expressive), as with Manessier or Lapoujade, the abstract takes a similar course, desiring to produce an original contact with the world, a primary truth of the perceived.[10] By inventing the abstract, Kandinsky and Malevitch attempted to return to the concrete. The same is true in the last works of Saarinen, Zehrfuss, or Kahn, all of whom give a truly expressive density and suppleness to the concrete; or Schaeffer and Philippot, who look for sonority even in noise; and similarly in Céline, Joyce, or Beckett, who return to the source of the "human" concrete, to the state of a primitive consciousness still immersed in dreams and traversed by elementary forces that are barely capable of being articulated in language. And what can be said of poetry? Poets can always be separated into those that plod and those that are inspired. Today it seems that the latter are the majority, causing the informal to prevail, and being themselves sometimes driven by the storm onto the shoals of death. "Poetry," said Sartre, speaking of contemporary poetry, "is a case of the loser winning. And the genuine poet choses to lose, even if he has to go so far as to die, in order to win."[11] He wants what is extreme:

> Cą a toujours kékéchose d'extrême
>
> Un poème (Queneau)

> There is always somethin' extreme in a poem and death is what is extreme in the Muse's shrapnel. (Audiberti)

This death is the death of the ordinary language, of the prosaic world, of the artist who renounces this world. But the loser wins: his death can be a transfiguration, the advent of a surreality and a new meaning. If the poet mistrusts rational constructions,[12] it can be in the name of a surrealism that leads us to one of the two roads explored by Bachelard. One is that of a non-Cartesian epistemology and the other is that of a poetry open to a world where the real still remains linked to the imaginary. It is the world of the origin, where Nature is the one who imagines. Poetry, then, "unveils, in all the force of the word, the space of a streak of lightning; *we see* a dog, a carriage, a house *for the first time*."[13] There are much greater images like those haunting St.-John Perse and Eluard, but there are also more humble ones. Whenever Ponge focuses upon the challenge of objects confronting language, it is in order to "define the truly unique qualities of the most ordinary objects" and to repair a world marred by utilitarian perception. "Careful mender of the lobster or the lemon, or the pitcher or the fruitbowl, such is the character of the modern artist."[14] Here, at the risk of formalizing itself, the informal serves the cause of existentialism. Look how many new domains are linked to art in this way; and look also at the extension of those domains that it had already won over! How can one fail to admire both the faith of these Argonauts and the golden fleeces that the most fortunate of them bring back? Informal art is not entirely realized under the mark of distress, and its return to the origin dissuades it from pursuing its own death.

Formal art also has two faces. It manifests the same transcendental will as informal art, but it proceeds from a reflection on the very work whose creator desires autonomy. He also ponders his production according to a method analogous to that of formal thought, namely, by keeping close watch on the dangers exposed in the reduction of the formal to the abstract. Certainly the word *formal* is equivocal in this case. Can the aesthetic form pervading the sensuous be confused with the logical form that formalizing thought obtains from it? Can an aesthetic formalism—that is, a system of norms destined to give in a practical way a form to a material object—be confused with a logical formalism that constructs an ideal object and a theoretical system of analytical statements? Tradition resisted this confusion for a long time. Formalism was employed by realism in order to promote, as much as it did beauty, the veracity of an object that was simultaneously highly structured and faithful to the real. Geometric perspective aims at representing perceived spaces, the rules of tragedy at representing the event, and the rules of harmony at imitating, as Eupalinos would say, architecture. The principles of architecture themselves, including the *modulor* of Le Cobusier, aim at imitating the proportions of the human figure as model.

But the formalism of contemporary art does not proceed from the same intention. Rather, it authorizes a union with formal logic. First, it is common knowledge that modern art has become aware of science. If architecture has always been aware of mechanics, it is only today that music and painting, instead of unconsciously exemplifying the laws of acoustics and optics, deliberately utilize techniques requiring knowledge of these laws. Perhaps the plastic arts propose to represent these laws instead of applying them. Is it not the scientific vision, regulated by the concepts of field and structure, that inspires them in an obscure sort of way? Are not the increasingly more refined cross-hatchings of Tobey an illustration of lattice geometry and the structures of Giacometti an illustration of structural analysis? Surely, and with good reason, a logician would see as illusory this materialization of the formal that only anemic signs are capable of representing. But formal art scarcely achieves a materialization, heedful as it is to mastering the sensuous to the extent of exhausting it.

It is in this sense that contemporary formal art seemingly imitates the procedures of formal thought. In works in which the material invites such things, it may give rise to highly organized pieces whose structures are striking. I am thinking of the works inspired by the *Bauhaus*, of the Cubist constructions of Le Courbusier and Neutra, of the paintings of Braque or Gris, of the sculptures of Pevsner or Arp. In each case the rigor of the forms bestows a brilliant presence and a sensuous plenitude upon the work. But elsewhere formalism seems to privilege structure at the expense of what is structured by the latter, and to the point where it seems to have nothing more to structure. Thus Michelis says: "architectural rationalism is transformed into an irrational myth of pure form, a form rendered abstract to the point of amorphism."[15] Whereas in the extreme cases of informal art, matter is without form and sometimes without grandeur; in this case we have form without matter, and therefore without necessity. Painting lends itself more easily to this type of sleight of hand than does sculpture. It is enough to cite Mondrian, but certain sculptors, such as Sophie Arp or Ben Nicholson, are headed in the same direction, as well as certain types of architecture strictly concerned with functional rationality. In this regard we can again think of that rarefaction of matter in musical scores lasting only a minute, or interwoven with *fermata*. This type of art is deprived of having a meaning in order to have too much, as if thought, in order to be pure, had to rid itself of any object. But only the object can have meaning there where form pervades matter (and we must not forget that even in logic a structure links the elements of a totality or the individuals of a domain). It is of little importance whether art is figurative or not, but in any case the object must not be exhausted to the point of losing all of its expressiveness.

We could also say the same for the new novel (and I will be more severe than Mouillaud, from whom, however, I draw my inspiration). The formalism of Robbe-Grillet, as with Faubert, stems from a kind of defiance or distaste with respect to the object, which is meticulously described solely for the purpose of resituating it, out of reach, inappropriate and meaning-less, and with respect to any nature, may it be conceived as a system of essences or as a nourishing power. All being is reduced to the work: *esse est narrari*; and the work seems reduced to nonsense. There is no continuity of time, fixed distances, lasting objects, or stable events (and this incoher-ence is not due to a consciousness whose narrative would adopt the particular viewpoint, as with Joyce or Faulkner). One can perhaps suppose with Mouillaud that this endeavor is inspired by certain concepts of scientific formalism. Here the objectively described elements can be related in structured unities: they oscillate around a center of gravity with a coefficient of uncertainty such that an object or an action can never be determined or fixed. But why introduce microphysics into the perceived world? Ambiguity and contradiction do not have the same meaning in history, or in *a* history, as they do in physics. To consider the two realms as identical is to strip the lived world of its meaning. Of what use is this, and why write a non-novel instead of seriously doing quantum mechanics?

In response to this question, it can be maintained that the construction of apparently insignificant structures ultimately gains a new meaning and offers us yet another face of the world: a moving and uncertain world that looks for its meaning. This is certainly true whenever formalism becomes expressive, by yielding to the power of inspiration and joining with the informal. It is also true that our analysis has perhaps unjustly isolated some extreme cases. Order and disorder most often tend to correct each other. Structure and the sensuous conjoin in order to prevent the self-destruction of the aesthetic object, a phenomenon that can be found in all art forms. There are kinds of art in which the material is immediately receptive and the creative gesture can be improvised or fortuitous. In this way poetry and the plastic arts lend themselves to the play of the informal. But even so, a control can be exercised on machine-made or involuntarily created products, in order to elevate to the level of the artwork only what is regulatively constructed and thereby assumes an air of necessity.

On the contrary, arts in which the material must be overcome, gesture developed, and the work premeditated are tempted by both reflexive ascesis and formalism. Thus we have certain types of music of which we would too quickly conclude that the sensuous easily disappears, as in painting. Completely new types of music, whether they enchant or disconcert us, and far from being left to improvisation (which is, moreover, impossible when there are no longer any performers) are achieved in two ways: either by the systematic extension of a traditional harmonic field or, in order to go further, by technical procedures that force us to define sound by its effects, and "in this way replace sound with morphology."[16] Moreover, this acoustic material is presented in well-planned scores which, to the present day, are borrowed from classical music. Thus, there is as much formalism in modern music before the introduction of the twelve-tone system as there is afterward and just as much of it in the first tumultuous and baroque works of Stravinsky as in his last refined and scholarly works. Furthermore, what ensnares this music is the fact that it often functions awkwardly in the mechanisms of a laborious construction and is thereby unable to yield to a state of necessary liveliness, or, as Jankelevitch says, to rhapsody. The luxuriance of the sensuous, however, gives this music an air of joyous spontaneity, and certain composers, following their initial efforts, rediscover the lyricism of inspiration.

As a matter of fact, the state of music is such that in many contemporary works, we will discover an unholy alliance between the most rigorous formalism and totally unexpected conjunctures. Boulez's *Structures for Two Pianos* allows its interpreters the freedom to order all of its composed measures. Pousseur was also able to determine fortuitously the order of entry of each instrument, but in respect to a preexisting score. Gilbert Amy and others also come to mind.

This interdependence also holds true for architecture. Even when it challenges the laws of mechanics, as in the Baroque age, it would be unable to ignore them completely. Today especially, it cannot ignore the imperatives of functionality, which, joined to economic exigencies, gave rise to the "misérablist" structuration of the anonymous cell mass produced *ad infinitum*.[17] Such is the modern face of the slum whose alienating effect would still be denounced by Marx. The industrialization of the building, however, and its recourse to machine-cast metal or reinforced concrete do not necessarily impose the paralyzing type of formalism that in the extreme case and often under the pretext of functionality, deprives the environment of its innate beauty and vital meaning. Today architects and urban planners know that we must also construct "buildings that do not respond to any objectively definable needs, but which are just as necessary to us as flowers in order to remain human."[18] Fortunately, certain pieces of architecture evade the obstacle of functionality; for example, the United Nations building or the Art Gallery designed by Khan at Yale. Not only are the structural elements on these works exposed, but also the mechanical equipment. This is done with such candor (the brutality referred to by brutalists) that they constitute without losing their meaningful form an element that could be called decorative if the term did not assume a pejorative connotation. Moreover, the irony so perceptible in Le Corbusier's works at Ronchamp or Chandigar where he deconstructs the rationality of an architecture which, desiring justifiably to ally itself with industry, made in fact a bad deal.[19]

Poetry is hailed by city planners such as Aillaud: it penetrates into the great apartment complexes as well as into monuments and private homes with harmonies more discrete than the baroque of Gaudi. The architect is rediscovering the Dionysian gesture of Painting. Zevi, invoking the Guggenheim, proposes the term "action-architecture." As Michelis says, the excess of formal rigor can flow over into the informal. In any case it is important that fantasy animate formalism and reintroduce into it a meaning susceptible of the semantico-symbolic interpretation proposed by Dorfles. This may represent the only salvation for art.

The layman, always a bit remiss in his knowledge of certain artistic styles and disconcerted by certain forms of modern art, sometimes accuses it of deception. This accusation is absurd, as the aesthetic object is not a fake, nor would it involve deception. It could only be deceiving in relation to an eternal essence or an absolute standard, and all of contemporary art in fact rejects such notions. Each work has its norm in itself, stolen from the unforeseeable by an insatiable and lively freedom.

Toward what type of future is this freedom committed? Does art dream of its own death, like the young Parca, "blind to outstretched fingers, avoiding hope"? If it were to lose itself, it would be owing to its quest for itself. If it were to die, it would be by dint of its vitality. Art confronts the same problem facing modern civilization: the development of reflection and mechanization can establish the reign of the impersonal, the abstract and the inhuman; but it can also establish the liberation and regeneration of man. Planning combats scarcity, authoritarian regimes become more flexible. The world forged by technology is a world in which man can still feel at home if education and the social structure allow him to become the subject of culture rather than its object. For the world, far from dissimulating or destroying Nature, still reveals it, as the bathyscaphe does the depths of the sea, or the plane the peaks of mountains, and so achieves it. What alienates man is his incommensurability with what he does. This temporary situation can disappear with complete automation and education, and making room for a new form of familiarity between man and the world, without having to destroy traditional forms of familiarity or the art that exalted them.

For the destiny of art can also be joyous. Certainly it can withdraw either by exhausting itself through its severity or by yielding to an endless search for pleasure. But extreme forms of pursuit are not necessarily sterile, and chance or delirium can be controlled. Moreover, a union can be formed between the formal and informal. Then art remains in the world, or rather, returns to the source of the world. It binds us and itself to the earth, which Husserl said, "remains as immobile as an *Urarkhe*." Formalism or abstraction are no longer ends in themselves. For science, they are means of adhering to the real; for art, they are means of celebrating the possibilities of the real through the creation of spectacular objects in harmony with man and his environment. Thus Saarinen's TWA Building at Kennedy Airport simultaneously signifies departure and arrival, just as the Doric temple expresses the Greek countryside. However refined it may be, syntax is *employed by* semantics—a sense is immanent in the sensuous, the more pregnant that the sensuous has become the richer.

This is perhaps the very sense of the world that we live. Art can always express this world, and not only because it inhabits it, or because it assumes its demands and utilizes its techniques, but also because it shows what cannot be said: how this world is still a face of Nature. Even in this apparently artificial world, which seems to require for its edification both a purely formal type of thought and the negation of all concrete singularity, such that its creator seems dispossessed of his creation, a landscape of concrete and steel is still a landscape, numbers and structures still sing, and the painstaking realization of the concrete universal represents the poetic unity of the ground. And man is still a being in Nature, traversed by desires and passions and always sensitive to the images through which Nature unveils itself. Art is always man's first response to Nature. As such, through uncertainties and downfalls, at the heart of a world in full gestation, he can still be joyous—and charged with a future.

Notes

1. From the proceedings of the International Institute of Philosophy held September 1964, at Aquileia, Italy.
2. Granger, "Logique, langage, communication," in *Hommage à Bachelard*, p. 46.
3. Ricoeur, "Le symbolisme et l'explication structurale," in *Cahiers internationaux du symbolisme*, 1964, 4:88.
4. See the article "Phenomenology and Literary Criticism" in this volume.
5. "Le symbolisme operatoire," *Cahiers internationaux du symbolisme*, 3:45.
6. The best discussion of this will be found in Maritain's *Creative Intuition in Art and Poetry* (New York: Pantheon Books, 1953).
7. See Mouillaud, "Le Nouveau Roman," in *Revue d'Esthétique*, August–December 1964, pp. 228–263.
8. "La Pizia, l'oracolo e la divinazione nell'arte contemporanea," in *Studi di Estetica*, 16:12.
9. From a recent pamphlet on *Dubuffet matériologue*, p. 5.
10. It is rather remarkable that surrealist art, on the contrary, has been most often meticulously realist. This is because, issuing from the world, it attaches itself less to presence than to signification, or rather to the power of bringing forth signs. With *Nadja*, Breton hunted signs; he takes a picture of a glove or a terrace of a café just as the Romans would have photographed the crow's flight or the entrails of a sacrificial victim. De Chirico and Dali are also photographers who create things addressed to them either in dreams or by chance. They are the sole interpreters of the meaning of these signs, and the sole judges of their importance. But as for us . . .
11. Jean-Paul Sartre, *What is Literature?*, trans. Bernard Frechtman (Secaucus, N. J.: Citadel Press, 1972), p. 37.
12. One must not allow intellectuals to play with matches:
    Quand on le laisse seul
    Le monde mental
        ment
    Monumentalement (Prévert)
    When one leaves it alone/ the mental world/ lies/ monumentally.
13. Jean Cocteau, *Le Secret professionnel*.
14. *Le Grand Recueil*, Méthodes.
15. "Contemplation et experience esthétique," in the special issue of the *Revue d'Esthétique*, July–December 1962, p. 238.
16. Revault d'Allones, "Technique et langage de la musique concrète," in *Journal de Psychologie*, 4, 1963. This article is an admirable introduction to the study of modern music.
17. See Françoise Choay, "Industrie et batiment," in "L'Architecture actuelle dans le monde," a special issue of the *Revue d'Esthétique*, July–December 1962.
18. Otto, "Construction legère et architecture," ibid., p. 328.
19. Ibid, p. 276.

8. Philosophy and Literature

The affinity between philosophy and literature has become more pronounced in our time, and it appears that existentialist philosophy has brought about a new understanding between them. In this regard we need only think of such figures as Gabriel Marcel, Sartre, Camus, and Bataille. Following the example of Alain, the philosopher not only refers to literature, in which he searches for his inspiration, but also attempts to express himself simultaneously through formal treatises and through the play or novel. Thus the barriers that French education, true to a set of strictly rational tenets, had erected between literature and philosophy have gradually been broken down.

This new alliance could perhaps only have been practiced by an existential philosophy, which, moreover, · renewed the tradition of its antecedents Pascal, Rousseau, and Nietzsche. It was a fact necessary to reveal the hidden relation between philosophical reflection and aesthetic creation: philosophy is now conscious of revealing itself by a voluntary act that is basically the same as the creative act of the artist. Philosophizing is neither a simple classroom exercise nor a blissful meditation upon an objective and absolute truth. It is an act of engagement and self-evaluation: for philosophy is true insofar as the philosopher himself is true, that is, authentically present in his work; even if philosophy in principle belongs to all, truth cannot be anonymous, and the sole means of encompassing or approaching it must primarily be, without reservation, self-initiated. It is thus by no means a betrayal but an act of faithfulness if the philosopher finds in philosophy a means of self-expression. But when he has made this discovery, how could he not be moved by all compelling forms of expression offered in literature, and in politics as well? Moreover, as he asserts himself he asserts a world that is consistent with him and borrows from him its structure and meaning; and why not give this world, embedded in abstraction, a fuller and more expressive countenance? Aesthetic creation may exemplify philosophical creation. Nevertheless, the two creative acts differ in one respect: the act of the philosopher is always incomplete and philosophy is always open-ended. Even when it is systematically organized, it has always returned to the very beginning, the veils close as soon as we glance behind them. In contrast, the artwork is complete, even if a hidden demand remains unfulfilled and thereby calls for another act: then he begins an "other" work, entirely new and different. The philosopher would delight in being able to find such a terminus! The Sisyphean task is sometimes exhausting for one who by no means views his task as absurd.

We can propose a number of reasons that, from the standpoint of the philosopher, justify and account for his recent alliance with literature. But we wish to pose here a more general question: What services does literature render to philosophy, and how are these fulfilled?

Let us sketch out the initial theme of our inquiry: literature straightforwardly offers what philosophy unsuccessfully struggles to attain, that is, the expression of a singular presence of man and the human world, a total meaning that would not evade us as we speak it. Philosophy indeed devotes itself to the basic task of seizing what we can call human essences. Now these essences, especially when they assume an ethical character such as freedom, conscience, faith, and love, admit of a fundamental deficiency: they cannot bring about objective knowledge, communicable and of universal value. On the one hand, these essences are deprived of any obligatory meaning: they only achieve full meaning through my echo and if I agree to live them as I think them. Just as colors are meaningless to a blind man, love has no appropriate meaning for the misanthrope who is closed to it, nor does freedom have a meaning for a fatalist who does not heed the unconditional demand of the "for-itself." The blind man may construct a theory of colors and the misanthrope one of love, but neither one can account for the original fact, for the direct experience—perhaps inexpressible—of colors or love, which concerns philosophy. On the other hand, the very status of essence itself is here uncertain. Can I speak in general terms of what exists only in the particular; of freedom when it is the subject alone that is free in his own way, of one human nature when there are many irreducible individualities? There is surely no essence of freedom, so to speak, since freedom does not coincide with any act that grounds it, yet it remains the foundation of all essence; it can be described only by focusing upon its singularity. And if it is true that freedom permeates all human actions, perhaps the destiny of every human essence is to disappear, to prepare or restore the experience of truth, *Erlebnis der Wahrheit*, and then to fade beside the singular act that it could merely indicate, the act by which there is an essence: beyond imagination, the act through which a consciousness gives rise to the imaginary or is trapped in it; beyond memory, the act through which consciousness descends into the past; beyond reason, the act through which a consciousness tries to synthesize a torn and incomplete world in which it is immersed. This careful description in all respects aims at substituting for the essence an act that grounds it, and that no longer has an essence because it is constitutive and not constituted, particular and not universal. (This remark, we note in passing, does not entail an attack on the legitimacy and validity of an eidetic. For it remains true that these incomplete essences are accessible to a direct look [*un regard direct*], and it is precisely to such a look that they reveal themselves as inadequate in displaying that their weakness is constitutive of their structure. At the very moment of speaking of freedom, I know that freedom is always someone's freedom and that my conception of it is but one approach. Since freedom characteristically yields only to approximate views, as long as it is not seized upon in its singularity, the knowledge I have of it is adequate at the very moment it appears to me as incomplete. And this is sufficient foundation for phenomenological enterprises.)

Moreover, even if human essences tend to sink into the singularity of the act, there is perhaps a need to rehabilitate them. But it was fitting to initiate proceedings against them initially in order to understand how we are led by the course of philosophy to invoke the concrete and singular presence of man, so that philosophy itself projects us into the domain of literature. Indeed, literature avoids the double flaw of philosophical knowledge, the inability to reach the singularity of self and the need for my complicity in awakening an echo or an appeal in me. First, literature always describes a singular being—Phaedra, Julien Sorel, Lamartine, or Rimbaud—for it is only around himself that the poet stages his production. Literature speaks to us of this unique being, its destiny, its world. The novel or the play does not attain the level of art as long as the characters do not appear inimitable, being enclosed in an undefinable singularity. Bardeche has stated that the overall development of Balzac's writing consists in the passage from an individualized type such as the hero, the traitor, or the young lover, to the typified individual such as Père Goriot or Vautrin. One can perhaps observe a parallel development in the transformation of the worlds of a literary genre—the pastoral, the courtly novel, the epic—into the particular world that bears the mark and name of an author—the world of Corneille or of Proust. Secondly, through its inherent power of suggestion, literature compels us to identify ourselves with the beings it depicts, and to live within their world. Philosophy can scarcely arouse this reverberation in us, and it has no right to do so, since its task is to reach us by the sober paths of intellectual understanding, and not to move us. Literature moves us immediately by poetic incantation, the illusion of theatrical representation, or by novelistic enchantment. Thus, the individual and his universe are immediately present to me.

They are an eloquent, luminous, irrefutable presence in which I am totally involved: I see directly what philosophy, in the final analysis, can only indicate.

But before considering how these presences become meaningful and instructive, we ought to address a preliminary objection. How can we assert that literature confronts us with a presence if the artwork is imaginary? It seems that Sartre's analyses are correct and that, indeed, the aesthetic object is unreal. It would be of little use to confront them with Alain's analyses, to which Sartre would agree, upon the substantial and full character of the work. For this perfection characterizes the work's material (*matière*), whereas we are concerned with its content, for which the material is but the medium, as photography is for a recent memory that is evoked through it. In the theater the performer is real, as are the staging, lighting, script, and dialogue; but Phaedra is not real, rather, she is an absolute being whom I focus upon through the actress, and for whom the actress, possessed by her role, is but the interpreter. Likewise, in the poem I focus upon an absolute type of Herodias or a young Parca who are offered to me in words, but as if they came from elsewhere to become embodied and visible within these verses; for they seem to enjoy an independent existence outside the poem, since I could experience and recognize them in a particular young girl at the side of the road. Thus the aesthetic object is unreal, but also a thing. "A thing which is before me, which endures, which remains," says Sartre; an unreal thing, but this time the thingness seems to prevail over the unreality. This imaginary world is capable of overcoming the real world. Thus I am not at all taken in by the material; I assign it its role as medium, and I proceed through it to confront the aesthetic object. This object, although affected by an element of unreality, is nonetheless present in the most convincing fashion. It is spared the imperfections deeply affecting the ordinary imagination, such as its essential poverty. It is rather a solid, vibrant, and meaningful object; I can observe, consider, compare it with others, and form a dialogue with it. It admits of enough density, indistinctness, and opacity so that I often have the impression that it is not entirely comprehensible and there is always something left unsaid. And so I can always return to it for I know that it will always be there for reexamination.

Why does aesthetic fiction have this privilege? Undoubtedly because of the intimate involvement of the unreal in the actual work through which it is given. If I sit in my study and merely conjure up Phaedra, her image is produced by a spontaneous act of my consciousness; and from this stems its fragility, wretchedness, and ambiguity. I create only a phantom, but Racine created a work. In the theater the image of Phaedra is imposed upon me, though certainly in order to apprehend it I have to assume a certain attitude, otherwise I see only the actress among the flats in a downtown Paris playhouse. But I am somehow compelled to adopt this image-forming attitude: Marie Bell, the scenery, the entire room completely enrapture me. Likewise, the verses of the young Parca are not given to me as verse, that is, an "exercise" in prosody, but rather as the vehicle for a vision: in light of this vision of the young Parca and her adventure, they disappear. All that concerns me—but decisively—is to acquiesce in the enchantment. But the real created by art is at the service of the unreal, and continuously sustains it; everything contributes to this enchantment during the aesthetic experience. In brief, an exceptional material sustains an equally exceptional unreality.

In order better to understand the privilege of art, and without exhaustive consideration of the tactics invented by each literary genre, we must consider the function that language assumes. Philosophy speaks, whereas literature names. Literature restores the primordial task of the word, which is to cause Being to appear before us and immediately present the phenomenon to us instead of waiting for it to be revealed in an ever-confused and equivocal perception. Ordinary language uses the word to speak, that is, to say something other than what it says. Whenever I say "the meadows are green," that means, depending on the context and intention, either these meadows need mowing, or it has rained recently, or green is a soothing color. This is because I am always occupied with some activity, involved in some project, and referred to some other thing. For the creatures of necessity that we are, always concerned with reacting or filling a void, the use of signs is to drive us toward signified things announced by, but distinct from, these signs. We have invented signals in which the distance between the sign and the thing signified is the infinite space of an arbitrary social convention; and we use words as signals as well. We have invented the idea of appearance because we are used always to look for something behind what is manifest to us. And so we must make an effort, when confronting a face or a landscape, to understand that the thing expressed is within the expression itself, as anger in contorted features, or majesty in mountains. Philosophy bids us to become again capable of wonder and innocence, to read the essence directly "on" the phenomenon. But philosophy itself is unable to exemplify this, as it cannot merely indicate but must rather substantiate what it sees. This is why philosophy works round, disputes, and refutes as much as it affirms; it cannot immediately express what it has to convey, and attempting to do so, it uses language that still risks betraying its intention. It uses lifeless words, which, in order to be universally valid and acceptable, have no more than an abstract signification.

These words convince, but do not show. They do not carry their significance within themselves, like an inner flame that would render them transparent. Instead, they still return me to the thing signified, as to a remote object that I cannot fully encompass. Philosophical language cannot produce the phenomenon it describes: when the description is thorough, the phenomenon is elucidated, but it is still not present. Perhaps, in truth, the reader was from the outset intuitively aware of the phenomenon, but the philosophical endeavor requires that the philosopher blithely pursue his analysis to the end. But we can once again conceive that he is inclined toward another language, such as that of the poet or novelist. Indeed when the poet says, "The meadows are green," these meadows unfold before me and I am transfixed by them. Kant has made us aware that aesthetic feeling is disinterested; I suspend my needs and quell my anxiety. When I attain to this pure moment of disinterestedness, I am completely present in the presence of the beautiful. Is this to say that my thought is empty because it is free of memories and expectations? Yes, but the presence evoked by the word is enough to replenish this void. The green of the meadow, along with all its suggestions, affective qualities, and symbolic value, is immanent in my representation. I live out these green meadows, all is given to me immediately, without further elaboration. The word itself embodies and brings to me a complete presence. Thus when Corneille's Augustus projects "I am the master of myself as of the universe,"[1] his freedom in the face of his own destiny is completely given to me. A single word that names reveals to me all that the endless enterprise of the philosopher can merely suggest. This represents the magic of words; it is easily understood how Claudel could assign an almost priestly vocation to the poet: he collaborates with the creator, and rivals him in his own power of naming and of consecrating every creature by naming it.

If the presence if the aesthetic object may offer these promises and motivates the philosopher, it must be more than dazzling, it must be meaningful. Now, can a presence be meaningful without indicating something other than itself, or furnishing a commentary or exegesis, or referring to some knowledge? In brief, without ceasing to be entirely a presence? How can we understand the immanence of meaning in presence? The poet or novelist at first sight is not concerned with meaning, for he presents enigmas rather than solutions; the beings he evokes have the density and opacity of things. He plays the part of a natural and immediately successful phenomenology, respecting the very character of the phenomenon, which is to render mute the one who experiences it. The green meadows, Augustus's freedom are there before me, without my being able to say anything about them other than what the poet has said once and for all. This presence is laden with meaning, but this meaning consists of being a presence, that is, something that inclines me to a certain attitude; what is required of me is to assume this attitude or experience it: I am what I see, my comprehension is absolute, without concept or knowledge. I do not know the green of the meadows or Augustus's freedom as the physicist or psychologist may know it, but I am in harmony with them and experience them in my own depths. I am completely a reflection of the phenomenon; my assurance is invincible and my feeling is infallible. Thus the meaning of the literary language is, so to speak, that it has no meaning; it does not designate a concept, it generates an object. Alain calls this absolute language, of which he finds the primary models in dance and ritual: these activities reinstate the primitive role of the sign, which is by no means to transmit meaning, but rather to summon a response. I respond to this sign, which cuts me to the core by echoing my experience; I do not have to understand, but only to be: being in accordance with the sign and as born by it is already understanding.

What is the significance of this meaning immediately felt because it is identified with presence? It is not developed at the moment I experience it; it is as a light that is not revealed by some shadow; it is not reflected on concepts, it does not call for reflection. In this regard we go beyond Husserl's adage "Return to the things themselves," for we are already within the things. But this is plenitude and not delusion. We are immersed in a meaning that is all the richer because it is undifferentiated! An attempt in explaining this meaning would call up sensibility as well as understanding, for the object is present to us with both its conceptual structure and its affective qualities. Both feeling and representation are germinal in aesthetic contemplation. Augustus's freedom is a freedom that I could understand and formulate, but at the same time adopt or refuse, like or dislike. Moreover, the structure of the object retains its ambivalence because its expression is strictly immanent to it; these green meadows *are* tranquillity or innocence, these mountains majesty, this freedom an upsurgence. Metaphor is not founded upon analogical reasoning, but upon the actual being of the object. The correspondences that the poet invokes are not laboriously established associations among heterogeneous terms but a manner of being of the object, immediately felt and evident,[2] and this is why the figurative sense and the literal sense are inseparable. This is sufficient to deflect every empiricist or materialist attempt to reconstruct a world of moral essences from a pregiven world of material essences. The world of majesty, freedom, unbiased justice is given to me at the same time and in the same way as the physical world, which science chooses as its object. Let us insist upon this: the problem of metaphor is not easily dismissed.

We must admit that the aesthetic object—and perhaps every object that is revealed in naive perception—is imbued with aesthetic and affective qualities composing its expression. It is perhaps on this condition that the object is *for me*, and capable of both questioning and answering me; this is why, as Bachelard says, the world is beautiful before being true. Is this a type of anthropomorphism? No, for I do not place a human mask on a primarily inhuman face of things; rather, these things offer themselves to my look as parts of the universe, speaking my language, having some affinity with me and some complicity in my project. They are intelligible not only to the intellect but to the totality of my being. The world is known (*con-nu*) because it rings (*con-sonne*). The in-itself is not irremediably estranged from the for-itself. This is how I read freedom in this act, justice in these words, love in this look, as well as pride in these pines and serenity in the music of Bach. Here we undoubtedly come upon a metaphysical question exceeding the limits of our study, and that can only be provisionally formulated: On what conditions can the world speak to me in a language? How is it that the world harbors this secret affinity with human essences? How is it that things also have the same affinity between themselves to the extent that they become identical, since I can speak of a harsh tone or a loud color? We should ask ourselves, then, what is meant by a unity of the world previous to its bursting forth into objects, and perhaps even before the in-itself and the for-itself were differentiated: can it be conceived after the body in which the in-itself and the for-itself appear precisely to coalesce, or is it necessary to employ the idea of creation and transcendence?

In any case, be it metaphorical or not, a meaning is immanent in the presence of the aesthetic object, and this is why literature in particular seems to fulfill the philosophical project. Nevertheless, this object is an unreality, albeit a privileged one, in literature at least.[3] Thus two questions are again raised. One of principle: Is fiction able to teach me about reality? And one is of fact: How is this possible? How do we effect the passage from fiction to reality? We partially answered the first question when we demonstrated that the unreality expressed by the object competes with reality in composing an almost viable world that at least remains sound as long as one does not, as did Don Quixote, subject it to the test of action. In addition we have to mention that the real occasionally rivals or mimics the unreal. We live in a cultural world, where real men learn feelings and virtues from the theater or in the novel. If we recognize Phaedra in a certain enamored woman, she has perhaps read Racine and lives in a world imbued by him. The imaginary is not merely a means of escape but also a collection of role models. But we must still examine by what right the imaginary informs me about the real as well as it informs reality. How can Phaedra teach me about love? At the heart of this prosaic world in which I call a spade a spade, how can a woman be an autumn sky? How is literature capable of a truth that may be its own—the truth of a dream—but the truth of the real world? The answer has to be sought both within the writer and within the reader. It can be said that the writer deliberately desires the truth of his work, but this is not entirely the case. If he truly is a writer, a poet, or a novelist, and not a reporter or psychologist—as Jules Romains is at times—he is seized himself by his fiction. If he is conscious of himself as creator, he does not care whether he be truthful or posit proofs or theses. He lets his characters speak, or the character he is himself as poet; they are in seach of a truth and sometimes seize upon it, but this is *their* truth, uniquely created by them, which is only true in this respect. Nevertheless, is this truth of the characters incommensurable with that of their creator, is this truth in fiction incommensurable with the truth in reality? No, for the imaginary in this case is a created imaginary, as we have said, and consequently cloyed with human sap—primarily because the author, at the moment when he was captivated and inspired by his fiction, unwillingly nourished it with his personal experience and his actual history as a real subject immersed in a real world. By contact with its creator, through an inevitable osmosis, the fiction becomes replenished with him, his humanity, and his era. For this reason Balzac and Malraux are for history valuable witnesses, and reciprocally, the worlds of Balzac and Malraux attest to the personality of their creators. Possibly, this is true of all imagination.

Tell me what you imagine and I will tell you who you are: such is the catch-phrase of psychoanalysis, searching for the meaning of dreams because they are laden with human experience. But the testimony of the aesthetic imaginary is incomparably more solid, because it is carried by a work, an *analogon* that is not uncertain and fleeting, but slowly and patiently formed with materials themselves laden with meaning—that is, words. This labor, necessary for the creation of the artwork, and not a battery of proofs, guarantees the truth of the imaginary. A work is primarily true insofar as it is self-sufficient and complete, forming a homogeneous and articulated totality—an Idea, as Hegel would say; it is a perfect object, rooted in and harmonizing with the real world in the same way as a rustic church is consonant with the thatched roofs of cottages, the voice with the throat, the rhythm with respiration. Nothing misleads, nothing beguiles, an end point can be fixed. Now, because the work is thus true, the image it generates must also be true; not fictionally but absolutely. This woman truly is an autumn sky because the poet says so in impeccable verse. (For if the verse were bad, it would no longer be true.) The unreal has weight in the real because the work itself is real, and it is true because the work is true.

But how can I know this truth? To experience a presence with a feeling of absolute understanding and to verify a truth by cognitive reflection are two quite different things. How do we reflect upon the imaginary? To reflect upon one's dream is to wake up. For reflection here implies a revolution: I must break the spell and regain control of the categories of reality; but as soon as I am reflecting, the imaginary fades. Nevertheless, the aesthetic imaginary still is privileged. While I cannot treat it exactly as a reality, I can at any instance return to the real without losing it as Orpheus did Eurydice. I can as well remain under the spell and simply live the presence that offers itself to me, or take a distance and reflect upon it. I am able to pass—in effect, I continuously pass—from the image-forming attitude to the rational one (in what Kant calls the reconciliation of the imagination and understanding), because the imaginary is in this case a presence that by no means depends on my spontaneity, and because the work bridges imagination and understanding. Whenever I am reading a novel, I am captivated; I participate in, I move along with the narrative, with the novel's internal temporality. But at the same time I can reflect, come back to myself and my own duration, call up in an instant my knowledge, without completely breaking the spell or losing sight of the imaginary; whether I stop or return to my reading, the work remains, guardian of the image. If I want to understand a dream, I wake up because all of its material resides in some bodily convulsions, some unconscious desires and blurred perceptions: no confrontation is possible between its closed world and the perceived world. But if I want to understand my reading, I can remain within the world of the novel or poem and confront it with the real world; the work permits me to keep a distance and verify its meaning without losing it.

The aesthetic world can be both lived and reflected upon—lived as an unreality, reflected upon as a testimony to reality. It is not a poor relation of the perceived world. I can exhaust the meaning of its presence.

In answering our first question, we have also partially answered our second. The literary object instructs us through its continuous movement from meaning felt in presence to meaning explicated by reflection. The only problem remaining is to discover how this information can assume universal signification and teach us about human nature or the world. For the privilege of literature, from the philosopher's standpoint, is to reach and manifest a singularity in which essence is consumed. Augustus's freedom is not Don Juan's, nor is Julien Sorel's ambition Rastignac's; the love of Tristan and Isolde is not that of Amphitryon and Alcmene, nor is the majesty of the Alps that of the Pyrenees, nor is the tragic of Rouault that of Delacroix. Can we understand what is unique in each of these experiences without referring to a general notion that clarifies them through subsumption? Let us first observe that the singular ways of an individual, though claiming originality, are always impregnated with objectivity and therefore definable by an essence. My own freedom appears to me not only as a unique freedom of a unique self, but as a freedom of which I am able to speak and which others are able to recognize. I am compelled to live an intersubjective existence (we know how Husserl used this idea). The gaze of the other as well as my own gaze when it mimics that of a stranger, compels me to objectivity. Moreover, my corporeal and historical condition immerses me in an objective world and I participate in the destiny of things, which is to become generalized and valid for all. Not that I make myself a thing; I could be it, but I refuse. Yet, from the very fact that I have intercourse with things, even if it is only to give them a meaning and to assert myself as irreducible to their status, I somehow participate in their nature: I am myself, but I am also a man, because I live in a world populated by men and things; and what is mine can be valuable to and extended to others, even what is most specifically mine, such as my freedom, my faith, my destiny. The essence of the individual is not a singular essence.

We can arrive at this idea by another route. Individual acts as literature displays them are reflected acts, or at least always amenable to reflection. Phaedra loves; that is, she has a certain enamored way of speaking to Hippolytus, thinking of him and judging the world according to his presence or absence; but at the same time she knows herself as lover and defines her love as painful, guilt-ridden, and ill-fated. Julien Sorel is ambitious, but at the same time continuously asks himself, "Am I ambitious as one ought to be?" Gide's Lafcadio, Malraux's Tchen, Bernard of *The Waves* want to be free according to their own conception of freedom, but what they conceive surpasses them. Thus there is a love, an ambition, a freedom that are the standards for every particular love, ambition, and freedom. There is a human nature. Reflecting upon oneself, one assumes a general essence through a particular act, one lives in his own way a universal destiny, one locates man in himself and takes man as a guide. One is a man in assuming the being of *the* man. So it is not suprising that literature discloses universal essences since, implicit or not, they are constantly defined by characters who take them as standards. And if they were not, we would define them when reading. As soon as this reading is reflective, and aims at understanding, we confront the characters with essences, and that is how we verify their singularity. Similarly, whenever I break away from the spell of the music in which I became Mozart's joy, I confirm the singularity of this joy in relation to the general idea I have of joy. I also confirm that this woman is an autumn sky or this mountain majestic, in relation to a certain idea I have of woman or majesty. The work itself, shaped by words, invites me to invoke these ideas. For the world itself substantiates knowledge, even when it is returned to its primordial function, which is, as we have seen, to name.

This type of analysis provokes many questions. We must admit that the intelligent understanding of a literary work implies a previous knowledge of human essences; that is, a veritable a priori. Moreover, this knowledge, like the Kantian a priori, is revealed and works only in an experience. For I know these human essences only in relation to a particular person or myself; and reciprocally, I know the singularity of a person only in relation to man in general. Similarly, on the ethical plane, I am a unique being only in identifying myself with man, and I undertake this only by assuming my singularity and not in living an inauthentic life oriented by anonymous models. I can thus discover human essences in the singular portraits offered by literature if I already have a priori knowledge of these essences. I cannot proceed by inference. For in order to be man one does not need to know the essence of a table, horse, or electron; he will learn gradually about it through empirical experience. On the contrary, man is man only through knowing himself as such, through a primordial knowledge. Indeed, literature can additionally aid us in this knowledge, since it presents fulfilled beings whose message is unequivocal and whose history is complete: here everything is said perfectly. But let us repeat, literature tells us about a singular being and we understand it only if we already possess a complete idea of man, that is, an unelaborated philosophy. I see man and his world only through what I know, and I know as soon as I see. The concern of literature is to have me see, to present me with what is more clear and precise than the object immersed in the world. The concern of philosophy is to make me aware of the knowledge through which my look is informed, and thereby the literary object meaningful.

We thus emerge at the antipodes of our point of departure. We wanted to demonstrate what literature does for philosophy, and now we find that literature is incomprehensible without philosophy, or at least without an implicit and universal philosophy by which everyone has some idea of "man." It is thus easily understood that in response to the question how is literature possible, we could furnish among other answers the following: on condition that it be clarified by philosophy.

Notes

1. Corneille, *Cinna*, act 5, scene 3.
2. One can easily see here the essential difference between philosophy and literature. Pascal writes: "Man is a thinking reed." The image is premeditated and contrived in order to express a clear meaning, which neutralizes the image. For I am not going to imagine a reed. It is enough that I know that a reed is feeble, a fact that Pascal wants me to consider, for he adds: "a reed, the most feeble thing in all nature." After which I must come to understand that this powerless being nevertheless has the capacity for thinking. But I have no need to dwell upon the image of a reed that thinks. I do not carry this image to its term. I do not think of the reed, but of man in terms of the reed; it is the man who is simultaneously feeble and capable of thought. The image is thus there only to captivate me, but without exaggeration, which would commit me to nonsense. The image fascinated me for a moment—that is, as long as I was tempted to evoke a reed—but I had to abandon this fascination: allowing the image to become fixed would have betrayed its meaning. It is thus that the language of prose can communicate with that of poetry, but without assuming its character. And where, on the other hand, does poetry lead? Baudelaire writes: "You are a beautiful autumn sky, clear and pink." Here I am not invited to understand, that is, to confront two distinct notions such as the man and the reed. I am required to recognize a profound identity: the verb "to be" admits of a precise exigency; with Pascal, it indicated an analogy, whereas with Baudelaire it affirms a community of substance. The woman he speaks of is truly an "autumn sky." It would be ludicrous to try to explain this image, and nevertheless it is true: I feel it, and now it is of little importance that my understanding be confused. The presence of the object, which imposes itself on me with this old structure, and the assent of my whole being are sufficient guarantee.
   poetry lead? Baudelaire writes: "You are a beautiful autumn sky, clear and pink." Here I am not invited to understand, that is, to confront two distinct notions such as the man and the reed. I am required to recognize a profound identity: the verb "to be" admits of a precise exigency; with Pascal, it indicated an analogy, whereas with Baudelaire it affirms a community of substance. The woman he speaks of is truly an "autumn sky." It would be ludicrous to try to explain this image, and nevertheless it is true: I feel it, and now it is of little importance that my understanding be confused. The presence of the object, which imposes itself on me with this old structure, and the assent of my whole being are sufficient guarantee.
3. Perhaps even natural beauty—a fjord or a sunset—is also an object rendered unreal through my contemplation. Reflection upon the aesthetic object has to meet this problem.

9. The Phenomenological Approach to Poetry

MANY approaches to poetry are conceivable. Indeed many are practiced—historical, sociological, psychological, psychoanalytic, formalist, semiological, for example. I would like to show here that the phenomenological approach is privileged. In a nutshell, the aim of the phenomenological approach is to describe the live experience of poetry and to bring out the meaning of poems revealed in the experience. I do not want to say, by calling the phenomenological approach privileged, that it should exclude others. The dogmatic proposal of any one method seems futile to me. Every kind of knowing is in process, not only because of its historicity but also because of the inexhaustibility of its object, which imposes a multiplicity of *Abschattungen*. As for poetry, every step of its process opens up to phenomenology. First, because the phenomenology of poetry lets us take hold of, if not define, the poeticalness of poetry. And second, because a phenomenology of poetry leads to an ontology, and thus provides a foundation for other interpretations.

There are two fundamental questions in the consideration of poetry: What is poetry, and who decides what poetry is. Scientists answer that poetry is a datum in human cultures. And since poetry is an object of knowledge, it is our privilege to determine what it is. This approach, perfectly legitimate and fruitful, is both eidetic and empiric. Eidetic because any research should be guided by some theory. And there must be a theory that defines poetry. Such definitions, the production of the concept, are—as the French say—somewhat the result of the study. Jakobson says that the science of literature is not so much interested in literary works as in the literariness of the works. Similarly, the science of poetry looks for poeticalness. It elaborates a method whose efficacy is measured by its ability to identify the poetic object. The semioticians call this a grammar of poetry. And quite evidently the theory is presupposed, as an hypothesis, at the beginning of research. To determine the formal properties of an object, we have to circumscribe the field where the object is to be found. We have to have some idea at least, if not a clear concept, of what poetry is. Actually, this choice is not difficult. In all literate cultures there is a tradition that tells us where to find poetry and who the poets are. And so the scientists go to the present tradition. They acknowledge the authority of what sociologists call the "instances of legitimation" in our field of interest. They study Shakespeare and Baudelaire. They do what Aristotle recommended, they commit themselves to the judgments of experts.

Now all this is all right, as long as we are aware that there is some danger in accepting tradition and the ideology that goes with it, as long as we do not trust them blindly. There are a good many studies today that alert us against dogmatically accepting the tradition. But this leaves us open to a relativistic perspective. Is it possible to hold on to such a relativism and still search for an essence? I think it is, on condition that we do not look for the essence in the grammar of a given corpus but in the *Erlebnis* of the poetic in poems or even in nature, or in what Valery called "the poetic state."

Laying out areas of reflection or research as outlined here has some shortcomings. First, concerning the poems themselves. It tends to leave a whole area unexplored. It seems to settle for a poetry that is too narrow, one that is without danger, more or less tamed, conformist, both good and pleasant. It would exclude the poetry of the fringes—and not only the poetry of the masses and the culturally deprived, who often make unfortunate attempts to imitate great poetry, but also the poetry of the madmen, or rebels and such. This is of concern because the periphery is possibly the place where poetry is most intensely made and lived, just because there are no academic norms that rule it and propose deference rather than enjoyment. The experience of poetry by the unsophisticated just might be the most faithful to its essence.

Second, literary scholarship does not pay much attention to how poetry is experienced. There are, of course, studies by physiologists and psychoanalysts that deal with the reading of poetry. But what the semioticians are looking for when they change a poem into an object of knowledge is its structure, its anatomy. Anatomists work on corpses, and here the skeleton is an abstraction. This abstraction has proved useful for the study of a given language. As Saussure has pointed out, a language is made out of differences. The phoneme is a distinctive unity, its features are pertinent only as opposed to others. Even for the signifying unities, the monemes, their meaning is defined by a process of differentiation.

Semiotics, inspired by structural linguistics, seeks out the interplay of differential elements in the poem, hoping to discover a grammar that, proceeding from a finite set of elements and rules, could generate an indefinite set of poetic objects. Some principles have been presented as tools for examining poetry along this line. One such principle has been proposed by Greimas in terms of the isomorphic relation of expression and content, which tries to show sense as immanent to sound. But Greimas admits that however sophisticated the segmentation and the systematization of the two levels may be, it is not possible to find a one-to-one correspondence between phonetic and semantic segments in poetic discourse. The same must be said for Jakobson's famous definition of the poetic function—the projection of the principle of equivalence from the axis of selection into the axis of combination, the promotion of equivalence to the constitutive device of the sequence. And hence the systematic analysis of contiguous similarities, reiterations, or regularities (and also of dissimilarities meant to frustrate our expectations) through all the technical feats of verse such as rhyme, assonances, alliterations, and so on. But, as a disciple of Greimas says, "no continuous discourse bearing on a whole poem, even a short one, has ever been able to begin to demonstrate this principle of equivalence." He proposes looking for analogies between different levels of poetic discourse. And this probably brings us back to the search for isomorphisms.

We must recognize, however, that the structuralist approach has inspired some very enlightening comments on certain poems. The study of Baudelaire's sonnet, "*Les Chats*," by Jakobson and Levi-Strauss comes to mind. But it can be shown that even such a study is truly penetrating only when, let us say, by an imperceptible shift it reaches an intuition, a kind of empathetic reading. Even with a good structuralist, if he is not an intelligent lover of poetry, his comments will not be of much help in understanding and enjoying poetry.

It is certainly interesting to develop the grammar of a language because we like to know the rules according to which grammatical sentences are generated, so we might understand and produce them. For the same reason we examine a grammar of poetry to know how a poem is generated, somewhat as a sonata is composed or a palace built. Such information helps in understanding structural practice and in explaining why a work looks the way it does. As a matter of fact, "*les arts poétiques*" were structuralist long before scientific and normative structuralism showed up. But poeticalness does not depend only on grammatical rules. We know that the poeticalness of a landscape or a face, which is not metaphorical, does not. And neither does the poeticalness of poetry. The rules may have been ignored or surpassed. They always are when genuine creation is producing novelty. And in any case, rules do not exhaust the poetic function. If we hope to grasp the poeticalness of a poem, we have to consider the effect the structure produces.

Before considering this effect, we should note that, as such, it must be experienced by a consciousness or a subject. Not until it is experienced does it exist, even if the structured object exists. We might say that not only the meaning but the very being is in the use. And in examining the effect as aesthetic object, we must also take into consideration a reader—not a critic or scientist, but a common reader. Ingarden distinguishes the aesthetic attitude, which makes the work into an aesthetic object, and the critical attitude, which sees the work only as a work. But even "common readers," owing to individual cultures, do not all have the same attitudes. And so a sociology of the work-as-experienced and of the ideology of art has something to say here, even though a certain permanent core in the work and a certain identity of the human race attenuate the divergencies. Our turning to the reader indicates that the phenomenological approach to poetry, like any phenomenological task, is concerned with both the noetic and the noematic, and that it follows these two paths to the point where they merge in the no-man's-land of the pre-real of savage being.

Let us consider first the noema, the poem. It is experienced and so enacted, made actual, when it is read, read aloud. A silent reading just does not do justice to a poem. Poetry is realizing its true, originary life when it is recited in the midst of an audience, and sometimes even taken up in chorus as at the *Nuits de la Poésie* in Montreal. We should perhaps not forget that in many ancient cultures, even after the invention of writing, it was forbidden to write poems. They were only recited, or rather sung, sometimes to the accompaniment of musical instruments. And because they were entrusted to the memory of trained singers, mnemotechnical devices, which justify the principle of equivalence and delight the structualist chorus, were employed.

Quite evidently in such recitations or singing, the structural skeleton and the sensuous elements are not separated. The words are savored by both reciter and listener. There is not only the ear's passive pleasure but also active pleasure of the mouth, of the organs of speech that dance rhythmically. A muscular delight, if you will. This dancing is like eating, as Ezekiel said. We can add, thinking of Melanie Klein, that eating is also being eaten, and that this ambivalent *objectal* relationship is a way of loving. The whole body is committed to the poem. It plays with the sensuous, which is experienced as totality and fullness. When we analyze this experience, we speak of elements and differences, differences in height and duration and intensity. But what is fundamentally given for our enjoyment is not such things but something irreducible, like the timbre of the sound, which is not experienced as differentiated. What is dancing within us is the flux of the melody.

We have been speaking of poetry here as if it were only music. It indeed is music, but music made of words. And words do not give up their semantic function when they are heard as sounds. Rather, they fulfill this function in a very special way. We know Valéry's remark: "Poetry is a prolonged hesitation between meaning and sound." In our ordinary use of language there is no such hesitation unless we are confused, either in our hearing or because of ignorance of lexical meanings. If you should say to me at party, "may I please have some more gin," I simply give it to you. The message is immediately communicated. Here we reach the meaning directly through the words, as if they were transparent. We pay no attention to them as special sounds. We do not perceive them as signs of a state of mind to be coded and decoded. These words as signs, so familiar that we are not aware of using them, and they are experienced somewhat the way a hammer is felt as part of a hammering arm. However, in the poetic use of language, where we hesitate between meaning and sound, it is the very sound that compels us, can even seduce us. In poetry, words are like things, palpable and tasty as a fruit. The kind of familiarity our body has with them is different. Savoring is not using. But these words that are as things are speaking-things. What about their semantic function? Saying that this speaking is musical should warn us that poetry will not produce something visible, like images. There has been a tyranny of the eye in our culture. Rhetoric has been concerned with what Gaston Bachelard calls "formal imagination." This is imagination of visual forms as opposed to material imagination where imagining is not depicting but rather feeling, as a sculptor playing with clay might feel the emerging of the statue-to-be with his hands. The slogan *ut pictura poesis*, is wrong.

In poetry, sense is totally within the sensuous. The meaning carried by the discourse is not signified, it is expressed. Signification becomes expression. In French, when we press (squeeze) an orange, we say that the juice is "expressed." The orange expresses itself in producing its juice. Likewise, a poem is expressive. It expresses itself in expressing its meaning. If you prefer, the sense surges within the sensuous in the reciting body as perfume surges within a flower in the heat of summer. Poeticalness realizes and actualizes expressivity. Here language is driven back to its origin. Here signs are not yet arbitrary; they somehow imitate the object they refer to and conjure up its presence instead of being merely representational. Onomatopoeia comes to mind here. But expressivity is more subtle than imitation. The sounds imitate and evoke some sensuous properties of the object rather than the object itself. Then too, visual effects coming from the graphics of the word also come into play. This can be seen in an analysis of Genette's "*Jour et Nuit.*"

There is a poetics of language. Words dreams, as Bachelard says. We imagine with the help of words, but words themselves imagine. Poetry exploits this natural poetics. It restores language to its poetic state. And I would say that this is its primitive state, where words name and do not wait to be articulated in a sentence in order to be expressive. A verse is not a sentence. It is itself a word. Mallarmé says, "out of several word-sounds verse creates a total word, new, foreign to the language and somehow incantatory." And we should note that in doing so poetry is not opposed to prose, as rhetoricians contend. Rather, poetry revivifies prose. Prose itself is poetic, and as long as rationality is not their only concern, many of their games of ordinary language are also poetic. Only in strict rational discourse, happily a rare thing, is a literal meaning achieved at the expense of a figurative one. But poetry not only invents new figures, it gives new strength to common figures by calling the reader to a poetic state.

We have been talking of a poetic state of language. Actually, this expression, "poetic state," was invented by Valéry to designate a state of mind. But not the mood, the inspiration of the poet; rather, the mood of the reader. We might say that poetry is inspired when it is inspiring for the reader. To understand the semantic function of poetry, we must go from the poetic noema to the poetic noesis. When I read "O seasons, O castles," it is *for me* that seasons and castles are there. And not in concepts, not even in images, but in words. To clarify this kind of presence, we might think of Kantian schemas. But here the schema is like a disposition of my reciting body, through which I am in harmony with a world. I say "a world" because the nouns in my mouth evoke rather than name. Seasons and castles are not conceptualized objects. They are elements that radiate into a world as all-pervasive perfumes create an atmosphere. In this enchanted world something happens: which soul is faultless? This is not a question. I do not have to answer. Nothing perlocutionary here, Austin would say. Rather, something is asserted: in comparison with this world of beautiful, regulated appearances sketched by the rhythms of seasons and solemnities of castles, every soul is crippled. It is the fault, the nonbeing in the fullness of being.

What about such an assertion? Is it true or false? We know well all the discussions in British philosophy from Russell on about unicorns or Mrs. Bardell. Is poetry referential only because it is an emotional game of language? Certainly, it is emotional. We have failed to stress the participation of the body, since we might well speak, with the help of psychoanalysis, of affects or drives. The sounds of poetic language are not mere phonemes. When my organs of speech move in uttering such sounds, my whole being is moved by them. These moving sounds carry an effective charge that is the same as their semantic charge. Long before psychoanalysis, Mallarmé emphasized this incantatory property of sounds. They give us something to feel before we know. And this "something" makes up the peculiar atmosphere of what I call a "world."

Positivists will say that this world is not *the* world. It is an unreal and subjective world, Mallarmé's world, for example. The poem is nothing but Mallarmé's self-expression. And if we pay attention to this, we are driven into the intentional fallacy. So if we need diversion, we may enjoy the poem as long as we remember that it is nonsense (*Unsinn*). However, phenomenology just cannot agree with this "condemnation." Perhaps poetry comes down to childish prattle, but through such prattle children become aware of their being in the world. How is the world given to us? At first, not in representation, from a distance, but in the experience of presence. Here the subject is still one with the object, our flesh is still symbiosis with the flesh of things: such is originary perceiving.

In the reading of poetry, our incarnate consciousness is in symbiosis with verbal sounds. Through the expressivity of the sounding words we communicate with a world. This expression is revelation. And poetry is true. Truth is understood here, of course, in the Heideggerian sense of *a-letheia*, an uncovering, an unveiling. Its contrary is not falseness but opaqueness, unexpressiveness. True is opposed to false only when a sentence pretends to achieve adequation, to be well formed, and to refer to reality or a determined field of reality. Poetry is not concerned with a presupposed and prefabricated reality. What poetry reveals is a *possible* of reality. It reveals an aspect of what I call the *pre-real* because it is given to us before we are given to ourselves and before the world as external and objective is constituted. The pre-real is the ground on which the real is founded. It becomes real by a process of objectivation, which implies separation and alienation. But it is neither unimportant nor irrelevant that poetry brings us this experience of the pre-real. It reactivates in us the forces of imagination and desire. And the possible worlds it evokes tell us more than rational thinking does about the world we inhabit as perceiving and loving people.

This phenomenological approach of poetry can lead us down two paths. The first path is a metaphysical one. In experiencing the fusing of man and the sensuous we have a presentiment of what the pre-real is. "The poem is of truth," Heidegger says. The very essence of being is unrevealing and founding. But phenomenology invites us to say "nature" instead of "being." Revelation reveals nature. Nature is the night that tends toward light, toward man as poet. And the possible worlds that poetry calls forth witness to the power of this ground, to its *poiesis*. There is poetry because a *poiesis* of nature acts through poets.

The second path, down which a phenomenological approach to poetry leads us, is a political one. Nature lays its own *poiesis* on men. The possible of nature calls for the human *posse*. I can denounce the real not only as constituted but also as instituted. I can change life, which is surely the wish of any revolution and perhaps the ground of every desire. Changing life presupposes a return in the direction of nature as origins, and thus a loosening of the chains of culture. It is possible?

If poetry is a means for such an enterprise, in order to experiment and discover its efficacy, we have to play its game. We have to be taught to play the game, and we are taught by culture. Culture gives directions for the use of poetry, which keeps us from falling into the Russellian dilemma that says discourse must be either rational or nonsense. But this need not trap us in the culturalist fallacy. Poetry can initiate a counterculture, especially when it is popular poetry, enjoyed in marginal places outside academia and its standards. Then, I would suggest, poetic praxis may be revolutionary activity. Poetry is a festival of language. And every festival that is not just ceremonious and ritualistic is a *re*establishment, a *re*-grounding. It is, for a moment, a sort of fraternity with the world and our fellow men. I feel pretty sure that phenomenology—if we bring out its ontological implications—will show itself in complicity with the utopian ideal of cultural revolution as post-Marxism might conceive of it.

10.   Why Go to the Movies?

"I've read all the books, and the flesh is weak." All the same, I was intent on becoming cultured (it's never too late to do the right thing). And I was on the alert, for it quickly became apparent that culture is a privilege that it would be scandalous to claim as one's own, since it mystifies those who have it just as much as those who don't. That's why I was so keen on getting to know the books that denounce culture. I must be given credit for that, for it seems that the authors of those books are actually very cultured, and their works are not easy reading. But the proletarians that read them are even more praiseworthy. Is their flesh weak? I don't know, but I'm not surprised that mine is; before this undertaking, on the whole, I was on pretty good terms with my flesh; anyway, my policy was to place my trust in my flesh, to leave things up to it, and it managed just fine. But now look what's happened: I discover that this familiarity is illusory, that the body is only a sign, or rather, a signifier, and that I was obeying the unconscious logic of the sign every time I had anything to do with it. It's no joke to find out that you can be so mistaken about yourself.

At this very moment . . . yes I'm writing in the first person, I'm talking about myself. What an illusion! I know, it's okay: just as the body is only a sign, so the ego is only a particular agency in a particular place (*topique*)—and not the first or the best established: reputable authors—who themselves are only names, but famous ones—deny that where the id was, there the ego shall be. And anyway, it's been firmly established that the individual is nothing but the product of society, or more precisely, the play in its relations of production. But this is all too much for me (exactly!), and so I'll continue to say "I." Bear with me: we're all trapped in ideology, and ideology is in fact the way the actual individual is produced and presents himself to himself as a subject. Hold on; we should say instead: how he would be produced and how he would present himself to himself if he did exist. For in the final analysis, I don't exist, and all those philosophies of existence have been well and truly misled by ideology.

Be that as it may, I had decided to go to the movies only for entertainment. What a trap I was heading for! Fortunately, just as I was about to join in and play the game of consumer society, I remembered several texts I had recently read. To begin with, how could I decide anything at all? I'm no longer as naive as Spinoza's weathervane, which thinks of itself as moving freely when actually the wind's pushing it. If I thought I wanted to go to the movies, it was only because I was under the influence of fashion or advertising: you have to consume a film as you buy a car, and as a car consumes gas. And if the car consumes gas, it's because it needs to to function. But do *I* really have needs? I only have them because they have been created for me, because the system wants to make use of me. Don't imagine that I'm going to satisfy needs that are the product of an ideological genesis, or that I'm going to let myself be persuaded that I needed movies. I hardly even had a desire to go to the movies, and the word says exactly what it means: "desire" arises in an intersubjective relation—let's says instead, to avoid any reference to the subject—in a social milieu—and it was a pseudodesire, the desire to be like everyone else.

Anyway, why do other people go to the movies? They think they know why; they say they want to kill time, enjoy themselves, see a good film . . . These are stock answers, suggested to them by the opinion polls: the film has to sell itself, so of course customers are given motivations for buying. It's social strategy, as usual. But what an illusion to imagine that one is self-motivated. What self? How on earth could one think and want on one's own, since—it's a fact—there is no self? As for me, I no longer listen to the sirens of ideology trying to convince me that I have one.

The worst illusion of these enthusiasts—that's what they call themselves (they pretend to be infatuated, and their passion gives them a certain status)—is their belief that when they go to the movies they can exercise their judgment, select and appreciate good films. Isn't it obvious that their critical opinions have been suggested to them by all the legitimizing mechanisms functioning in the cultural field? And how do you define a good film anyway? Don't give me that old line about aesthetic value; Voltaire put it very well when he said what's beautiful to the toad is his toad wife. But I am nevertheless prepared to admit that there are sometimes beautiful films: certain very discerning critics says so, and I trust them. But who's the judge of this beauty? Only those fortunate few who have the rare privilege of escaping the clutches of advertising and ideology. I hope I'll be among them one day, but until then I don't want to take any risks. I don't want to join the crowds who see the films as a consumer item, who talk about aesthetic value as if they were capable of appreciating it, and who don't seem to be aware that this value is a value-sign and nothing more. For under the domain of generalized exchange that applies the law of equivalences to all things, nothing is valuable in itself. Do you know which films are considered respectable by those who are perceptive enough to avoid seeing the aesthetic object as an ideologized one? Precisely the ones who renounce the artificial beauty of masterpieces, and who deconstruct film instead of fulfilling it. If you have to go to the movies, don't go looking for an eternal essence of film; at least go and see a nonfilm.

This nonfilm is the film of an nonauthor. For the author doesn't exist, or at any rate he must be effaced, as we have previously said. Why speak of authors? In order to give certain productions a label of quality; since a Fellini or a Picasso will sell well they make you believe that Fellini produced *8½* and *Roma*, and you're quite pleased to go and see a genius's congenial Rome. What you're in fact seeing is the Rome of the system: a Rome determined by a particular ideological condition (the eternal Rome that is dying, where nothing beyond the banal expectations of the tourist could happen, where nothing could disturb the reassuring images). This Rome is also determined by a certain technological state as well as by the state of the film market (there are enthusiasts who, accustomed to a certain style, invest in the price of a ticket just to find this style and to find themselves in its midst once more).

So that's the story: you think you're going to the movies of your own free will and for your own enjoyment, and it's all a trap. They present you with all those beautiful images, but only in order to lure you: while you think you're having a good time, you're actually absorbing the ideology necessary for the reproduction of the relations of production. They conceal historical reality from you, camouflaging it under a facsimile of convention—which is not only tolerable, it's fascinating. Therefore you no longer need to dream, nor do you have the right to do so, since your dreams might be nonconformist. A ready-made dream is given to you, consisting of ready-made fantasms, an agreeable fantasy life that puts you in tune with your unconscious. For of course, you must give your unconscious its due, since you know enough to put demands on it and make demands for it. Movies today provide for your pleasure a veritable house specialty, that is, a perfectly ideologized unconscious.

Moreover, it is not only the content of the film that permeates you with ideology, but also the form, according to the material conditions of its production. I am talking about financial conditions, of course, for the filmmaker does not obtain his millions with impunity. But we must certainly consider the degree of technological development as well. The camera is not the innocent device you think it is, but rather an ideological one. For a long time I thought it was enough just to open one's eyes in order to see; now I understand that sight is not that closely connected to the eye. We are in fact dealing with a perceptual code, and I see only according to the system, or rather, the system sees via me. It's the same thing at the movies, where the camera dictates what I see. For the camera mechanically reproduces the perceptual code handed down since the Renaissance, and its diffuses the ideology of that code—what has been termed the "theology of the third dimension." The Renaissance ideology is still ours today. You think you see things with your own eyes, but do you know whose eyes they really are? They're the king's! It's true that when you take your seat at the movies, at the required distance from the screen, and look at the image produced in the little box, you are sitting on the king's throne. You are invited to play the king, so as to forget the situation assigned to you by the relations of domination.

Taking all this into account, what pleasure would I get out of seeing a film? Even if I were not inhibited by my lucidity, what would this pleasure consist of? A pseudopleasure, at the antipodes of *jouissance*, where desire is realized. For desire cannot be realized, since lack is essential to it. My pleasure would be a fake pleasure—not even the reward you give a good student, but the seductive bribe offered me by the system on condition that I bow down to its demands. So what? Well, I cannot resign myself to being fooled: I prefer to give up movies. Too bad if the flesh remains weak.

We have not been playing the fool without good reason; we wanted the reader to be able to separate the wheat from the chaff. For it is quite obvious that you cannot be too careful in disclosing ideology. Merely being in the world is living a world already always ideologized. The temptation, therefore, is to equate ideology with culture, and all the more because etymology suggests the definition of ideology as any system of representation, anything that is remotely related to ideas. But in the case, two questions arise that the denouncers of ideology too frequently evade: How and why do you locate and denounce this ideology?

If we are inside it, how do we find a neutral spot from which we can talk about it? How do we get out of it? We invent an epistemological break, a critical leap, in the same way as Aristotle invokes a thought about a thought. And it must be true that all consciousness can fold back on itself, reflect upon itself; it is just a matter of changing its intentional object, and changing an object is hardly changing its nature (that is, if you can talk about the nature of a consciousness). Now, shifting from ideology to knowledge—that is, changing our space—would also in some way involve a change of being. Is this possible? Or to put it in another way: Ideology has in the past been equated with the cultural unconscious, as Panofsky puts it, rather than a libidinal unconscious—but that is not really the point here. Well, we would not be able to tell if the unconscious were the whole reality of the psyche; we would not be conscious of it because we would not have a consciousness at all. It is true that since the death of

God, contemporary thought continually invents new ones: just as religion saw only appearance in this world, so the new theologies pledge that the real is "impossible," and instead hypostasize everything within their grasp: id, structure, signifier, reactions of production. Similarly, if ideology were the whole of thought or culture, we would know nothing about it, and no one would fabricate theories about it. Whoever in fact denounces ideology thinks himself immune, and lays claim to the truth: *verum index sui et falsi*. This sense of immunity holds even if he claims that we are all contaminated, even if, at least when he is moralizing, he accuses anti-ideological discourse of being ideological. The concept of ideology is essentially polemical, and there are opponents on all sides. But on what account is the polemicist spared?

True, he may be spared, want to be spared, and even could be, but only on condition that he thinks of ideology without hypostasizing it. To begin with, ideology is definitely an operative concept: it allows us to name and describe certain cultural realities. And the way we make use of this concept is certainly axiological or normative. In order to define the pathological, the physiologist identifies with the patient who wants to get better, and similarly, the man trying to define ideology as essentially linked to the actions of the dominant class identifies with the oppressed. At least, that is what Marx suggests and what makes the concept operative. It is all the more so in that it emphasizes an operation that is itself relegated to a particular function. This function is defined by Althusser as an inherent conservative function of the reproduction of the relations of production. The operation is harder to define. First of all, because we are tempted to locate ideology in contents rather than operations; in what is transmitted via a kind of resigned wisdom, in such ethnic stereotypes as "all Arabs are lazy," in cultural models such as "the woman is the heart of the home," and of course, in precepts of official morality and in norms of good taste: in brief, in all those prejudices forming part of our behavior like a second nature. And ideology works through these contents. But the question is to discover how these prejudices have such authority while remaining unnoticed, to find out what mechanisms produce the ideological effect.

The essence of ideology is to create illusions, disguise the real, and substitute something unreal for it without this substitution being apparent. Barthes reveals this very clearly in showing how contemporary myth—one of the key expressions of ideology—naturalizes the historical, bestowing a character of necessity and eternity on what is actually contingent and debatable: "It goes without saying that . . ." or "It's a matter of course that . . .," for example, "youth passes." Thus by the introduction of false historicity, what could disrupt the system is disarmed and made harmless. Nothing distorts the real more surely than this essentialization, but the illusion is not possible unless some "real" is first given before it is travestied. The operation of ideology does not consist in inventing another "real" but in tampering with the old "real," in making it seem other, in making it say something else. Not only does it transform the object into a sign for the possessor—a distinctive sign of a certain "status," as Baudrillard says—but also into a sign for itself. The Citroën DS 19, at the time of its mass promotion, when Barthes was writing his *Mythologies*, not only signified the social class of its owner but also the power, the elegant sobriety of "automobility." It referred then to a certain lived experience of driving a car. And it is in these terms that we must understand Althusser: Ideology is the system of imaginary representations expressing our lived experience in relation to the world. But this relation to the world is not ideological any more than it is false, any more than the images, desires, and emotions evoked by this relation are false. But it can be falsified, just as our vision can be falsified by means of distoring glass, or our taste by the residue of a past flavor. It is a lie, but one that depends on the truth, on that first truth that situates man in the world. There is thus a relation prior to ideology: a relation to the world that does not deceive (before you deliberately *make* it deceitful), a use-value in objects that becomes sign-value, a quality in objects exposed to adverstising, a beauty in those objects that become status symbols. And we cannot ignore this if we want to understand the efficacy of ideology. If good wine did not make men happy, there is a good chance that they would not drink it. It could nevertheless be said that even the most basic experience is not innocent. The only reason the palate and the ear register and assimilate information is that they are themselves formed by culture; we learn to perceive and taste through our familiarity with multiple codes. But even so, you must admit that these codes are cultural rather than ideological: they *do* help us see, and do not necessarily transmit the vision of the dominant class. Musical dictation, practiced in the days of tonal music, was not part of the ideological model according to which young, well-brought-up girls had to play the piano.

Consequently, we will propose three rules for an antiideological strategy.

The first is to circumscribe clearly the field of ideology; to find out exactly what it is we are combating, what mystification has been imposed by the dominant class (perhaps without its knowledge, without Machiavellianism: to what extent is the dominant class itself dominated by the ideology it harbors? It is a question worth looking at, but we will not attempt to answer it here). Consequently, we must clearly distinguish the mystification itself from what is based on: the lived experience, be it savage or already culturalized.

The second is to return to the things themselves. Let us uncover the "real" camouflaged by ideology. The difficulty probably lies entirely in defining this "real." It is not immediately present, known, controlled, and available; it must always be understood, worked on, and interpreted. Negatively defined, the "real" is what is hidden, disguised, and denied. Positively defined, it is what we live, neither the sterile "real" of knowledge nor the ambivalence of the symbolic. It is rather raw being (*l'être brut*), but what is important is to return our attention to the moment when this being is given, intermingled with the imaginary, in a confusion of object and subject, but precisely before it has been tampered with, tamed, and normalized.

The third rule is to bring the individual back to himself, to appeal to him: Do not allow yourself to fall into the trap of biases; exercise your judgment! Return to harsher reality! And if you find pleasure in this reality, let it be yours, a true pleasure that is not mere convention!

This third rule allows us to answer the question Why: Why combat ideology, if not to free; and free whom, if not the individual? Otherwise, why invest so much ingenuity and fury into denouncing ideology? We sometimes get the impression that it is a question of an ostentatious consumption of intelligence; you have to be smarter than the other, yet the other is not necessarily the adversary who has to be fought, but also the partner who must be surpassed. Sometimes, however, the denouncers of ideology talk about liberation. But free whom, and from what? The unconscious, from an immense and continual enterprise of repression? But this does not make sense, for it is a very naive kind of materialism that conceives of the unconscious as the supreme agency calling for a defender to get recognized and freed. Insofar as the unconscious speaks, no one can speak for it; insofar as it is active, it can manage perfectly well on its own. If Artaud had developed a theory of the unconscious, he would not have been Artaud. Only the individual has to be freed, and precisely because he is alienated. It is not a matter of freeing something *inside* him, such as desire or fantasy, nor outside of him, for in turning desire into an anonymous and unassignable agency, we revert to a philosophy of history where this desire is substituted for mind. A revolutionary project—I do not say a program—a project for liberation only makes sense because there are in fact people who need to be freed, and because, for example, ideology holds them captive. Men will never be finished freeing themselves, and what will result from their liberation no one knows. It will still be objected that this antiideological discourse, calling on the subject, remains within the confines of ideology. We can only respond with a counterattack: the passion for code also haunts the discourse of those who denounce it; a similar terrorism rages in the interpreters of the system, as in the defenders of deconstruction. But what can I tell you?

Let us get back to the movies. Just as everywhere else, ideology insinuates itself there too, and all the more insidiously in that it creates that famous impression of reality. Here the image has more authority, more credibility than in theater or painting, for its message is more readily received and accepted. For a host of reasons, which Metz has analyzed very well, the public is ready to swallow the ideological pill, to believe that the screen shows things, people, and events "as they really are"; that film is always "direct," and fiction always "documentary." So there is justification for once again repeating that film takes and editing produce deliberate images that are not at all reproductions of the real. But let us get this straight: the camera faithfully records, and allows us to reproduce what we give it to see. It does not depart from optical laws, and if, for example, it shows the spectacle in perspective, it is entirely without Machiavellianism, and quite simply because it is unable to do otherwise. It does not have the freedom of the painter, who can alter the perspective at will. It is therefore something that functions innocently, like any other tool—Mallarmé's pen or Xenakis's computer. It is the filmmaker who is responsible: in this case, responsible in that he can use the camera in such a way that the third dimension can be eliminated on the screen: for example, by using particular lenses or lights, by darkening the background or by tampering with the film.

And in any case, perspective is not an ideological trap in which the spectator could be caught. If ideology had to be discussed here, it would be far better to leave it to the critic who ignores the reality of the spectator's perception, who thinks of film in the same way as theater and painting, substituting represented space for a theory of the representation of that space. He also pretends to believe that we see the image according to the laws operative at the time of its recording, and which, during the Renaissance, were in force at its creation. For the spectator does not see space, he sees objects and events; he does not perceive the coordinates with the same cyclopean eye of the camera. With his entire body, desires, and fantasies, he perceives the existential dimensions by which the world is organized—the above and below, the near and the far. No ideology is involved in this relation to the world. Perhaps culture is, insofar as even the body learns to perceive and is initiated into perceptual codes.[1] But surely ideology is not involved in this relation, unless it is with a certain use of perspective, as in Della Francesca's *Duke of Urbino*, who imperiously surveys and claims the distant lands comprising the painting's background. Similarly, a close-up can be charged with an ideological message.

And so can every image, insofar as it conveys information, and even in the way it expresses things by its very substance; its composition, framing, and color can all imply an ideology. And for a more important reason, so can the content of an image: "Has it ever been noticed, for example," writes Noguez, "that in recent supposedly 'protest' films Hollywood manages to slip us, undercover, a reassuring message about the fundamental stability of the American system by showing us students drinking *Coke* or doing their washing with *Tide*, like any good Nixonesque housewife. Students protest, the cops beat them up, but *Coke* and *Tide*, the popcorn thingamajig and the TV watchamacallit are always there, offering us satisfying evidence of indestructible guardian spirits . . ."[2]

Thus the application that certain criticism employs to disclose ideology is legitimate. But we may well wonder whether it is not rather a waste of energy. For can we really be sure that ideology, no matter how present it may be in films, is really continuously operative? We would say that its efficacy is all the greater because it is acting in secret without the knowledge of the receiver. Yes, but it preaches only to its converts. If the spectator does not perceive it, it is because he is in his element—that is, the air he breathes, the world he lives in; in which case, it does not matter much if he downs an extra dose. Of course, our task is to open his eyes to ideology, and the critic's function is, once again, salutary. But theory is not enough to immunize or cure a film enthusiast, nor can the theory of realism in general or the theory of ideology of film. Perhaps we should have recourse to two other therapeutic aids. First, to the production and distribution of other films, which are not mystifying and which highlight, by contrast, the mystification operating elsewhere. Is it so impossible that good money be thrown after bad? Second, we can employ the pleasure of films meant purely to entertain. In those, even if ideology does infiltrate, it is relatively inoffensive; the awareness of unreality neutralizes the impression of reality; whoever participates in the game knows he is only playing. Thus the Western can rightly be suspected of ideology. The reality it represents is totally artificial, but, as Metz observes, inasmuch as it flaunts all conventions peculiar to the genre, it does not cheat, or it cheats with such simplicity that we cannot help noticing it. We enjoy it as a story, and thereby have a good time. But our era, or at least those who interpret it, generally despise pleasure. And at times it is difficult to understand our era, since it offers so many different faces. But there is perhaps a feature common to most of these faces; it is the pleasure elicited by play, which is also the key to what we call aesthetic pleasure.

The enthusiast who does not value his pleasure is immune to this experience. Leave him to his own pleasure! Do not tell him to adopt a different attitude, and in particular, suffocate his pleasure under blankets of knowledge. There is a right time for everything; a time for unmasking ideology, a time for the semiology of film, but also a right time to savor films. Let us give the go-ahead to those who enjoy them: maybe they know nothing about film, but they are free to grasp what is singular in a work. For the film is a singular system and its structure is "a particular combination realized through a singular selection chosen by this film from the resources of various non-singular systems, be they cinematically oriented or not."[3] The system is never laid out; you have to discover it. This is the test of the semiotician, to unravel and reweave the various threads of the fabric constituting the text. But the text does not get its meaning only from its structure. It remains to be seen whether it is not *jouissance* that introduces expressivity into reading, which is not the same as intelligibility. For the search for intelligibility does not lead to an understanding of the meaning expressed. Of course, this understanding can be questioned: it is well known that any work is open, polysemic. But the semantic dimension is sometimes too easily and willingly neglected by a certain type of structuralism: all meaning is then reduced to significa-tion, the intelligibility of the message is reduced to the readability of the texts, the work lends itself more to structuring than interpreting. How-ever, structuralism does not necessarily imply this approach; on the contrary, one can try to see how a meaning—a meaning irreducible to the literal message, a "symbolic" meaning of the kind referred to today by structuralists like Todorov—is invested in the play of structure and in the use of codes. In that case, the analysis is revealing. But perhaps it reveals only what the analyst has already at least suspected, if he is sensitive to the expressivity of the image of the sequence; for there perception is irreplaceable. Thus we would say to the individual who was speaking a moment ago: If you want to go the movies, go. There is only one rule: Go for pleasure, and if you are bored, leave. Treat it as a game; that is the right way to use the movies. But games are far more intensely experienced by the participant than by the observer. If you really want to set the spectator free, it is not enough merely to give him films that do not alienate him; give him a camera. The day that films will be a popular art form—an art practiced by the people and not subject to commercial constraints or academic models—there will no longer be any ideology to track down in them. And perhaps there will be fewer structures to disclose, for codes will no longer decide the norms and invention will be the norm. Must invention be vacuous and naive? You say that popular films will only be a clumsy imitation of authorial commercial films? Wait and see! But you will need new eyes, open to a new culture.

Notes

1. We have to look more closely at this use of the word "code"; for if the code is in fact a system of established constraints, then certain objects are well coded, like road signs and graphic signs, but the world is only metaphorically a type of writing, and perception decodes the world in this manner. We must not confuse the cultural system of signs with the habits the body develops in commerce with the sensuous. We might say that the body, when it is in harmony with the sensuous, decodes, but it does not decode a text that must first have been encoded.
2. D. Noguez, "*La dimension politique du cinéma*," *Champ libre I, Montreal,* p. 16.
3. C. Metz, *Language and Film* (New York: Praeger, 1973), p. 73.

11. Painting, Forever

Kinetic art, conceptual art, body-art, earthworks, little personal mythologies . . . Today art bursts into a cluster of unforeseen forms. And yet how many painters still set up an easel and apply colors to a canvas! In this essay we would like to understand the astonishing perseverance of this quasi-immemorial gesture. Before describing it, however, let us suggest how it affects us. By experiencing how painting is both born in us and we in it, we can ascertain how the act of painting arises and what it means to be in the world as a painter.

Being given to us, painting invites us to see. Most often we do not see: we do not refrain from acting; we only register signs that call for knowledge and action, summoning concepts and tools. Even a painting we rarely see: we pass by it too quickly. For the painting to live *in* us, it must live *with* us as a familiar object, but one that is striking and inexhaustible. Sometimes, however, we heed its call, we respond and begin to see. But if we take this initiative, it is soon taken away from us and the painting takes control. Certainly perception is active, and, as Klee remarks, our eye grazes over (*broute*) the painting, and our entire body takes part in this exploration: vision does not involve the eye alone, it summons all our psychomotor powers; and this would motivate us to touch the surface of the canvas, the tactility of its paint, the glaze that flattens it, unless some museum guard interferes with our curiosity. But if we remain immobile, the entire body is gathered up in the eye, which becomes its representative, so that vision may be "devouring," as Merleau-Ponty has said in regard to the painter; but it also applies to the spectator. Yes, painting "celebrates the enigma of vision," but then vision is in some way transcended: it focuses on the enigma of *appearing*, which is also celebrated in a nonvisible register by poetry and music. The eye is the principal requisite with painting, for the sensuous is dependent upon it, and not only the visible, but also the tactile, and even the audible (since Delacroix speaks of a music of painting).[1] This is why we can speak of seeing as a kind of touching, but without reducing seeing to touching, as Descartes did, and above all without reducing touching to a mechanism, stressing on the contrary the fact that touching is itself a type of seeing. All the sensuous brings itself together in such a way that appearing makes sense, and that means that a *Logos* inhabits the sensuous and is known to our body prior to any cognitive operation. Painting shows us how.

It takes the initiative, as we have previously said. It dissuades the subject from placing himself at the distance of representation as a sovereign; if he stands at this distance, it is because painting, as in the era of *perspectiva naturalis*, invites him to assume this position. Whenever the eye grazes over the painting, it is the painting itself that maps its movements according to the structuring lines of force (Lhote's "preliminary tracings"), unities of form, play of volumes, and color modulations, or whenever the painting is figurative, according to the articulations of the objects it represents, or even of the narrative it relates. Moreover, this inquiry is not that of the expert, who, desiring to identify the painting in terms of what he knows, looks for the pertinent details characterizing a particular style. This investigation of the eye is directed by an initial massive vision of the whole, which has recorded a certain effect that it seeks to expand, deepen, and justify, but by an understanding belonging to heart or senses rather than reason. This examination, however, may be rationalized through an immanent analysis of the eye, and the object of *jouissance* may become an object of knowledge. But, following what Ingarden calls "initial emotion," this examination is at first a lover's one. We speak a great deal about desires today; one of them is *concupiscientia videndi*. This desire for seeing is a desire for justice, for doing justice to the object, and since we are intuitively aware that the object is just: justice is beauty. This desire is at the heart of all desire, and expresses itself in the same way as "physical" desire. Grazing over the painting is like kissing, simultaneously eating and being eaten, being caught up in the game, losing oneself in being possessed. Far from claiming an abstract freedom, the eye only surveys the painting in order to stray into it, and to likewise be seen in its turn. Merleau-Ponty says, "rather than seeing the painting, I see according to or with it."[2] But if the art-lover gets lost in the ambivalence of seeing, he also finds himself: the eye experiences and asserts itself in complying with the painting. We need not say that the visible eliminates the seer, that it is "the visible of a vision without subject, the object of no one's eye,"[3] so that it would call for psychoanalysis instead of phenomenology. If the visible is tinged with the invisible, as we will maintain, it is not by voiding the subject, but rather by inviting him to feel beyond seeing, in the very act of seeing. We need not say either that the subject displays a death wish whenever he desires the fullness of this presence in which the visible unfolds. The realization of desire sometimes mimics death, but only so as to experience life. Such is the paradox of our being-in-the-world, which childhood never relinquishes: oscillating between daytime, when it is separated from the world, and nighttime, when one is lost in the abyss. But the night can be illuminated by dreams and the day can darken. In the aesthetic experience conquering and losing oneself are co-given, as in the singular moment of birth or awakening. In front of the painting, the eye is born to itself as seeing; but in some way vision is invented only by denying itself, as if the desire for seeing could in fact only be realized in a movement beyond seeing. But not in nonseeing, for the identification of the seer with the visible is—would be—the culmination of vision: the luminous night of a presence without distance. If the eye therefore dreams of abolishing distance and settling within the painting to be devoured by it, it is in order to be itself, and also for the painting to be. For painting both requires the birth of the seer and the birth of the visible, a simultaneous genesis of subject and object within presence.

Which object? What is promoted to appearing? At first, must the visible be manifested in the seen?[4] As long as painting is figurative, we are inclined to answer affirmatively. This painting gives something to see: it teaches us to see not the seeing but the seen. Its value is then measured by the faithfulness of its imitation, and what it represents or copies is a real already given, acknowledged, and known. To give something to see is to give something to *recognize*. As soon as the object is recognized, painting has accomplished its task, and our interest is in what is represented, as when we look at a photo on an identification card. But do we actually look at a painting, even the most successfully representative, in this manner? Whenever we are sensitive to resemblances, is it not in the same way as Giacometti, who states: "What interests me in every painting is resemblance, I mean what for me is resemblance: that is, what causes me to discover a little of the outside world"? To discover, not to recognize: what we see, even if we can name it (a sunflower, a tree), even if we can assign it a proper name (Mt. Sainte-Victoire, Old Ballier), is seen for the first time; because before viewing the painting we did not know how to see, and now the object reveals itself to us: it makes shape, it becomes visible through what does not resemble it: ink strokes, splashes of color, planes, surface textures, a "sowing of flourishes." This visual medium that ordinary perception does not see because it is anxious to posit and master the thing, thereby affffirming both itself and the world, is now seen and savored by the glutinous eye. The painter shocks us into seeing it: he shatters appearances, breaks lines, multiplies planes, distorts volumes, plays with local color (we will discuss later whether these distortions could have another meaning). Through this visual, by the double affect of that operation that gives to experience the sensuous and neutralizes any practical interest, the thing enters the eye's light and accedes to vision. It originates in the painting, in our look (*regard*). Klee Says: "*vom Vorbildlichen zum Urbildlichen"* (painting must go from the presented image to the originary image); this motto is reflected by Merleau-Ponty: what the painter demands of the mountain is that "it reveal the merely visible means by which it becomes a mountain for us." Cézanne's painting "shows how things become things and world becomes world."[5] Similarly, Lyotard states: "What painting shows us is the world in the germinal states."[6] It is the birth of the world, which is not represented, that is, copied, but rather brough back to its origin, transfigured into itself.

The world, or *a* world? Where does this world stand when the painter is no longer Poussin, Cézanne, or Klee, but the later Kandinsky, Fautrier, or Newman? In describing the aesthetic experience of painting, perhaps we are still prejudiced by the model of figurative painting as well as our concern for representation. We say that the mountain truly becomes one only when it is painted; in granting painting this power of revelation, no matter how broad our concept of figuration may be, we are privileging figurative painting. Nevertheless, there is another "true" mountain: not the one the geographer studies, but the one we discover in another type of aesthetic experience when we climb it. Perhaps we must define the operation of painting in another way, a way that would take abstract art into account: then what painting realizes is the truth of seeing rather than the truth of the visible. The essence of the pictorial, let us repeat, is in presenting something for my seeing. But this genesis of the seeing keeps being linked with a genesis of the visible, for seeing is intentional, and so implies a visible; and this visible is originary, *urbildlich*. What is engendered in our vision, however, is not the real, but a possible. It is not *the* mountain Sainte-Victoire that exists in the countryside near Aix-en-Provence, as well as on the map, seven kilometers from Le Tholonet. It is *a* possible mountain among thousands of others that could be evoked by other paintings of the same mountain, a mountain that exists nowhere outside of the painting, having in it its own space without reference to other previously known places. This mountain is the here-and-now, according to which a possible world is ordered. After this experience we can proceed from the possible to the real; if, for example, our eye has been sufficiently educated by painting, we can be inspired by the inherent minerality of this possible mountain whenever we perceive a mountain landscape. Painting offers us a possible that informs us about the real. So does abstract painting: it does not represent *the* real, but announces a possible, a world that is not populated by determinate objects, but remains open and yet singular, being, rather, the atmosphere or tonality of a world. Abstraction has been a necessary moment in the history of painting: it teaches us by a retroactive effect to realize that even figurative painting also expresses rather than represents. Cézanne's canvases are not photographic reproductions of Mt. Ste-Victoire, they show us essential mountain-ness, they give us to feel a certain minerality, which is clearly the essence of the mountain, but which can readily dwell in other objects, including the folds of a tablecloth or facial wrinkles, so that it expands into the dimensions of a world. Abstract painting teaches us about the expressivity of painting in general.

This power of expanding into a world belongs to all painting. But the possible expressed by it is neither imaginary nor unreal; at least, it is not opposed to the real as the subjective is to the objective. The subject whose gaze realizes the painting is not called upon to imagine on his own account, and even less to produce free associations. When Ingarden asserts that the concretization of the aesthetic object calls upon imagination in order to fill in what is "indeterminate" in the work, he insists that this activity must be controlled to remain faithful to the work. But this restriction is not sufficient: whenever we look at the Venus de Milo we do not have to imagine an entire woman, as Ingarden supposes: nothing is missing in this truncated statue, no more than in a torso by Rodin; the statue appears fully, gloriously, and faultlessly. What remains in a state of nonbeing without acceding to appearing is the world that the statue opens, the indefinable world of grace and serenity; and if our imagination had to come into play, it would be to penetrate into this world and crystallize it into objects. But this is unnecessary; let us allow the work to be, to imagine for us and within us: it imagines by expressing itself.[7] Certainly we always have this occasionally delirious power of imagining, but in its own way the real also has this power. The object can emit an aura, and the mountain can appear as titan. There is a polysemy for the object, as for the word. What readily becomes culture originates in nature. But we must qualify two points in this regard.

First, this world, as it is only a possible world, remains in a nascent state. The imagination, even if it were compelled to do so, would not succeed in completing this world, that is, rendering it full and closed, filling it, in Husserlian terms. One can thus understand that our experience is that of a genesis symmetrical with the genesis of the look: the world of the work, no matter how energetically it may be expressed, no matter how decisively its singularity may be asserted, is still not a fully natured world; it remains in gestation, and this is why, while we can always give it the name of its creator, we are at a loss to verbalize and conceptualize it, for we can only feel it. What expression offers us is a matrix; what appears to us is an aurora, that is, the appearing of an apparition that never reaches the threshold of reality.

The second point is: From where does this possible originate? Is it in some sense the possible of a real? It is what the painting expresses, as the nymph—also always a possible—is what is expressed in the hidden spring in the forest. Now, this painting is completely real: if you have any doubt, just ask the painter. Is it therefore the real of the painting that engenders the possible? But perhaps we are proceeding too rapidly. No matter how real the painting may be as a product of praxis—a controllable object delivered to commerce and ideology—it calls upon vision to become what it is; and the painter who made it exhibits it in order to have it realized in this vision. Is it in fact realized? Every perception certainly experiences the reality of the perceived object, that is, its presence (let us refrain from stating that it posits this reality, for that would involve a theory of constitution). But this object always escapes us at the same time that it is revealed, as if by some malediction, presence had always for ransom some form of indetermination. This indetermination, however, is less essential than that of the possible, which can only be represented in the imaginary, whereas we are always able to go round the object present to us. Thus let us not meditate too much on this absence at the center of presence, my dear Lyotard, all the more since *thanatos* has nothing to do with it. Moreover, whenever the visible gives us to feel beyond seeing, this "negation at the heart of seeing" is abolished. Aesthetic experience tends to correct the deficiency inherent to perception. In this experience, the eye attempts to attain a fuller presence, to somehow coincide with the painting, and, as we said, to become lost in it. This effort is required for the eye to gather what is expressed in the painting, and also for the simultaneous genesis of the seer and the visible to be effected.[8] Both must discover a kind of communication more primordial than the real, and join together, in order to be paradoxically reborn, in what can be called the pre-real, what Merleau-Ponty calls "savage being"—the orgasmic union in one and the same flesh of the subject and object. *Pre-real* and *non-real*: such is the visible when the gaze is made one with it (such also is the seer when he yields to the fascination of the visible). The pre-real will become real when the spell of presence is broken, when the pre-real stops seeing itself as well as giving to see, when it is held at a distance of representation, as an object of knowledge or discourse, by a subject who is henceforth separated from it.

But this pre-real, inasmuch as it does not attain the level of the real and is not negated by determinations constituting it, is an archi-real or, if one prefers, a surreal. Here we have the answer to our question about the source of the possible: It is the pre-real that is pregnant with the possible, that expresses a possible world. Lacking expression—incapable of producing aesthetic experience—are the objects that do not call upon us to grasp them as pre-real, that will never be anything but real.

As for abstract painting, if it invites us to be present to it, it also opens a possible world for us. And it teaches us what figurative painting represents, which is also an unfolding of the pre-real into the possible. So we perceive how the figurative tempts us: it can too quickly satiate our desire to see by overwhelming us with the represented, and thereby dissimulating the opening to the possible, which unfolds in the intimacy of presence. But can we say that abstract painting also attains a kind of resemblance? It resembles nothing in the real, but rather the pre-real, precisely because it *is* the pre-real. In the case, should we not define resemblance in another way than Giacometti did, and say that "resemblance is what causes us to discover a possible world"? No, it is not necessary to go so far, and we can agree with Giacometti on condition that the term "exterior world" be elaborated. For we must return to the idea that the possible can shed light on the real, since it implies a *posse*, a power of the real. But again, what real are we talking about? It is a real that is the basis of everything given, according to which the visible and the seer are in the world as being founded within it. This real is the hearth of all possibilities; it is Nature as *poesis*. So we can say, as does Lyotard, that painting is a workshop in which primary processes exhibit themselves, but if these processes are in effect unassignable to any particular subject, it is because they are the very movement of appearing, and must be attributed to Nature. Of this Nature, since it is prior to man—it produces him—man has no idea: as soon as he is there, and he is always there, Nature becomes world. But in this experience of the pre-real, in which he almost returns to the moment of his birth, man can sense that ground sustaining him. Nature is a kind of pre-pre-real, and the possible worlds evoked by the expressivity of the pre-real attest to its depth and power; they give us a sense of Nature, and thereby cause us to discover the exterior world, since this world is the visible, that is, the face that Nature assumes when man is there to see. Thus the appearing of the painting to some extent mimics the appearing of Nature, the advent of being to appearing. Now, leaving painting and returning to things,[9] we can still sense Nature in the experience of the world. Each time we visit Le Tholonet, if Cézanne has enlightened us, we will experience how Nature is expressed in Mt. Sainte-Victoire. Painting will not have really demonstrated how *the* world becomes world, for it only invites us to see the event of *a* possible world through the visible, but it will allow us to sense in the world how Nature becomes world.

Is the painter completely aware of this? Unless he is Klee, it is doubtful. But no matter, since he is producer of this sense. Does he always produce it? No, not always. In order that painting manifest the event of appearing, of which it provokes us to be simultaneously agents and witnesses, in order that it gives us to sense Nature in the pre-real, it must itself have a natural air, it must have the thickness, opacity, and inexhaustibility of a thing. Before saying by what means it has these qualities, let us try to say when it does not have them. We may observe once again that the opposition does not lie between the figurative and the nonfigurative, nor between a painting that realizes desire and one that does not. In order to substantiate the latter opposition, Lyotard evokes a history of painting as a history of desire. Why not? But if there is a history of painting, it is also a history of a quest and its various instrumentations; we need not discuss this history here, for we want to focus only on the permanent.[10] What is opposed to the natural is the artificial, and there are many ways for an artwork to appear artificial. It does not look such, let us note, because it bears the evidence of labor: the artifice resides rather in erasing this evidence, as occurs in classical painting. But the labor must itself appear natural: a struggle between the artisan and his materials. Whereas a reflective and sophisticated labor produces an "artifact," as is the case with certain works of serial or kinetic painting that seem to call for the tests of experimental psychology, thereby deceiving the eye rather than enlightening it. Painting also risks being artificial when it chooses to serve causes other than the pictorial—religious, political, and so forth—thereby becoming a discourse. The emphasis is then put on the represented, which must teach, convince, or simply please whenever, all violence being repressed and all delirium forbidden, a conventional, ideologized, and theatricalized visible summons a well-educated eye: we must admit that this is sometimes the case with "classical" painting. Painting may again be artificial for the opposite reason, that is, when by sheer reflexivity it denounces itself, exhibits means without producing ends, and thereby denies the eye its pleasure. And it is the same for an overcalculated painting, that is, one that gives us the impression that it has nothing to say and repeats itself ad nauseam.

Painting can only be "natural" if the painter is himself, so to speak, "nature" (or inspired—it is the same thing), if he proceeds as a craftsman. Let us therefore speak about the painter, but just as the man of a praxis. The painter has a privileged relation with painting; and at first with the works of others, which incite him to say: "I too will be a painter." At the Louvre, Cézanne is spellbound by Poussin's paintings. Both Malraux and the culturalists emphatically state that no one could invent painting if it did not already exist, no one would look for the pictorial if others had not found it. (This is why it can also be said that one painting refers us to all others, that it is a "plural text," or constitutes a closed system in which all painting is gathered.) But is this stimulating relation, itself in some way competitive with the world of paintings, sufficient to form the painter? Through this pictorial Oedipus the painter establishes a relation to the world, and undoubtedly in the same way that he encourages us to do so. He does not try to master the real, but to reach the heart of the visible. But this desire for seeing does not make him a voyeur, for it is linked with a desire for making: the painter sees only as long as he is making; and it is not in the painting, but rather in the act of painting, that he becomes lost, that is, realized. And probably this desire for making is foremost in all individuals. In giving paper and pencil to a child, you are providing him with cultural materials, but his desire to doodle is not cultural. This desire, which makes man as *homo faber*, more deeply rooted in him than basic needs—and which will make him a revolutionary when it becomes a desire for justice—is perhaps not the last word on desire. Does not making in turn manifest desire, and perhaps a more profound one, which gives us the key to why we make in the first place?

We will return to this point, but let us first observe that the desire for making, in this case painting, is aroused by the world. The world offers itself to be completed, and at the same time, the body is experienced as a means for this completion. In contrast to animals, which can only adapt to their environment, going sometimes as far as celebrating it through the grace of song and dance, man alone actively transforms his environment, and not solely for his own comfort: for the human hand is an instrument for both grasping and understanding. This is true even for the writer: "Dear poet, take up your lute." And the pen in Hugo's or Michaux's hands serves alternately to make drawings as well. The painter sees the world as subject matter, and this becomes his compelling focus; his vision is regulated by his desire to render visible, as Klee says.

We can understand the term "render visible" in a way that leads to the rehabilitation of the decorative. Whenever a Québecois paints his barn door with bright colors, what was formerly only part of a functional and inert real offers itself for the first time to a joyous vision without losing its functionality. Easel painting, however, is not applied to an object in the real that already has its place and function; it brings into the world a new object, which must find in it its place and function. Does it find its place in a museum? Perhaps . . . for lack of a better one. Or in an apartment, as formerly in a palace or church? In this case we can see the object more assiduously and familiarly, but it also risks being reduced to a decoration. In truth, it has no place anywhere, because it is in the world without belonging to the world. Instead of perfecting the world by situating itself in it, its function is to remake the world elsewhere, that is, on the canvas where it expresses itself, in order to render the world visible. Is this to say that the object reproduces the world in its own way? No, and not even when the theory of imitation predominates, or when a painter works from real life. Perhaps at art school he was taught to copy models, thereby practicing and perfecting the use of his hand and eye. Cézanne copied Poussin before being Cézanne. But for others, the danger lies in going on

practicing all their life, and in the end the means for seeing not being used
to see, nor the means for making used to create. The true artist, however,
maintains an essential relation with the world. And this is also the case for
the abstract painter, as Picasso points out; it is because he is a seer that he
feels himself confronted by the invisible. And what else does he see but the
world? But what provokes him within the world is not necessarily the
subject matter he has chosen; it may be surroundings (and, for example in
a certain technological era, electricity or machines, as Le Bot has so
admirably demonstrated). What the painter wants to render visible from
the real is what is not seen, that is, what appeals to a more originary
vision, the pre-real according to which being arises in appearing prior to
its humanization. Even if the painter wants to repeat the real in a
conventional and acquiesced form, which he is often asked to do, he
cannot really do so, he can try optical illusion, but in the end his canvas
will be only two-dimensional, and it is by dint of craft that he tries to
dissimulate his craft. (This is why the eye is not duped: the desire
animating it is not caught in this trap; it becomes invested in the pre-real
and in the possible it suggests.) Moreover, it is precisely a possible that
the painter proposes, that is, not the world, but *his* world as a possible of
the world. And it may only be that his gesture is his own; that he stamps
his singular mark upon the work—the mark, his own fantasmatic, his
personal myth, as Mauron says.

The painting comes into being by this gesture, and the painter is aware
of this. As long as he is working, he watches the painting in gestation. He
sees not only what it is, but what it is not, what it lacks in order to be a
painting. Is not this the lack that concerns the world: the still unseen in
the already seen? But now this lack is a determined one: a certain color
awaits its complementary one in order to become radiant; a volume, a
certain tone to find its density; a line waits for another by which it will
gain its force. Thus we can speak, along with Souriau, of the painter as
called upon by the work to be done; what is to be done is already there as a
possible or, let us rather say, a virtual, in order to distinguish its status
from that of the world open to the spectator by a complete work. This
virtual will eventually become actualized to open a world for us. Does the
painter already see, or at least imagine, this final product? No, no more
than the mother can see the child she feels being formed within her; he
sees his work revealing itself as he works upon it. Such is the secret of his
making: the painting is not before his eyes, but in his hands.

Thus the painter, like the spectator, responds to the call of the work
with his entire body; but it is to be present to what he is making, and not
to what is made. This making, which produces the painting, will be
inscribed within it. Our eye will see it by grazing across the painting; we

will only reach this possible world the painting opens by feeling how the virtual was actualized in the painter's gesture. In other words, we have to relive the work's gestation. This experience is entirely different from analyzing its structure: what we relive is its structuration, that is, the movement by which the work is composed. (And, let us note, as well as chaotic, it may look harmonious, violent, or pacified, complete or incomplete.) We take part in this gestation by a type of carnal familiarity with the painter's gesture.

Thus we can now understand the surprising endurance of easel painting. It is with it that, in order to produce a spectacular and expressive visible, the most intense presence becomes lived, the greatest proximity between the working body and the worked is realized. Let us consider the canvas at first: this flat surface is hardly an object; it does not have the thickness, density, or coarseness of the thing; it is there neither to be embellished nor completed. Everything must begin with it, on it; it is almost the *nihil* from which creation issues. But how enticing is its whiteness, like that of the page for Mallarmé! This white can hardly be seen, just like unreflected light.

It is not yet a color, although it contains all colors, and elicits them in order not to become an embellishment, but to disappear, to make room for an object for which it is only an imperceptible support (unless it appears as transfigured among and under the colors, having become a color itself). There is, however, one important qualification: although the frame always indicates the canvas it delimits, figurative painting may cause the support to remain unnoticed, since representation negates the canvas by making it a window open to the represented. But whenever painting focuses attention on the representative, to which the power of expression is accorded, the canvas is no longer only a support, but rather an element of the painting. Instead of the painting being on the canvas, the canvas is in the painting, and the painting reveals its world without having to tear open the canvas. In any case, for the painter the still virgin canvas is white. Only the "alphabet of stars" indicates itself "on the obscure field," like the constellation, that manifests the place at the end of Mallarmé *Coup de dès*, when "nothing will have taken place, save the place." But it is on whiteness that man writes or paints, fixes his thought, or creates some visible. Whiteness is not a place, for a place unfolds in three dimensions, whereas the canvas is flat, it lacks the depth of the starry sky, it is a skin that is not deep because it covers nothing. The canvas only becomes a place for the painting that will cover it, and to which it will become identical. Just as it is not a place, it has no place—at least no proper place of its own; it has only this arbitrary but decisive position on the easel, within reach of the eye, and especially of the hand.

The function of the easel is to place the canvas in a workable position. Let us not forget that the pliable thinness of the canvas calls for the work of painting. It does not offer any resistance, as does stone, nor does it awaken a type of fury, as marble did for Michelangelo; we cannot say of the painter what Alain said of the sculptor: "Fortunate is he who sculpts in hard stone!" But the canvas provokes the painter's gesture, just as the void provokes vertigo. And, in truth, for this gesture the canvas definitely has this type of material reality that must be prepared and, so to speak, tamed before one can apply color to it. The easel places the canvas at eye level of a tense person whose body, entirely mobilized to be truly present, is gathered in the movement of the hand. Whereas in writing the hand is under the command of silent thought or speech, here it takes control and is not the sentinel of a body at rest.[11] Certainly the body sometimes takes precedence over the hand in working the canvas. Pollock, for example, stretches the canvas on the floor and dances upon it while simultaneously splattering colors; his is a savage painting, born from a type of drunkenness. But generally the painter prefers to maintain control. The hand exercises its powers with more reserve, and its contact with the canvas, albeit discreet, is perhaps the most intimate.

This contact, however, is indirect, for the hand is equipped with a tool—a pencil, brush, or palette knife—that touches the canvas. Let us pause for a moment and think about this mediation. The painter's tools are seemingly like all tools. They are extensions of the body, which improve and increase its powers, on condition that we know how to use these tools, and to the point of being unaware of using them. Whenever the painter just looks at things, it is as though he caresses them with his hand, thereby suggesting the movements by which the invisible in them becomes visible. But in front of the canvas he sees with his hand, and this hand is a pencil or brush: it seems to be in direct contact with the material, like the hand of a sculptor with clay or a basket weaver with wicker. So we can evidence the difference between the painter's tool and the everyday tool: the everyday tool does not create, but rather transforms; it is determined in relation to a specific medium offered to its act in a pregiven world, as, for example, the relation between the axe and wood, shovel and earth, hammer and nail. The tool acts upon the material by increasing man's power, and thereby produces a result upon it: the wood is cut, the earth overturned, but it does not produce a work. In contrast, the pencil or brush carries its medium with it; it is through its action that the visible is rendered: the inert canvas is obliterated, line vibrates and is amplified beyond the preliminary tracing, and color becomes luminous and radiant. Painting conquers color in this way: color becomes a type of material with which the painter can wrestle, and this struggle is crucial in rendering the visible sensuous. What Bachelard calls "material imagination" always takes part in this struggle, no matter how devouring the painter's vision may be. For color is definitely a medium, and following Bachelard, it can also be an element. It is in color that the drawing will take on form and the forms are drawn out; it is in color that the dimensionality in which these forms are articulated arises. But this medium becomes meaningful because it is already worked (and the painter must foresee that itself also works on the canvas). Like the canvas, color is prepared; the palette is the workshop where it is produced. What industry today puts at the painter's disposal must still be reworked and transformed by an artisan's labor; if it is not so, if color is "industrial," we will have another type of painting, the painting of an engineer. In the traditional art of painting the color is a heavy paste that the painter works, and with which he struggles in the same way as a clay modeler. This element elicits material imagination before being employed by formal imagination. And it is perhaps for having been worked by hands that color becomes a dimension on the canvas, as Merleau-Ponty says. What the painting gives us to see is in the color as in the water is the fish, born out of the aquatic element. If everything on the canvas takes form and exfoliates in color, it is perhaps because the painter has established an intimate familiarity with it, thereby according to it this texture of the flesh and this power to give birth to things by its vibrations.

But color only gradually gains this power, for the painter works only by retouching. If he is interested in breaking a speed record, his strokes will only be paraphs, something like a signature, but not a mark in which something hidden and profound is revealed: it is nothing more than an exercise by which the hand becomes dextrous and the fingers nimble, without the body being fully engaged. On the contrary, the true painter (after all, we all have to make judgments!) is in no hurry. He allows being (*étant*) to be, he gives it time to appear, since the event of appearing cannot be rushed. Appearing is not an explosion, but a genesis. And in the same way that the spectator requires time to achieve a genesis of vision, the genesis of the visible needs time to appear. Let us repeat that the painter does not produce a particular seen, and even less an already seen, but the visible. He shows us the world as offering itself to be seen, raising itself to appearing, and expanding to the expression of a possible that escapes vision. The type of painting that shows us the coming of the visible into vision requires a slow gestation, and the entire being of the painter is at work in this effort. To see this, we need only witness the painter at work.

But must we say that, rather than affirming himself, the painter loses himself in the act of painting? We must indeed understand how painting, sketching out a possible, leads us beyond the actual paint, how expression

transgresses representation. Is all of this possible because something
enters into the gesture that the painter always repeats, in the patient
dialogue between the hand and eye that mobilizes the mute powers of the
body into a stationary dance? Is not that something the fantasmatic of the
painter, which appears in the matrix-like figure of which Lyotard speaks,
haunting the visible while keeping the invisible for itself? Would the
possible world that we enter unawares be the unfolding of this matrix-like
figure? We must then invoke the idea of desire. The event, argues
Lyotard—and by event, we must understand this upheaval of a visible
animated and overturned by the invisible—"cannot issue from this
world," nor from the body; it only issues from the force of desire, from
desire as force. Only desire can open this vacuum—"this space of
dispossession,"[12] As Kaufmann says—where the fantasmatic could inscribe its figure. Only the force of desire can break down the "good form"
so as to open up this space.[13] "The infraction," to cite Lyotard again,
"issues from primary processes; it is not at all due to the gesture engendering a sensuous space, it is due to the mobility of desire."[14] But Lyotard
makes this statement apropos of poetry, that is, of a verbal gesture.

We must then pose the question: Can we similarly deny the pictorial
gesture so as to do justice to desire? Should we not, on the contrary, desire
with gesture, that is, the activity of a desiring subject? We have discussed
elsewhere the type of philosophy that makes desire an absolute by simultaneously detaching it from the desiring and the desirable, which in turn
locates it not only in the unconscious, but also in the anonymity of a
history without agent, thereby invoking "the visible of a vision without
subject, the object of no one's eye."[15] Possibly this kind of romanticism
may be justified, desire may arise from the ground, a mountain existing
prior to man may need someone like Cézanne because, in the end, it
"desires" to appear. But this desire comes to live in a man, in whom it
inspires a singular fantasmatic; whether they are originary or not, my
phantasies are not yours. And the desired upon which the energy of desire
is invested is also singular. In the man Cézanne, desire requires the name
that we have already given it, that is, the desire to be a painter. This desire
is undoubtedly something more than the wish to produce and sell canvases, to attain a certain status and recognition. It is the desire to be
present to the world, and to render it justice by rendering it present to
others, that is, visible. What animates this desire, and is at the center of all
desire, is undoubtedly the desire of a world other than this one—of this
world as other, such that the subject can find and lose himself in it because
perception returns to the originary. Discovering the pre-real through the
real is approaching the fulfillment of this desire, it is rendering justice to
the world by annihilating the distance imposed by representation. The

desire to paint and the desire to see converge at this point. For seeing, as we have said, is to be present to the visible, to feel the world that the visible expresses; and painting is to express this world while being present, in the making, to the means and problems proper to painting. This world produced by painting for our seeing it a singular one: not the real already seen, but the one that the painter lives in an inextricable mixture of imaginary and real, of affect and concept.

Is this to say, as is commonly thought, that the painter expresses himself? Yes, but not in the same way as a child whose drawing becomes the delight of the psychoanalyst. It must be his work that expresses the painter while expressing itself: no matter whether the work is a work or a nonwork, what matters is the laboring process. Labor is the condition for the singular to be promoted to the universal, instead of being engulfed in particularity; then we are given access to the sensuous and not the intelligible, and the visible is for us pregnant with a world. What seizes the spectator is this opening rather than the private fantasmatic of the painter. This fantasmatic has also undergone a transformation: the painter has his fantasies, as does everybody, in which the avatars and investments of his desire are manifested, outside of the act of painting; but he is also a painter, and his desire is above all desire to paint, as in others it may be to know or have power. The painter finds both his pleasure and anxiety in the act of painting; it is his life and death. This fixation does not prevent him from dreaming about sexual difference, absolute knowledge, revolution, or any other investment of desire, but it forces him to confront the reality of the problems and tasks inherent in pictorial praxis. And his fantasmatic is limited by that; it is only in the working process that it may introduce itself; to paint the revolution will be to revolutionize painting. It is painting that creates fantasies, and thus opens a possible for us. But this fantasy, because it is at work within the painter and is itself worked or, more precisely, becomes part of a practice, loses its particularity, and the possible that is issued from it is offered as a possible of the world. This possible originates in the pre-real, to which his labor brings back the painter; it is a possible invisible of the originary visible whose labor summons presence on the canvas.

Labor is always necessary, in order to produce a painting in labor, heavy with a possible world, a painting that has an air of Nature, naturing itself by virtue of being natured. This labor is precisely that of the artisan who has an intimate knowledge of his materials, so that, for him, this material is never merely the indifferent means toward an alien end. The painter does not use color, but rather serves it. He restores the world to color, for it is in color that things are drawn out. If the painter has a particular color theory, it is a theory that serves to give colors a soul. This understanding with matter is not broken by the tools he uses when these tools are the palette knife and brush; for they are the extensions of his body, they do not shackle the freedom of his gesture, nor do they require a gesture that would break contact with matter. Although these tools are entirely real, they do not claim a separate reality; in other words, in the relation that the painter has with them, so as to create the visible as pre-real, they themselves are in some way pre-real, returning to their originary being. And they are undoubtedly at the origin of painting. So we can understand why a great many painters remain faithful to this origin. It is in this regard that painting retains all its force: with the achievement of an inexhaustible gesture, at the end of the brush, the seen is metamorphosed into the visible, a possible germinates in the real. Is this genesis still effected when the painter works with another type of material, with other tools, or when he shuns actual work? It is not so certain.

P.S. But it would probably still come about if painting, retaining the same means, were to stop being a monopoly of a caste of painters in order to become "popular" painting. The desire to paint would then no longer be repressed by the institutionalization of painting, and the painter's gesture would flourish and increase without for all that losing its virtue.

Notes

1. Is this only metaphorical? For there is a sonority of colors, just as a color of sounds. See Messiaen.
2. Maurice Merleau-Ponty, "Eye and Mind," trans. Carleton Dallery, in *The Primacy of Perception* (Evanston, Ill., Northwestern Univ. Press, 1964), p. 164.
3. J. F. Lyotard, *Discours, Figure* (Paris: Klincksieck, 1971), p. 56.
4. Merleau-Ponty, "Eye and Mind."
5. Ibid.
6. Lyotard, *Discours, Figure*, p. 28.
7. We will have to examine later if the artist's imagination has been necessary to produce the work, to summon this world to which we willingly attach his name, and if, for example, his fantasmatic takes part in the creative labor.
8. This presence is not that evoked by intellectualism to define clear and distinct knowledge. Presence in which the sensuous is experienced is not the presence of the *cogitatum* to the *cogito*, which is still representation.
9. But will it always be necessary to effect this movement? Today art dreams and attempts to become mixed so integrally with the everyday world (as it undoubtedly was in the past) that we no longer must deny the surreal to remain in the real.
10. Certainly we must consider history, since our present does not repeat the past. Cézanne and Mallarmé were innovators, and Lyotard is justified in invoking the notion of a revolution in painting, as does Kristeva, following Barthes and others, concerning poetic language. But a few questions remain:
    1. Is the true revolution not initially a social one? Must it not be directed toward the institutions of painting and literature, toward the social conditions of painting and writing?

    2. Is subversion a privilege of our time? In throwing off the veils of culture, would we not find in every age, *mutatis mutandis*, Cézannes and Mallarmés?

    3. How is it that in every age, whether they be privileged or not, revolutionary or not, there are people who take up the brush and pen? This is the only question we are confronting here.

11. The monk who illuminates the manuscript is also seated, but his painting is more closely related to writing. It is to be read as a text, and does not introduce into it any alien or explosive elements.

12. Lyotard, *Discours, Figure*, p. 21.

13. This is true, at least in modern painting. And this proper form is subverted only if it is still present in some way: the pure disorder of entropy is not disorder, noise is only noise in relation to information, there is still a savage harmony in Pollock's drippings. And conversely, if proper form is clearly elaborated and abundant in classical painting, is it not secretly contested in certain instances, even if it be only in its excess, as representation is contested in optional illusion.

14. Lyotard, *Discours, Figure* p. 290.

15. Ibid., p. 56.

PART THREE

CRITICAL ANALYSIS

12. *Literary Criticism and Phenomenology*

Skimming through the contemporary history of philosophy, phenomenology appears to be one doctrine among others, perhaps stumbling against the same difficulties as the others. But what does it offer us? It proposes a method that introduces a new style into philosophical discourse. Thus no wonder that it can inspire disciplines not properly philosophical, such as literary criticism. To justify this, let us immediately evoke phenomenology's motto, "back to the things themselves." But why, one will ask, return to things? Is their presence not always assured? Must we learn to see a spectacle, use a tool, read a book, and do we learn this from philosophy? Now, this motto is all the more strange inasmuch as Husserl proposes that, as a condition for all philosophical reflection, we suspend our naive belief in reality of the world. Is this not an invitation to turn away from things? To reduce, however, is to neutralize belief without taking anything away from the thing. Reality continues to belong to the perceived object, unreality to the imaginary object, ideality to the conceived object, as positional characters of the noema. Even if this radical conversion of our attitude might convert the real into the unreal, into what would it convert the unreal? And, on the contrary, in forbidding the realist attitude, in which action risks sealing off thought, the reduction makes the object appear more clearly, whatever it is, with its proper characteristics (*caractéres*). Nothing of the object is lost when it becomes, under a new and disinterested look, an intentional object.

Yet is it in this object alone that phenomenology takes interest? Noematic description serves as a guiding thread for an intentional analysis that explores noetic-noematic correlation, that is, that shows to which conscious acts or intentions the object's characters correspond. Here the major theme of Husserlian phenomenology appears: constituting subjectivity. This theme puts idealism back into question and can lead, as with Fink, to metaphysical speculation. But we will consider its echoes in a thought that refuses making subjectivity into a separated and transcendent instance. If one incarnates the transcendental in the empirical, and if one identifies subjectivity with man's being-in-the-world, the theme of constitution amounts to saying that it is on the world that one can read the figure of constituting subjectivity, on the world where it lives, or on the works it produces. Thus it is that Sartre seeks to detect the activity of image-forming consciousness on the figures of the imaginary, or the person's fundamental project on the meaning objects have for him. But the accent cannot be put on subjectivity alone. In considering the subject engaged in the world, one comes to consider this subject's intentional life as itself engaged and somehow relativized by the world. Husserl was already led, through the analysis of conscious acts at work in logical thought, to the idea of an archeological phenomenology that discovers the hidden foundations of this thought and describes its genesis. To be sure, this genesis is genesis of the constituted, but it seems to bend the idea of constitution toward the idea of solidarity and affinity between subject and object, dampening the idealistic accent. This return to the origin or the immediate, to the most primitive relation between man and the world, also seems to be a fundamental theme of phenomenology. One can develop it in another sense than Heidegger's, in seeking, on this side of the foundation that is precisely the reciprocity of man and the world, the ground that is perhaps Nature, and that announces itself in the primary forms of the man-world relation. In any case, without even speculating on the origin of the origin, one can say that in returning to the immediate, phenomenology remains faithful to its initial motto: the thing it describes is entangled with man, but it is precisely the thing that is proposed to man before an objectivizing thought takes its distance from it and undertakes to reduce and explain it. We will have to recall this soon.

On the other hand, what is the function of literary criticism? Or, in other words, what can one expect from the critic? For we cannot separate criticism from the critic. If there is perhaps a realm and history of art or philosophy, in which artists and philosophers are subjects, integrated into an open totality that summons and justifies them, there is no realm of criticism; there are only critics, men of taste, experts, who are the deputies and informers of the public. When these critics are in the presence of works—what are they going to do with them? If they address themselves to the authors they are adopting the attitude of a judge, or in any case an adviser; such was the professional behavior of the Académie Française in its youth. Today artists are more conscious of their vocation, and they are more tempted to see their critics as failed artists who seek a compensation for their impotence in their function, rather than as sovereign judges; they respect critics only to the extent that they exert an influence, often inordinate, on the public. Thus, the critics address themselves more willingly to the public. Their mission can then be threefold: to clarify, to explicate, and to judge. And it is rather remarkable that these three activities are not held together among themselves by any necessary relationships.

To clarify is to instruct the public by bringing out the work's inner sense. One assumes that the public lacks the critic's competence, and left to its own resources is incapable of understanding the work. For one assumes that the work—we are limiting ourselves to the literary work—is intended for the understanding, that it has a meaning, but one that can be obscured or dissimulated. And the function of the critic is to decipher and translate this meaning into a clearer language in order to place it at the public's disposal.

To explicate is something else; it is to consider the work as an object, as the product of creative activity, as a product in the world of culture. The critic, who was a moment ago erudite, now becomes scientific. He invokes a causality, the work is determined, whether by psychological processes or by historical circumstances. Obviously one can take the edge off causality by speaking of conditions or influences, as well as by distinguishing between proximate and remote causes; but one always affirms that the work is explained by what it is not, by the author's personality or the milieu that determined that personality.

To judge, finally, is something else again; the work as object, as with any product and consumer item, has a value. But in the name of what? The critic is modest; he no longer pretends to speak in the name of the law or to know the canons of beauty; he has an open mind, welcomes every novelty, is even ready to resign by saying the works judge themselves and that instead of being a judge he is only a witness. But he insists on being a good witness, impartial and prudent, in whom the aesthetic judgment attains the universality Kant recognized. How can he achieve this?

Let us see what phenomenology can teach us. The critic can take in his own account phenomenology's motto. Returning to the things means returning to the work. Why do this? To describe the work and say what it is. Straight off, this instruction limits the mission of criticism to the first of the three terms we evoked. Explaining and judging are, if not excluded, at least postponed to the extent that their tasks introduce something foreign to the work. But on the other hand, it seems that phenomenology, inasmuch as it inspires criticism, must also renounce certain of its tasks. For Husserl, phenomenology returns to things only in order better to grasp the intentional ties that unite the object and the subject. Now, it is the object alone that interests our inquiry. Moreover, who is the subject one could correlate with the work? Is it the critic who reads the work, or the author who produces it? In point of fact, phenomenological criticism cannot eliminate all reference either to one or the other: the very inquiry into the work requires this.

Indeed, let us consider the critic who places himself in the presence of the work. A preliminary remark: This decision he takes has somehow a phenomenological character. There is some analogy between the aesthetic attitude and the reduction. To practice the *epoché* is to suspend spontaneous belief in order to turn attention toward the way in which the object offers itself to us. Now, the aesthetic attitude also implies a neutralization; at the moment I approach the work, in some way I abolish the exterior world, and on the other hand, the world of the work into which I penetrate seems itself neutralized. I would not call a doctor or the police when I read or view the scene in which Othello strangles Desdemona. The reader of a poem, says Bachelard, has no business with things, but with words. Nevertheless, the analogy between the two attitudes is not identity. For, on the other hand, the aesthetic attitude is entirely turned toward the object and not the subject's constituting activity, and on the other, if the exterior world is neutralized, the world of the work is not: there is no neutralization to the second power of this neutral world. The phenomenologist alone, when he observes the critic in his turn, performs the reduction. The critic is not a phenomenologist, but he can be taught by him.

The work such as it offers itself to critics has two specifying characteristics: it is for reading and it is written. First, it awaits a reading. Why is this necessary? Does it not fully exist as that book on the library shelf? Has it not acquired a definitive existence when the writer puts the last period on the manuscript? Let us not proceed too quickly. A play waits to be acted—it is made for that—and its existence is only completed when the performance consecrates it. It is in the same fashion that the reader acts the poem in reciting it and the novel in sightreading it, for the book as such has as yet only an inert and opaque existence: words, signs on a white page, the significations remain in a potential state as long as a consciousness does not actualize them. The literary work, says Ingarden, is heteronomous; it waits for the subjective operations that actualize it. To the four strata of the work that Ingarden distinguishes—material signs, verbal significations, represented objects, and imaginary aims—there respond the acts of consciousness whose system constitutes the reading. The reading is a "concretization," it makes the work what it wants to be, namely, an aesthetic object, correlate of a living consciousness. In this sense the critic—and every reader as well—has the right to feel some pride, for he promotes the work to its true being. He collaborates with the writer, but also rivals him, for in making the work be he takes it away from its author. This work, born in torment and sometimes bearing its trace, finds peace and joyously blossoms out in the reader's reception. This is why, says Blanchot, the Yes of the reading must be airy, innocent, and in some way irresponsible.

But this irresponsibility is the true way of assuming responsibility without ostentation. The reader must devote himself to the work, without playing or using trickery.[1] Before each new work, the critic must have a new and entranced look, infinitely receptive. He must be entirely present to offer the work the vastest openness (*le séjour le plus vaste*) and the deepest echo, yet be entirely absent, to mix nothing of himself into it. For he betrays the work by weighing it down with his own memory or measuring it by his own experience. But does he not betray it anyway by making it an object? The reader exposes the work to the same danger as I am exposed to, as Sartre said, under the gaze of the other or the gaze of God. The work takes its place in the world of objects, cultural values, and consumable goods; it enters into history, where it finds itself confronted by other works, tied to a past and pregnant with a future; and this history of works is one history within history: it may well happen that one does not respect the work's novelty and that it finally appears as the product of historical causality. Thus the consciousness of the critic proceeds to the death of the work through impatience to explain.

But does the work not call for this treatment? Its status is ambiguous, like that of the subject or of a quasi-subject. It is true that it must become an object, affirming itself with the mute and closed obstinacy of things. It is also true that it is historical in that it testifies to its times. But it is also entirely true that the work shields itself against an objectification that would place it at the mercy of the reader. Like those portraits whose gaze follows that of the spectator when he passes before them, the literary object defies the reader; it affirms its freedom while keeping its secret—its meaning is always infinitely distant. C.- E. Magny writes: "The intuition the critic seeks (when he seeks the interior coherence of the world the novel presents) is made here similar to what is the *Wesenschau*, the vision of essences in phenomenology."[2] And precisely the essence is not always grasped in a single look, and if it is, it is sometimes in a feeling that does not permit itself to be conceptualized. Phenomenology invites the critic not only to prudence—how can the work be read objectively?—but also to humility—where is the truth of this object?

But we must take into consideration another of the work's characteristics: the work is written by someone, it has an author. What can phenomenology here assign to the critic? Criticism, it seems, has no use for a phenomenology of creation; it is interested in the work. Nevertheless, when it pretends to explain the work it willingly evokes the writer, it has recourse to biography, psychology, or psychoanalysis, as it previously had to history and sociology. And the titles of many works of criticism bear the name of a writer rather than a work. But the scientific knowledge whose dignity criticism again claims does not introduce us to the comprehension of the work; it stretches the ties that unite the author to his work, it seeks on the outside of the work elements of information about the author, and finally retains from the work only what is necessary to comprehend the author or verify a general theory of creation.

Undoubtedly, again, the work calls for this new avatar; it is signed, sometimes lightly and sometimes heavily, with happiness or pain, it carries the stigmata of creation on itself, it designates its author. But who is this author? For phenomenology, the writer is also a phenomenon, he shows himself to the reader—but in the work and nowhere else. Everything that the reader might know of him from elsewhere does not show itself; it is perhaps a truth about the writer, but not the truth of the writer. This is why the writer shows himself only in dissimulating himself. Homer shows himself better to us than those contemporaries of ours whose life and person are forcefully advertised to us. The writer is in his work as we said the reader must be before the work. He is never better present than when he is absent, when he refuses to speak of himself, to deliver his world to us, or when, if he speaks of himself, it is of this "I" who is another, this "I" who only exists as a task or a dream. What good is it to confront the *Confessions* of Jean-Jacques with the life of Rousseau? Does one ask the self-portraits of Rembrandt or Van Gogh to be good likenesses? They are undoubtedly likenesses; they are like that world that Rembrandt or Van Gogh inhabited, they are like their works. The writer also is like his work; he is nothing other than this likeness, the look that has illuminated the world that the work delivers to us. All that we can do when we penetrate this singular world is give it a name attesting to its singularity; we give it the name of its author, we call it the world of Balzac or of Verlaine. And Balzac or Verlaine are nothing but this name, this name is laden with all their work.

Yes, the imaginary writer is indeed the truth of the writer. Does one believe justice is rendered the writer by questioning his doorman, his doctor, or his editor so as to write his biography? It is not even he himself who must be questioned to get at the writer within him; if we had interviewed Claudel at the dress rehearsals, we would have had a bizarre idea of *Partage de midi*. To seek the writer elsewhere than in his work, even in his personal thoughts, results in substituting for him an empirical man who is undoubtedly not imaginary, yet one who is not in the likeness of the work, so that we are sometimes astonished that the author could have written it. One thus poses an interesting problem of psychology, but renounces criticism. One may also substitute man in general or the writer in general for the individual writer, and thus expound a theory of creation, renouncing criticism. If Blanchot, as penetrating as he is, and without resorting to anecdotes, evokes Kafka's *Journals* or Rilke's letters, it is to the extent that he is interested less in Kafka or Rilke than in the metaphysics of creation suggested to him by them. It is the same with Sartre, when he does existential psychoanalysis in connection with Baudelaire or Genet: he knows well that he must understand the man through his world, that he must "determine the free project of the singular person from the individual relation which unifies him with the different symbols of being."[3] that is, from those images of the world heavy with a metaphysical tenor, as the viscous or slippery, and thus that he must know the writer in his work; but because he is interested in the man within the writer he never truly gets at the work; nothing he says of Baudelaire is indifferent to an anthropology, but this tells us nothing of *The Flowers of Evil*. Suppose, however, that the study of man does rejoin the work and even clarifies it; then it is because the critic will have tampered with his project, that is, because he has read the work first and then sought the man in relation to the work. And perhaps there is another bit of trickery in every attempt at objective explication of the work. The psychology to which one resorts is not just any psychology; it is a psychology that the work's reality induces in order to take account of the man's creative power. Likewise, the history to which one can also appeal is not just any history whatsoever; it is a history that takes into account works as well as events, in which the truth of a people must be sought in the testimonies of its culture, and in which the sense of becoming resides in the dialectic of world visions. So the itinerary that goes from the work to the writer and from the writer to the man in history can be followed, but not the reverse. Beginning with the man, one would not know how to find the writer, one would not seek him if one had not already found him in the work.

The writer's truth is in the work, but the work's truth is not in the writer. Where is it, then? In the very meaning of the work. Here again phenomenology teaches us that every phenomenon bears a meaning within itself, both because the subject is always present to the given to organize and comment on it, and because the given is never given as brute and unsignifying in the manner of the *sense data* empiricism imagines. Thus the work always has a meaning; the writer speaks to say something and the virtue of the work is in its power to say. No matter if what is said cannot be measured according to the ordinary criteria of true and false; the truth of the work is always in its telling a meaning. And it seems that the fundamental task of criticism is the explication of this meaning.

This task must be oriented by two characteristics of meaning that phenomenology draws to our attention: meaning is immanent to the sensuous, and it is lived by a singular consciousness. Let us examine these two points. That the literary work has a meaning is evident from the fact that language is the bearer of significations. But how is this so? Here one must introduce a distinction between two forms and two uses of language: prose and poetry. In the everyday use of prosaic language it seems that thought precedes speech; language is treated as a tool both so available and so efficacious that it disappears in the use one makes of it. No one thinks of the dictionary or grammar when he speaks or listens; he gets right to the idea across words, and words have for him only a discrete, transparent, and inconsistent existence. But whoever reads poetry, or rather recites it with the respect that is its due, finds that the words suddenly take up a consistency and brilliance; here they are relished for themselves, or for the happiness they give to the voice uttering them; they are restored to nature, charged with sensuous qualities, and they regain the spontaneity of natural beings; they break from the usual rules and associate to form the most unexpected figures. At the same time, meaning is transformed. It is no longer what is understood *via* words, but rather formed *on* them, as an image takes form on the surface of an at first agitated water; it is an undetermined yet pressing meaning that cannot be mastered, but one feels its richness, which has to be felt rather than thought. This meaning inhabits the word as essence inhabits a phenomenon; it is there, held in words, and it cannot be extracted from them to be translated or conceptualized. A new dimension is added to meaning; expression is added to representation.

What we are saying of poetry can be said to some degree of all literary works. What defines these works and opposes them to documentation, the science book, and the philosophical treatise is that in the work the meaning remains immanent to its language and formal structure. Being inseparable from style, meaning assumes the density, but also the opacity of things; as do things, it deploys what Husserl calls an interior horizon, it expands into and opens a world. A world to which feeling gives direct access, but which reflection has never finished exploring. The singular essence of the work is infinitely remote; what can be said of every perceived object, and particularly of the aesthetic object, can be said of this immanent meaning of the sensuous, for which each reading is an *Abschattung* that both gratifies and frustrates us. The represented object, henceforth subordinated to the expressed object, becomes a symbol, like those archetypes that myth develops, or like the image of stain expressed in the myth of original sin, or the image of the poet in the myth of Orpheus. Every great work is a myth, the exfoliation from a symbol into a world. And if the symbol gives rise to thought, as Kant said, it is also refused to thought. It seems that the fullness of meaning is a nothingness of meaning, as if meaning became annulled in being expanded.

Hence certain critics, such as Blanchot, take up again, in a Heideggerian context, the Hegelian thesis of the identity of being and nothingness and the death of art. The work seems in this case to transcend itself toward its negation. And if, on the contrary, it dwells in being in order to become a substantial object, they will say that it has betrayed itself unless this objectification still attests to the power of nothingness, as *rigor mortis* attests to death. The work's meaning is to not have meaning; its being is beyond all determination, not in some glorious positivity, but in the incessant negation of all positivity. Art lives through the death of artworks, as history lives through the death of men; and the phenomenology of the work is intent on uncovering in the work the active presence of nothingness. One could find for this strange enterprise many a justification: in the status of the aesthetic object, which exists like a quasi-subject for which every objectification is both an accomplishment and an alienation; or in the inaccessibility of meaning whose plenitude and indistinction thwart every exegesis. I believe, nonetheless, that only an unjustifiable perversion of meaning invites confusing a positivity that escapes grasp with a negativity, and that the work's plenitude in the radiance of the sensuous must be relished for itself, and not as a message of death. The silent force of the possible, which justifies the interpretations and metamorphoses of the work, does not proceed from nothingness; the possible is a potentiality inscribed in being, and proposed to the reader.

The principal justification of aesthetic nihilism, however, resides in a certain conception of the act of writing. The meaning is indeed lived by the writer in a spiritual adventure, of which the work bears the trace. The writer is here not the empirical man, but rather that phenomenal author we previously invoked, whose work invites us to grant a certain experience; at least certain works, for it seems that Blanchot founded his theory of writing on several privileged works, namely, those of Kafka, Hölderlin, Mallarmé, and Rilke. The work's aspiration to nothingness would then be founded less on its status than on the experience of nothingness lived by the writer. Today the writer knows that every work is a defeat, and he desires this, for he wants to be situated at that point of language where everything begins, but without going beyond this beginning, allowing speech to be possible that is not actualized. Here we find various stirring themes intermingled: the return of language to its origin, which is poetic speech; the experience of inspiration as a quasi-mystical test making it necessary to traverse the arid night of senses and mind, the obsession with death, where, everything being consummated in a kind of ecstasy, only the grave and full presence of things remains; the experience of the image as nonbeing, where the thing accomplishes itself through its absence, as if the real were only delivered over through the magic of the unreal. These themes are given rise to by certain torn, violent, unfinished works, in which it seems that the writer has indeed in some way refused to accomplish himself in order not to renounce a bewildering contact with depth, as Orpheus has chosen to look at Eurydice in the night and lose her forever. One could say of all contemporary art that it manifests the same excess, the same desire for death; while reflecting itself, it wants to go beyond itself, aspiring to a mortal purity, convinced of its own impossibility. But perhaps it is mistaken about itself and about what inspires it. The writer claiming to live a spiritual adventure is exposed to the worst dangers— Maritain saw this clearly. What saves him is that he remains a writer; writing, he tampers with nothingness. Orpheus reascends to the light of day, and sings; if the Maenads tear him apart, he has not willed it. The vertigo of silence is abolished in the joy of speaking. And finally, once having traversed desert and night—if this trial was necessary—what inspires the writer is not always "the inexhaustible murmur" of nothingness, but perhaps the clear voice of light, the glorious images of Nature. And it is Rilke who writes, "*Hiersein ist herrlich.*"

Far from the writer being abolished in the work, the work tells us what he is. And for us he is nothing other than this response to a certain call provoking him to reveal a certain world; and this world defines his existential a priori because it expresses the faces of the world to which the writer has been sensitive. As important as it is for the man who lives it or the psychologist who studies it, the experience lived by the writer, as by Rimbaud becoming "a seer," is of little import: this experience would be strongly equivocal if it were not guaranteed by the work. What has import for us is what Rimbaud saw: "and I have sometimes seen what man has believed he has seen"—because his work says it. The meaning of the infant is not in the pain of childbirth, and there are some labors without pain. The meaning of the work is in what it says, and it always says more than the experience from which it issues and from which it is uprooted in order to be: it expresses a world.

What is this world? Here again, phenomenology, or a phenomenological ontology, can throw some light. It can show how an inspired consciousness is open to certain possibles that are not logical possibles, but potentialities inscribed in what one may call Nature. Each possible world signed by an author is not an unreal world invented by the creative imagination, it is one possible of Nature, an aspect of the inexhaustible real that wants to be actualized in the work. Something of Nature is said in every work. And if I had to distinguish between poetry and literature, I would suggest that poetry says properly the ineffable: Nature before man, the depth, density, and power of being; the prose work talks of man, but man as he takes part in Nature, that is, insofar as the force of being is manifest in him, neither the real nor an imaginary man, but the possible man, whose possibility resides in Nature as the place of all possibles. This reference to an inspiring Nature guarantees the truth of the work.

But the task of the critic is less to philosophize on the truth of meaning than to clarify meaning. How does he clarify it? How does he say better than the writer what the writer intends to say? Is the critic not in the end dismissed? No, for if he indeed cannot add to the work, he can at least speak of himself. As a reader, he can communicate to us his reader's experience. It is of little import that this experience is personal; C.- E. Magny has denounced with good reason "the illusion of the absolute observer," according to which "true criticism would be objective and universal."[4] To do justice to the work, it suffices that the critic say what it inspires in him. For a work is inspired only because it is itself inspiring; the poetic state, Valéry loved to say, is for the reader of the poem and not for the poet. Thus the critic does not betray the work by saying what it inspires in him. How can he accomplish this?

If he reads a poem, he can quite simply dream along with it; this is the position assumed by Bachelard. He allows himself in some way to be penetrated by the image, and he savors it like a fruit forbidden to one who seeks knowledge, he says how its charm affects him. He would condemn himself to silence, if he were content with dreaming. But he expresses his own reverie and those images of the world revealed to him. His phenomenology is a dreamed cosmology: the description of a world caught in the nets of poetic language.

If the critic does not too strongly dissociate the dreamer and the thinker in himself, he can explicate the world vision latent in the work. This is, for example, what Alain does in his *Propos de littérature*. The writer has not undertaken this abstract elaboration of meaning; he has felt the meaning rather than having conceived it, and he has left it indeterminate—by excess and not by default—in expressing it. The reflection on the work that privileges and develops one meaning is not a betrayal, since, as we have said, the work in incarnating itself in the reader becomes objectified and opens itself to a history. Each reading maintains the work in this history in which the work's meaning ceaselessly enriches itself. More precisely, each reading partially discovers the richness of its meaning. Thus the critic adds nothing to the work, but he adds the work to itself.

Finally, it may be that the prose work elicits action in us. Even if, as Magny observes, "one laughs at Don Quixote who takes the books of chivalry seriously,"[5] literature does not propose to us merely an imaginary or gratuitous experience. We know how much Sartre has insisted on this point: the writer does not address some doubtful posterity, he is a freedom who intends to communicate with other freedoms to summon them to a communal enterprise; he can awaken in man a new outlook on the world in order to invite him to feel engaged, or to take cognizance of his responsibility, or to work for the liberation of mankind in every man. The critic can say how he hears this call, how it appears to him that the writer's world is also a task for the reader, and how he feels moved to this task. Seeing is already a task, before doing; the critic can say what the work gives him to see, and how this vision can orient and stimulate the will.

Thus phenomenology does not leave the critic without purpose. Of the three functions we discerned—clarifying, explicating, and judging— phenomenology primarily justifies the first, which should orient the others. It does not disavow the second, but it invites us to distinguish between a subjective explication, which seeks the origin of the work in an author already defined by the work, and an objectifying explication, which makes creation amenable to psychology and history. It does not even invalidate this second form of explication, since the work by itself tends toward being subjective, but it does disclose its insufficiency. Finally, what can we make of judgment? The critic does not voluntarily renounce this function, which confers authority and prestige on him! Phenomenology does not forbid him this, but it limits its practice of it and moderates his presumption.

In fact, to judge is perhaps first to appreciate the way in which the work is produced. The question then is whether the work is truly what it wants to be. Does the play come across? Is the poem truly poetic? The danger here is measuring the work by some preestablished conception of what it should be, in which case all novelty would be unrecognized or condemned. The critic must recognize that the work has in itself its own norm. The question the work poses is to know if it truly actualizes its singular essence, in particular if it says what it wants to say, if the form is adequate to the meaning, and if it realizes that immanence of meaning to the sensuous that characterizes the artwork. Nonetheless, it is true that the work's singular essence is in accordance with a general essence, as the essence of red is in accordance with the essence of color, and that there is indeed an essence of the novel, the drama, or the poem that assigns general conditions to the work. But one must readily admit that these conditions are general enough so as not to impose a determinate technique or style, and that they allow the flowering of new forms. They only determine the nature of a genre and the means by which a work can have access to the reader's consciousness. To take one example, I would like to show, if I were a critic, that the new novel risks missing its mark: first, because it is not what it desires to be, that is, the objective report upon a world whose only signification is not to have signification, and, second, because it bores or uselessly disconcerts the reader for want of respecting the general structure of the narrative.

But judging can also be comparing and classifying works. The difficulty is then to establish some hierarchy while constantly respecting the principle that the work is for itself its own norm, and so must spontaneously confront itself with the others. It seems to me that the sole criterion that can be instituted in this case is that of the depth and, primarily, the stature of the works. A comedy, madrigal, or piece of light music can be perfect, and thus beautiful in its own way and at its level, but without for all that being a great work. But every great work tends to be deep as a consciousness is deep, through its relation to a world itself deep, that is, laden with being and meaning. To penetrate into this world is, for the writer as well as for the reader, to live a more or less serious and engaging adventure. The quality of this experience is immediately apprehended by the reader; in expressing it he judges the work, and once again, judges it on what it is; the work judges itself through him if he knows how to open himself to it. Letting the work be, is in the end the task of the critic, and this is no easy task.

Notes

1. Forgetting this is the danger that Bachelard never stops flirting with. At some moments he is too good a reader, I mean too innocent, for he responds to the work with the most generous but most heedless fantasy—the work is always a pretext for reverie. Certainly, his reverie is a co-reverie, elicited by the image. Insofar as he seeks the faces of the world through the reveries of the "material imagination,"Bachelard accounts for poetry. But he must be cautious when he mixes his own childhood with the world's!
2. C.-E. Magny, *Less Sandales d'Empédocle* (Paris: Payot, 1950), p. 28.
3. Jean-Paul Sartre, *Being and Nothingness* (New York: Philosophical Library, 1956) p. 326.
4. Magny, *Les Sandales d'Empédocle*, p. 11.
5. Ibid., p. 272.

13. Structure and Meaning: Literary Criticism

Since writing was first established and works were collected, it seems that literature has always been accompanied by criticism, either preceding it or following it, for while works quite often provoke criticism, criticism, in turn, sometimes inspires works. This obstinate presence of criticism is not surprising: to criticize is to judge—if not to render judgments, at least to exercise our judgment—and each reader is potentially an influential critic, including, when he reflects upon his work, the author himself. But as it has become institutionalized, criticism has tended to confirm and justify its authority. The critic has become the "man of good sense" (*honnête homme*) who speaks in the name of taste, of established values, of the church or prince. He has now usurped the title of scientist. Can he claim this right? Criticism, like today's science, is ceaselessly questioning itself, entering into an impassioned and fascinating debate as to its meaning and function. With regard to this debate we cannot present its protagonists, nor can we relate its complex vicissitudes, but can only attempt to shed light on its meaning.

The objective consideration of this debate is amenable to several interpretations: 1) A psychological interpretation that claims to reduce it to a conflict of personalities, but the liveliness of their resolutions and the rigidity of their attitudes does not justify an interpretation that is so reductive. It is just as well explained through the gravity of options. 2) A sociological interpretation, in which the conflict is between related but different institutions, unequally progressivist in any case; but the participants are not distributed according to their institutions, and what separates them is rather their own conception of the function of criticism. Should we state that the conflict is between epistemological differences, and that it primarily turns on problems of method? Yes, but it seems that the diversity of scientific conceptions appropriated by each participant always involves a philosophy. Thus, what is really at stake in the debate is of a philosophical nature, and I wish to outline these philosophical options

here. I shall not, however, invoke the philosophy of those who have tilted
against the new criticism, for it seems to me that they are more concerned
with common sense than philosophy. It is rather the background of this
new criticism that I wish to examine, for two distinct tendencies can be
discerned—the philosophy of thematic analysis and the philosophy of
structural analysis.

In the field of scientific practice, structuralism is the often conscious
expression of what one might call "a philosophy of concept." This
philosophy is bound to the extraordinary progress that formal thought has
enjoyed for decades. In the English-speaking world, which perpetuates
the empirical tradition, its principal form has been and still is logical
positivism. In France, where the tradition, animated by a number of cross
currents, had devised a different climate, this positivism has remained
virtually ignored. Wittgenstein has only appeared on the scene recently,
and that is when universities have begun to take the teaching of logic
seriously. But in its somewhat brutal acculturation to French philosophy,
logical positivism has found a new accent; oddly enough, it quickly
assimilated Heideggerean ontology, which had already ensconced itself,
and then shielded itself from Sartrean existentialism. In any case, it is no
longer limited to reflecting on the formal techniques of logic, on the
distinction and the conjunction, in scientific praxis, of the formal and
material or of the analytic and synthetic. It rather reflects on the being of
the formal, on the movement that animates it; in its own way it reminds
one of Hegel's interpretation in the *Logic* of the being of the *Logos*, and in
the *Phenomenology* of the relation between the experience of consciousness
and the object of that experience. It finds its form in a philosophy of
concept, or a system, itself opposing a philosophy of consciousness. (That
philosophy of consciousness, today violently repudiated, has found itself a
new avatar: it is no longer the Brunschvigean philosophy of the progress of
consciousness, to which Cavailles has opposed a dialectic of concept; it is
the Sartrean philosophy of the for-itself or praxis, to which one today
opposes a thought that is in-itself in language and in unconscious structures.)

In regard to this neo-positivism, we can only put forth two interrelated
themes that are reflected in structural criticism and inspired by a deep
fascination with formal thought. The first is the setting aside of meaning.
But what is this meaning? One is well aware of the debate raging over the
"meaning of meaning" in Anglo-American logicism. This was initiated by
Frege, and after him by Husserl, in that they distinguished between two
types of meaning, *Sinn* and *Bedeutung*, and, more precisely, Husserl distinguished several notions of meaning. On the one hand, he determined a
kind of reverberating meaning: of any given judgment I can determine the

meaning by the state of the thing it designates, since this judgment is *Sinnvoll*, as *Experience and Judgement* states.[1] But I can also abstract its content, take it as an object belonging to the "region of meaning," and so consider it as "simple meaning," without orienting myself toward the object it intends. But on what condition is this meaning? On condition that it is correctly articulated. Thus Husserl, on the other hand, distinguished three other types of meaning: first, a purely grammatical one, proper to morphology, and that defines itself simply through its opposition to nonsense (e.g. man, therefore yes); second, a meaning proper to a "distinct" judgment that is opposed to the countersensical (e.g. all S is P, except some S); finally, a meaning that, calling for the content of judgment, rests on its possible unity, that is, on the material homogeneity of the core (to which we might add is opposed a false meaning or an incorrect sense, which Blanché exemplifies with a judgment such as "3 is oviparous"). We can see that the first two types define meaning through grammar, through an accord with the rules of usage and transformation, whereas the third implies a reference to a content of judgment and defines meaning by an adequation to that content. This duality of meaning is perhaps best expressed by logicians, especially Quine, when he distinguishes a theory of meaning and a theory of reference, or again, grammatical and referential meaning.[2]

Now, what I called setting meaning aside—a protest of Quine's as well—is the exclusion of the second type in favor of the first; a reduction suggested by formal thought, which strives to foreclose all intuitive content, and more precisely, by the process of formalization, which takes into consideration only the logical form of the statements it takes for objects or of the languages whose properties it studies.

Besides, philosophy has been invited from various sides to encourage this reduction. For example, by information, theory, which being concerned only with transmitting messages, remains indifferent to the meaning they convey and is interested only in their form and the codifications such a form requires. Information, then, is measured in terms of the properties of that form, and is defined by the probability of the occurrence of certain indices, in much the same way as logicism defined signification through the structure of the statement. By Saussurean linguistics, which has always privileged syntax over semantics, language is studied as a combination of elements, and each element—whether it be a phoneme or morpheme, according to the analysis dealing with one or the other of two linguistic articulations—is differentially defined—that is to say, by the relations that connect it or oppose it to all others, whether in a systematic phonemic table or in a statistical table of the different occurrences of morphemes within the chain of speech. Thus, the signifier is an element within a system of signifiers defined without reference to its signifieds: assigning a meaning to a word would amount to lending an intrinsic quality to the morpheme, thus rendering the element an in-itself, indiscrete and alien within the system. Semantics, of course, when practiced, cannot help taking meaning into consideration, but rather strives at times to reduce it according to the principle of distributional analysis formulated by Harris: "two morphemes having different significations also differ somewhere in their distribution."[3] Semic analysis either seeks to constitute meaning from elements of meaning that it can combine or exclude, so that it avoids referring to the object signified by the word, or apologizes if it cannot avoid it.[4]

Thus philosophy arrives at the idea of a solely contextual meaning—a meaning immanent to a system that does not open on anything, a meaning that is neither meaning-of nor meaning-for. On the one hand, it does not itself refer to object, as in a propositional function where the place of the argument does not need to be completed by a variable; it consists only in the relations between empty places. Thus the structure of a system of exchange can be formulated without the objects of exchange being specified (they may be wives, mythemes, goods, and so on). The meaning is in the relation, not in the terms the relation unites. On the other hand, this meaning does not have to be recaptured—reactivated, in Husserl's terms—through a singular consciousness that would be present to the object as it is present to the world. The logician disappears facing the logical system. This system posits and deploys itself through an atemporal history proper to it and outside human initiative. Language thinks in our stead—"myths thinks between themselves."[5] In brief, man dies in order for the system to live. And the prophets of the new philosophy announce with a deafening roar that the reign of man has ended.

It is this philosophy that orients structural criticism. The critic approaches the work in exactly the same way as a logician considers a formal system. He considers the work to be a language and criticism to be a metalanguage. In fact, the first axiom is that the work is a consistent, autonomous, and pregnant object. On this everybody will agree—or nearly everybody, for certain contemporary works of informal art appear to express a desire to compromise the aesthetic object to the point of destroying it. But most of these works protest with all their brilliance and density that they should be rendered justice. The being that criticism confers on the object, however, is the being of language, or more precisely, the being of a specific language carefully distinguished from speech, that is, the subjective use of language. The work is a discourse, but a discourse that is not held by or addressed to anyone. This decision made by criticism has negative and positive consequences. Negative in that one refuses to "explicate" the work in terms of its author, through the circumstances of his life, his changing moods, sentimentalities, or even the intentions he proclaims. Nor can one explicate a work through a historical context—political, intellectual, or artistic; at least, if this context is invoked, there is no causality lent to it. In other words, in the same way as logicism tends to substitute a dialectic of concept for a history of ideas, epistemology proposes a history of science without historicity, and linguistics privileges the synchronic over the diachronic, criticism refuses to explore the origin and genesis of the work. The object is merely an object, as Husserl has said of formal objects, if not atemporal, at least omnitemporal. Criticism thus severs the umbilical cord connecting the world to the writer and the writer to the world. But there is another way in which the work enters in relation with the world: it intends it, and in that intention it finds the condition of its truth. This relation is equally set aside. Structural criticism denounces what Mouillaud, commenting on Robbe-Grillet, calls the "realist illusion,"[6] the naive idea that the work can witness the world and perhaps at the same time invite the reader to act in it. The work is a complete and given totality, a blind spot, a closed system, cloistering its meaning in itself without that meaning ever requiring reference to external reality. For that meaning resides entirely within the organization of signifiers, as the meaning of a sentence resides in the arrangement of words (but has one the right to add: without the words having an independent meaning outside the sentence?).

The task of structural criticism, then, is to disclose the elements and the structures articulating them. These elements are signifiers, but they receive that quality from their insertion into a system rather than from their direct agreement with a signified. In themselves, these elements are merely nonsensical, and starting from nonsense, structuralism tries to generate meaning through the operation of structure. Moreover, the meaning is never essential—just listen to Barthes:

> . . . literature is entirely a language, that is, a system of signs. Its mode of being is not in its message but in that system. And in this regard the critic need not reconstitute the message of the work, but only its system, as the linguist has not to decipher the meaning of a sentence, but rather to establish the formal structure allowing meaning to be transmitted.[7]

Or else: ". . . it is much more the attention granted the organization of signifiers which grounds a genuine criticism of signification than the discovering of the signified and the relationship uniting it to the signifier."[8] Taken literally, these statements suggest that criticism deals with the work like an algebra in which semantics is radically subordinated to syntax; or like a picture puzzle in which the meaning only becomes apparent when the elements, through a kind of *bricolage*, are manipulated in such a way as to introduce an order. At least this game aims at restoring meaning in the midst of nonsense; and algebra . . . does it not expect to find meaning in isomorphic models that justify it? Does the logic of consequence also have the right to be, as Husserl says, a logic of truth and, as such, claim a signification that is not entirely linguistic, which is properly a meaning? It is thus impossible indefinitely to defer an examination of meaning, and we shall see that modern criticism by no means eludes this task. The question is of knowing whether meaning is produced out of nonsense, or if, prior to structure, it does not need to be carried by the elements.

Now, structuralism can doubtlessly offer us a first and valuable access to meaning when meaning does not reveal itself to an immediate approach. To begin with, this is clearly the case with myths, for which Lévi-Strauss deliberately invents a structuralistic apparatus: these enigmatic works, orbiting in a foreign sky, keep us at a distance and deliver only a small part of their innermost sense on condition that they be brought together and analyzed until one discovers in them the equivalent of a code. In the midst of the impenetrable, the sole penetrating vision proceeds through a combinatory logic, and decoding consists in discovering a logical organization.[9] To understand an element of myth, then, is to determine its place and function within a system; to understand the myth itself is to grasp it as a structural system.[10] It is also the case with works that have, in our own familiar skies, the same disconcerting opacity, if not the same bewitching brilliance, as myths—the new novel. It is not surprising that these works appeal to structural analysis; they have been "written for" and the critic has preceded the writer. Notice, after all, with Genette that "the part of literature lost to meaning is much greater than the other, and that it comprises before our very eyes an extensive realm which is in some way ethnographic": the realm of juvenile and popular literature that criticism has always ignored and that structuralism could take in hand. And why not add that: "certain works which are officially recognized but which are in fact becoming in great part alien, like those of Corneille, perhaps would speak better in the language of distance and strangeness than in the language of false proximity which is continuously imposed on them, often without any results"?[11]

There are two more cases in which a structuralist method delivers what it promises because the meaning it must reveal is the empty meaning of a schema or network of relations rather than the full meaning of an object or world. First, when it is involved in what Barthes calls a "theory of literature," that we might also call a typology of literary genres, analogous to a typology of musical forms or an architectural order. Well before the advent of structuralism, Etienne Souriau illustrated such an undertaking by a study of what he called "the two hundred thousand dramatic situations." Propp has also done the same for Russian fairy tales, and Brémond now applies this order to narrative, while Metz uses it for film narrative.[12] One then proposes a model both in the normative and logical sense of the term; a schema that can clarify the construction of certain works and inspire others. Second, the method is fruitful when one wants to explore what Genette calls "the literary field" of a given age, "a coherent ensemble, a homogeneous space within which works articulate with and penetrate each other."[13] It is a kind of Imaginary Museum of literature, but one that is conceived in terms of an indefinite series of synchronic strata. This idea of a literary field is analogous to Foucault's notion of an epistemological field (and the problems of its mutations and its relation to a social context would raise the same difficulties). In the same way as the sciences define themselves and determine their objects by a certain position in an epistemological space, the works are no longer considered for their own virtues, their power to signify, fascinate, and exemplify, but solely according to relations of contiguity or resemblance ordering their totality.

Thus one sees that structuralism is not entirely useless. Moreover, it can substantiate its claims, and certain critical works stemming from it are exemplary. But perhaps they are misleading because without recognizing it they betray structuralism. In this regard we would want to show that structuralism is not self-sufficient and that it leaves certain problems in suspension that find their resolution elsewhere. These problems concern meaning and subjectivity; formal thought does not pose them, and rightly, since it constitutes and determines its object on that very condition; but a, so to speak, empirical thought does not have the right to reject them whenever it focuses on human objects, for the study of which formalism may be a means but could not be an end.

Structuralism intends to treat the work or, more precisely, the field of works as an ensemble of signifiers. Yes, but in what circumstances is that ensemble significant? And what is then the nature of signification? Beginning with the second question: What do we expect and what does the critic expect of a work? We wish both to understand and taste it. Taste it? That is to say, both to sample its flavor and propose a judgment of taste. These two operations are in the expert—the man of taste—only one, less perhaps because he is capable of judging than because he leaves the work to judge itself. A criticism is only fair if, far from imposing its norms on the

object, it leaves the object to conform to its own proper norms and
acknowledge itself as successful or not; the act of tasting registers that
judgment which the object pronounces on itself. But what is important
here is that understanding and taste be bound up in a single operation
rather than two, one essential and the other inessential, as Lévi-Strauss
suggests:

> . . . what is meaning for me? A specific flavor discovered by a
> consciousness when it tastes a combination of elements of which
> each is incomparably set in its own particularity. Like a laboratory
> scientist, one tries to reconstitute a meaning by means of devices,
> one fabricates it, one dissects it. And then, just the same, because
> one is a man, one tastes it.[14]

But this is somewhat gratuitous, and Lévi-Strauss goes on to say "that the
recapturing of meaning appears to me secondary and derived." This
statement is all the more emphatic because it decides the lot of meaning
and subjectivity. For, in following Ricoeur, Lévi-Strauss claims that the
recapturing of meaning brings back subjectivity; it signifies that "since we
are men who study men, we can offer ourselves the luxury of putting
ourselves in their place,"[15] something Lévi-Strauss, let us admit, has done
admirably. Now I do not deny for a moment that "it is essential to disclose
the mechanism of an objective thought," that is, the structuralist enterprise. But it appears to me that this enterprise can only proceed in an
atmosphere of an already perceived meaning, or at least an adumbrated
one. And that meaning is understood only on condition of being recaptured, that is, tasted. But as a specific flavor? Yes, but we could say as
well: as a certain face of the world unveiled by an involvement in the
world.

That we mention the world here—a world open to a consciousness by
the work—suggests two properties of meaning. First, that it be overflow-
ing; that it be independent of the elements we can reveal in it in the work,
as Gestalt psychology has sufficiently demonstrated. Rising out of the play
of elements, meaning itself indulges in a kind of play and remains forever
ambiguous. But this ambiguity should not delude and force criticism to
sever itself from the pursuit of truth, as Barthes proposes: ". . . if criticism
is only a metalanguage, it can be said that its task is by no means to reveal
'truths' but solely 'validities.'"[16] The ambiguity proper to aesthetic
symbolism is a sound one; as Dubrovsky says: ". . . it is not what tends
toward a kind of degree zero signification, but what implies an overabun-
dance. Not what supposes the absence or effacement of contents, but what

rests on their inexhaustible density."[17] This is the very density of things such as they are offered to the eye or hands. And, in fact, to speak of meaning as overture to the world, is also to say that it always has a referential character. The world of the work is created in the world's image, and abstracted from the world, so that a philosophy of nature can conceive it as a possibility of the real. The work enters the world to speak to us of the world even if it transports us to an unreal realm, even if, to enter it, it invites us to neutralize the real and open ourselves to the imaginary, for the imaginary still bears witness to the real. In any case, even if one decides that the unreal is totally distinct from the real, that unreal would have some meaning and the work would convey something.

It is always language that is in question. One cannot assign to literature "an inevitably unreal status"[18] because it is constituted in language. Structuralism is too quick in deducing the function of language from its being. That language constitutes a system and an institution, that it is at the same time coherent and, to some extent, arbitrary, does not imply at all that signification itself be entirely situated within its perimeters, and that speech does not employ language as a snare with which to capture the real. Wittgenstein has stated it, and the poets have always known that the primary function of language is to name. Poetical naming persists to conjure the very presence of the object, the presence of the Mallarméan flower, or "the presence of the fire on the horizon of my life . . . as an active deity endowed with powers."[19] The writer, according to Sartre, "has the object he describes enter into the sentence,"[20] with, floating like a halo around it, all that it can signify. For the meaning that literature garners, where speech is not directed toward a formal object, at first attaches itself to objects or to words naming it. The writer does not speak merely to hear his voice, to construct a coherent discourse, to pay homage to that new god of language. He speaks to say something. He is always to some degree writing. Language is his implement.

There are thus three conditions for the literary work to have meaning. The first is that language not be onanistic, that it in some way refer to the world, if only to deny it or make it a background for the imaginary. An ensemble is significant only if it indicates a signified, if it is directed at an external reality that the signs name. In order to describe, we first need to name, and the meaning described is directed toward the objects named. Speaking is still a mode of being in the world, present to the very things through the mediation of language. For the speaker, language is not that infrangible and transparent barrier enclosing him within the finite universe of significations. An ensemble is significant only if it summons the world, and if it finds its source of meaning in the world.

The second condition of meaning is that the elements of that ensemble be themselves meaningful. It has been said often enough that only clauses or sentences make sense, and an isolated sign signifies nothing unless it is itself an implicit statement. Does that not mean that it is a totality that is significant, and that literary work ought to be read in the same way as a *Gestalt*; for example, a plastic work? Signification is, then, what I call expression; a means by which the work, expressing itself in us, produces its flavor and allows us to savor its meaning. But the way structuralist assess meaning defers that pleasure, and we are limited to an analysis verifying expression and producing a genesis of meaning. How can one not respond to such an invitation.?[21] But can one engender meaning *ex nihilo*? No. The sentence is not able to give meaning to words (nor the myth to mythemes, nor the melody to notes, nor the film to frames nor the painting to colors). In order for the sentence to make sense, the words must already have a meaning. And one can paraphrase Husserl here: it is necessary that the material nuclei of words have some affinity between them, joining all terms, and even respecting grammar, you do not necessarily get a meaning unless that meaning is summoned by the meaning of words.[22] But, going from the whole to its part, is it the same meaning? To be sure, the sentence says something that the word itself cannot say. It establishes a relation between terms, and its meaning resides in that very relation. The meaning of terms consists in designating objects that lend themselves to that relation because they themselves have a meaning. The primary meaning, the meaning proper to the element, belongs to the thing-itself: it *is* the thing-itself insofar as it appears to me when I perceive it or when I know it. The man climbs the valley; that makes no sense, at least in the nonpoetic use of language. The man climbs the mountain; that makes sense, and creates a meaning that is new in comparison with the meaning of each word taken separately because the word "mountain" already has a meaning by itself, since it designates an object that is itself given for climbing. If one asks me what a mountain is, I would probably respond by using a sentence like "It is something that one climbs." But I then verbally express an immediate knowledge of the mountain, a primary meaning, certainly insufficient, often suspect, and yet irreplaceable in that it is imbedded in perception. Thus we rediscover the notion that meaning belongs to the world. Before being elaborated by a speaking subject, meaning is garnered by perception; of course, the two moments in the history of consciousness are neither successive nor entirely discernible. But what must be discerned is the meaning founded by the relation, and the meaning proposed by the being of the object. The former is only made possible by the latter. And so, in the interior of a totality, or a structure, the element is already significant.

The third condition of meaning is that there be somebody not only to express it in words, but to read it on the things carrying it or on the words relating it. This reading is largely creative, of course, for we do not pretend that the meaning inhabiting things or words should be complete and summon only a mere passive registry; it is born at the encounter between man and the world, for the world only announces itself in the natural light of the human look or human praxis. Without some form of human mediation, the object is simply not an object. But conversely, we know since Kant's refutation of idealism that there is no subject without an object, and even less a dialogue between subjects. If literary criticism concerns itself within illuminating meaning, it implicates a philosophy that takes into account subjectivity and intersubjectivity; for the very being of the work requires such a dialogue. It refers, as Dubrovsky claims, to the *cogito* of the writer and the *cogito* of the critic, which is delegate to the public. The work itself is in fact never anonymous. There is certainly no question here of returning to psychologism and explicating the work by invoking the writer as historical subject. The true writer whom the critic can appeal to is he who, far from being the truth of the work, has his truth in the work. All his reality—a very pregnant reality—consists in being the correlate of a singular world that that work discloses, but that is enough to make him present and familiar—even closer to us than those who assail us with empty words. But it is necessary that we be the receptive ear that the speaking work calls for and by which it realizes itself; and the critic must be a good listener. Are we trying to say that meaning is given through a receptive consciousness? No, rather that it is recaptured and in the same act interpreted—without, however, that interpretation being inevitably a betrayal, for it is the essence of authentic works, as well as symbols, to suggest an inexhaustible meaning. There is not one and only one truth about Racine; but Racine himself is rather a principle of truth, rendering most diverse *Sur Racines* true. But are there any that he renders false? Yes, all those that in fact do not actually deal with Racine, do not proceed from a true reading of him. And perhaps it becomes apparent that the diversity of the true ones is more apparent than real, because all their itineraries converge toward the same uniform nucleus of meaning without ever definitively encompassing it.

In opposing a phenomenology of meaning to a structural formalism, we are not proposing that the two share a mutual affinity, but rather wish to become aware of their complementarity. Certainly there are works, as Genette has said, that appear to call for a choice between the two approaches; but that choice could not be exclusive or dogmatic. On the one hand, phenomenology cannot totally divorce itself from structuralism, for structuralism is a modern formulation of a very old imperative—namely, that in order to clarify thought one must analyze and discover elements and correlations between elements. What is new about structuralism is that, in certain privileged cases, structure can draw its expressions from the rigorous language of a new mathematics. But literary criticism has not arrived at that point, nor the study of myths, and the novelty of structuralism resides in its philosophical presuppositions rather than its methodology. Nevertheless, this methodology remains the necessary condition for the explication of meaning, and consequently the condition of its being tested. But is this also the condition for its being produced? Yes, in its explicit form. No, in its primary form, when it is felt before being tested by the very elements composing it.

Here, on the other hand, structuralism cannot put aside phenomenology, and indeed does not. For we can always counter Lévi-Strauss with Lévi-Strauss and Barthes with Barthes. Barthes knew how to describe the "myths" that mystify our contemporaries, and his *Critical Essays*, inasmuch as they go beyond his *Mythologies*, do not deny this work. Even if Lévi-Strauss, practicing ethnology, recovers in primitive thought unconscious categories that belong us today, he still knows how initially to leave his own culture behind in order to communicate with that thought and describe the meaning lived by foreign consciousnesses. *Tristes Tropiques* offers us an excellent model of a phenomenological approach to archaic societies. When he analyzes a myth, Lévi-Strauss is quite aware that its elements are already meaningful; that high and low, Heaven and Earth, the bird and the bison are from the outset, at the same time they are enmeshed in the warp of a formal network, objects laden with meaning: symbols for an hermeneutic as well as for a logic. Similarly, a typology of narrative or drama, like the one suggested by Brémond, will have to question the elemental meaning of archetypical elements such as pact, betrayal, redemption, and so on, which punctuate fables, forming all the peripities of an endlessly meaningful odyssey.

The most penetrating, subtle, and suggestive works of contemporary literary criticism appear as a result of the influence of Bachelard. Jean-Pierre Richard's thematic analysis is exemplary. The themes that Richard's analysis discerns, conjured by the work itself, are those objects or incidents that so vividly evoke daydream and at the same time assure us of being at home in the world. This type of criticism is then both co-dreaming and deciphering. It reeffects the primary meaning of images and narratives; it animates and articulates it in following "the subterranean ways" of a personal labyrinth.[23] The adventure of the critic doubles that of the writer. But are these networks structures where the themes are linked, transformed, sometimes confounded? Yes and no. They represent a moving and varied totality, the face of a singular world, of an "imaginary universe." Is it necessary that the structure be formalized to the point of diminishing its contents? Yes, if that world, as Wittgenstein would say, possesses a "logical form," if the operations of its understanding are already present in it and if the writer, like certain aborigines held in high regard by Lévi-Strauss, is already, unknowingly, a logician. No, if the imagination constitutes, as Kant has suggested, the profound source of intuition and concept, and if the literary work is seen as witness to its primacy.

But how do we decide with precision between fantasy and intellect? How do we separate structure from meaning? Genette says that Richard's criticism is ambiguous. But perhaps all criticism is ambiguous, because the meaning it intends to clarify depends upon both man and the world: upon the individual who elaborates structures and the world that at first announces itself through images. It would be absurd to propose a methodological option that would ameliorate this ambiguity. We have only wished to say that meaning does not entirely reside in structure, and that there is a savage state of meaning that speech presupposes, that literature revives, and that structural criticism cannot ignore.

Notes

1. Edmund Husserl, *Erfahrung und Urteil: Untersuchungen zur Genealogie der Logik* (Hamburg: Claasen Verlag, 1964), p. 324.
2. W.V.O. Quine, *From a Logical Point of View* (Cambridge: Harvard University Press, 1953), p. 130.
3. Zellig Harris, *Methods in Structural Linguistics* (Chicago: University of Chicago Press, 1951), p. 1.
4. That one is, according to a certain approach (that of Pottier or Greimas in France), obliged to begin with the reference of words rather than their meaning is held as "a difficulty" (Todorov, "Recherches sémantiques," *Langages* 1, March 1966).
5. Claude Lévi-Strauss, *Le cru et le cuit* (Paris: Plon, 1964), p. 20.
6. Mouillaud, "Le sens des formes du nouveau roman," *Cahiers Internationaux du symbolisme*, 9–10: p. 63.
7. Roland Barthes, *Essais Critiques* (Paris: Editions du Seuil, 1964), p. 257.
8. Ibid., p. 268.
9. See Lévi-Strauss: "In the myths of the Western Pueblo, the logical organization remains the same." In *Anthropologie structurale* (Paris: Plon, 1958), p. 254.
10. But Lévi-Strauss goes much further: "logic is not only an access to myth, it is also the soul of myth, as it is of scientific discourse': 'the object of myth is to furnish a logical model to resolve a contradiction." (Ibid.)
11. Gérard Genette, *Figures, I* (Paris: Editions du Seuil, 1966), p. 160.
12. See the article by Christian Metz in the preceding number of the *Revue d'Esthétique*, 1966, 19: nos. 3–4, pp. 333–43.
13. Genette, *Figures I*, p. 164.
14. Claude Lévi-Strauss, "Réponses à quelques questions," *Esprit*, no. 322, November 1963, p. 641.
15. Ibid., p. 640.
16. Genette, *Figures I*, p. 255.

17. S. Dubrovsky, *Pourquoi la nouvelle critique?*, p. 93.
18. Barthes, *Essais Critiques*, p. 264.
19. Y. Bonnefoy, "La Poésie française et le principe d'identité," *Revue d'Esthétique*, 1965, vol. 18, 3–4, p. 337.
20. J-P Sartre, "L'écrivain et sa langue," ibid., p. 306.
21. I have tried elsewhere, without having at my disposal the resources of structural thought, to show that analysis was a necessary moment in aesthetic experience (see *Phénoménologie de l'expérience esthétique*, vol. 1, part 2).
22. "Criticism loves the subterranean ways," says Richard, *L'Univers imaginaire de Mallarmé* (Paris: Editions du Seuil, 1961), p. 17.
23. Genette, *Figures I*, p. 99.

14.   Valéry's Leonardo

Leonardo is fascinating. The crowds that line up in front of the Mona Lisa obey cultural norms, but beyond this mere observance of social rituals they are seized by a sense of awe. This fascination was evident during Leonardo's lifetime as well. At the time of his death in France, he was already a legend—and he still is. Even the most positivistic of men—historians who subsist on hard facts—partake of the aura of Leonardo's fascination. They are, however, disconcerted by the strange fate of many of his works: the *non-finito* and *non-publisho* of an astonishing mass of his *oeuvre*. There is a *sfumato* surrounding his written work as well as his paintings, and through this *chiaroscuro* Leonardo both reveals and dissimulates himself. The thinker meets with the same mystery as the historian. Valéry is among those thinkers. He has attempted to understand Leonardo throughout his life. His *Cahiers¹* as well as three small penetrating texts, "Introduction to the Method of Leonardo da Vinci" (1894), "Note and Digression" (1919), and "Leonardo and the Philosophers" (1929), attest to this concern.

Let us now look at Leonardo through Valéry's eyes. We will not have recourse to erudition any more than Valéry himself does; nor will it be necessary to establish what Valéry read from or about Leonardo after 1894. Valéry is clearly not interested in what positivists would call "facts" about Leonardo, e.g. his historical milieu, the way he lived, loved, or worked. Valéry does not approach Leonardo as an historian, sociologist, or psychologist. Does this then indicate that he is concerned only with what is given to us as an object, that is, Leonardo's works? Such a dehumanizing approach, which attends exclusively to the artwork—its form and content, its place and function in the development of a specific style—and dismisses the author entirely, would indeed be fashionable today. It is, however, unnecessary to dwell upon such a method, which had been so amply illustrated by the "New Criticism" before it invaded European studies under the name of structuralism. In fact, this method was largely initiated by Valéry himself as early as 1894, in the "Introduction to the Method of Leonardo da Vinci."

Valéry is nevertheless also interested in the problem of literary or artistic creation, and to such an extent that he has coined a new term of its study. He calls it *poietics* as opposed to *aesthesics*, both of which fall within the field of aesthetics. But creation itself is merely the most spectacular aspect of mental activity, and in the final analysis may not entirely differ from everyday activity. On this, Valéry writes:

> If we could fully understand the inner mechanism of an idiot and that of a man of genius, perhaps the difference between them, immense as it often seems to us, would be reduced to insignificant differences in their *inherent* structures and modes of functioning—by comparison with which the great external differences would be mere *accidents*.[2]

In order to study this mechanism of creation, Valéry is not forced to return to the history or the psychology of a singular being. The creative operation of a mind should be described in the way that a philosopher approaches the acts of perception or imagination. Kant, for example, describes the three syntheses necessary for the cognition of an object as anonymous mechanisms at work in an impersonal consciousness. Of course, we might say that producing a given object implies a given subject whose behavior must be empirically described. Valéry, however, emphasizes that the mind, in order to be powerful and creative, must attain a certain purity, and thus abstract itself from all its peculiarities. The result of this kind of asceticism is that self-consciousness becomes self-possession, and thereby gains a universal status. Leonardo has himself stated: *"facil cosa è farsi universale"* (it is easy to become universal).[3] Observing the acts of this ascetic mind may be said to be psychologizing, but without concession to psychologism. This mind, which Kant would call *Gemut*, is inhabited by an "I," that is, an *ich denke* as synthetic unity of apperception. Yet this "I" is merely the power of thinking rather than an ego; or at least it posits itself in an effort to expel its ego. This "I" may nevertheless be given a name on condition that it not carry any concrete denotation or connotation. This name is Leonardo, which later becomes M. Teste. We must, however, understand that this Leonardo has nothing to do with Freud's Leonardo, nor with that of any other psychologist or historian. Valéry's enterprise is, as he notes, that of a mind that wishes to imagine a mind. This Leonardo is an artifact, a *créature de pensée*, and Valéry says that he has constructed him but does not live him. This is undoubtedly false, for Valéry lives Leonardo, but not in a psychological sense. It is rather the act of one mind experimenting on another, and at the same time dreaming that it *is* that other mind. Valéry, however, never explicitly states that his *concupiscentia sciendi* is a *concupiscentia essendi*—the disguised manifestation of a Will to Power. Yet this is unimportant, for the Leonardo that he constructs has never lived. The only life that Valéry lends to his Leonardo is an "intellectual life," which is expressed in displaying a method. But the term "method" should not here deceive us, and we will refrain from trying to discover rules and precepts in this essay, as we would in Descartes's *Discourse on Method*. Speaking about method is a way of putting aside shallow terms such as "enthusiasm," "inspiration," "genius," and so on, which merely serve to lend a mystifying prestige to the problem—and Valéry hates to be mystified.

Our real task here is to detect the mechanisms at play in an intellectual act, or the intinerary *meta-odos* that a pure mind might follow. Is this possible? Reading Valéry, we are tempted to answer negatively. For he seems to succeed only in producing brilliant variations on a theme that remains undetermined, elegant circumnavigations around a point that is never reached. Let us not, however, blame him for these shortcomings— the operations of the most lucid mind are as deeply hidden and obscure as what Freud called "dream work." These operations might be sufficient in themselves to justify the word "inspiration." In fact, Valéry becomes increasingly aware that the "I" *qua* pure consciousness can never realize its identity, and that it thus remains unachieved and vulnerable. As a subject it is vulnerable and open to objectification by others, a relationship that Hegel termed "the struggle of consciousness."[4] These problems inevitably appear because there is no pure mind, and because of the relentless movements of this "I." An awareness of the distinction between "the work on one hand, and the accidental circumstances which engender the work on the other hand"[5] begins to unfold in Valéry's writings. He becomes especially sensitive to what he terms "accidental circumstances," and among these we should include not only chance occurrences of social conjuncture and artistic environment, but those occurring within the "I" conceived as a psychic totality. These are the obscure movements of the soul that have their source or, more precisely, their substance in the body. Valéry's inquiries into this phenomenon culminate in Eupalinos's famous prayer addressed to his body'[6] and in *Dance and the Soul* in the marvelous image of the dancer Athikté.[7]

I would not go so far as to claim that Valery completely renounces his ideal of the intellectual life as lived by an impersonal "I" transcending the peculiarities of an incarnate ego. He did, however, come to understand that it is not often that the mind soars high enough to gain access to a luminous summit where thought is thoroughly aware of itself and free from all commitment. In 1894 he wrote: "But this final clarity is attained only after long wanderings and inevitable idolatries."[8]

Valéry's shift in thinking from intellectualism to a kind of naturalism

does not move us away from the central issue—Leonardo. The mature
Valéry might have portrayed Leonardo as he did Eupalinos (and I wish
that he had). In fact, as we shall see, he is not far from doing so when he
deals with Leonardo in the act of constructing. Nevertheless, Valéry's
principal concern is with the operations of the mind, and as secret and
unpredictable as these may be, I find in his essays two interesting themes
concerning the privileges of a "great intellect." The first is the power of
reflexive anticipation or "prediction," so that psychic developments may
"expand to their limits."[9] This produces very quick and formalizable
thinking, since it is quite easily generalizable. Valéry is here referring to
recursive reasoning or mathematical induction, and I find it interesting
that he proposes a psychological foundation for what is intrinsically a
logical process. The second privilege of a "great intellect" consists in
finding hidden relations between apparently heterogeneous or, as Valéry
puts it, discontinuous things, that is, things that do not ordinarily coincide
within our cognitive system. I would call this privilege the aptitude for
grasping or imagining unexpected analogies. The art historian André
Chastel emphasizes the term "analogy" in his study of Leonardo, and
reminds us that Leonardo's insistence upon the analogy between macro-
cosm and microcosm stems from the continuity of phenomena and nature,
and links science with art.[10] Thus, for Valéry, an "I" can universalize
itself, Leonardo constructs a universe whose structure forms a meshed
fabric of relations. Every void can be filled with analogies: "Wherever the
understanding breaks off he introduces the productions of his mind."[11]

Analogies build unexpected bridges between phenomena and world,
unifying and molding them into a coherent universe. These analogies are
dependent upon imagination or, more precisely, an imaginative logic. Yet
Valéry shows little interest in mental imagery: "It has hardly been
studied," he says, "but its laws are essential." Unfortunately, he does not
offer us the least hint as to what these laws might be. It seems that for
Valéry psychical creations, even if they fall under the category of method,
are undetectable. He must therefore return to Leonardo's works, for he
can only exhibit the product and not the act of production. Thus we must
confront those beautiful passages that are concerned no longer with the
tree, but rather only with the fruit, for they invite us to judge the tree by its
fruit:

> This *symbolic* mind held an immense collection of forms, an ever
> lucid treasury of the dispositions of nature, a potentiality always
> ready to be translated into action and growing with the extension of
> its domain. A host of concepts, a throng of possible memories, the
> power to recognize an extraordinary number of distinct things in the

world at large and arrange them in a thousand fashions: this constituted Leonardo. He was the master of faces, anatomies, machines. He knew how a smile was made; he could put it on the façade of a house or into the mazes of a garden. He disordered and curled the filaments of water and the tongues of flames. If his hand traces the vicissitudes of the attacks which he has planned, he depicts in fearful bouquets the trajectories of balls from a thousand cannon; they raze the bastions of cities and strongholds which he has just constructed in all their details, and fortified. As though he found the metamorphoses of things too gradual when observed in a calm, he adores battles, tempests, the deluge.[12]

But Valéry does not abandon his overall purpose of disclosing Leonardo's mind at work. He no longer attempts to describe those mental acts escaping his grasp, but rather characterizes mental activity with the aid of a typology. He confronts Leonardo the painter with Leonardo the philosopher and scientist.

The third of Valéry's essays on Leonardo is entitled "Leonardo and the Philosophers." But what is a philosopher? Above all, he is an individual who is in love with language, and who, by the same token, is prepared to fall into the traps he himself has set. Valéry, however, does not think much of language, as he is principally concerned with a linguistic function that Jakobson has classified as pragmatic, a function in which language serves as tool for intersubjective praxis. In this respect it is useful and efficient, but also dangerous. Valéry would agree with Cassirer that language orients and structures our perception, or, in other words, we see what we can name. The Eskimos, for example, who can choose from among ten different words for snow, depending upon its various aspects and properties, tend actually to see snow better than we do. This verbal equipment can, however, also produce some unwieldy problems, for although it makes for more efficient perception, it can also be more abstract. The name suggests the concept, in a crude sense of the word, and that is why Valéry says: "Most people see with their intellects much more often than with their eyes. Instead of colored spaces, they become aware of concepts."[13] On the other hand, he also says: "The words of ordinary speech are not made for logic."[14] Of course, the philosopher scarcely makes use of a concrete vocabulary. He prefers inventing his own form of slang, but he is also moved by some of the most common words, such as existence, truth, beauty, and above all "that neutral and mysterious verb TO BE."[15] He makes icons out of these simple notions, which are functional in everyday speech, but meaningless outside the context of their practical use. The philosopher's move from pragmatics to ontology is a *saltus mortalis*; and the logic of his discourse is only a ruse. No philosophy, argues Valéry, can resist a precise examination of its definitions, and therefore any philosophy can be, and has been, refuted by another.

Should we then dismiss language games as useless and deceptive? Socrates, dialoguing in Hell with Eupalinos, deeply regrets not having been an architect. But actually he was one, or at least, thanks to him, Plato became one. For the philosopher as writer builds an architecture of words. The system to which every classical philosophy aspires cannot be recommended for its logical value, but, so to speak, for its artistic value. A philosophical system cannot be true in the same sense that a scientific treatise can be, but it may be beautiful. "If we refute a Plato or a Spinoza, will nothing remain of their astonishing constructions? Absolutely nothing—*unless it be a work of art.*"[16] So the question does not seem to be: Can the artist be a philosopher? but rather: Can the philosopher be an artist? The answer to this latter question is yes. Classical philosophers might not be pleased with such a response, but I wonder if modern philosophers, beginning with Nietzsche, would not be ready to accept this conception of their status and function?

Nevertheless, the lingering question of whether Leonardo is a philosopher cannot be avoided, for two very good reasons. First, this universal mind, expressing itself in so many ways, occasionally employed the philosophical language of the time. Second, Leonardo's work was so vast and all-encompassing that his total output perhaps constitutes a system. Yet we must answer this question negatively. Valéry does not state it quite so categorically, in that he prefers to say that Leonardo substitutes painting for philosophy. Painting is an activity that produces the most intense impression of his own power. For Leonardo, painting replaces the need for philosophical reflection. As a painter, Leonardo is strong enough to resist the seductiveness of language, which, by the way, is something that Valéry greatly admires: "But for Leonardo, language is not all."[17]

Now, if Leonardo is not a philosopher, is he a scientist? Although Valéry does not explicitly formulate this question, it is nevertheless a legitimate one. As long as they remain aware of themselves, of their objects, procedures, and results, the sciences will be opposed to philosophy. Valéry, whose intellectualism entails a certain positivism, subscribes to this opposition. Thus, with him, philosophy receives the same laudatory respect as a work of art, but where knowledge is concerned, science stands in its stead.

The question of whether Leonardo is a scientist can once again be evidenced in his work. So many statements in the manuscripts appear to be scientific assertions, and enthusiastic interpreters have read a number of them as surprising anticipations of recent developments in physical theory. His numerous drawings also indicate a refined concern with a technology that is not mere *bricolage*, but applied science. Everywhere that Leonardo traveled—Florence, Milan, Amboise—what interested him even more than painting was his commitments dictated by the two great practical demands of the time—preparing for war and preparing festivals.

Thus we can maintain that Leonardo may be called a scientist—or more precisely, since the science of his time remained uninstitutionalized and unofficial, we might say that he possessed a keen scientific mind. This is true not only because he developed a method of discovering or inventing unique analogies, but also because he was far more concerned with making than with thinking. For Leonardo, thinking is merely a step toward making. For Valery, the truth of science also lies in its various applications, and even the pure sciences require us to do something:

> The propositions of this true knowledge should be simply directions for performing certain acts: do this, do that. All this amounts to *power*, in other words, to an assured external transformation that depends on a conscious internal modification.[18]

The power of the mind is, in the final analysis, measured by its degree of participation in worldly things. Valéry's Leonardo might well subscribe to Descartes's famous *"cogito ergo sum"*, or Comte's well-known slogan "Knowledge is power" (*Savoir pour pouvoir*). He might even identify with Lord Kelvin's statement: "To understand is to build a mechanical model." For Leonardo is surely the weaver of schemes that would give us the necessary means with which to exercise power over nature.

At this point, allow me to indulge in a brief aside. This kind of Will to Power, expressed as well in the ideology of progress, should awaken our suspicions. Since Max Weber, we tend to see its sources in the spirit of capitalism. The Frankfurt School has warned us that man's domination of nature not only leads to its blind destruction but also to the domination of man by man. We must therefore be suspicious of the very word "power," and even the intellectual power that enchants Valéry is not entirely innocent. It is easily transformed into social power, which coalesces with both political and economic power. This is precisely how science and technology have become ideologies in the service of the dominant class. But of course Leonardo cannot be held responsible for this abuse of power.

A passage from Valéry clearly summarizes what I have previously mentioned about Leonardo as a precursor of modern science:

Another characteristic of Leonardo is the extraordinary reciprocity between making and knowing, as a result of which the former is guaranteed by the latter. This reciprocity stands opposed to any purely verbal science and has become dominant in the present era—to the great detriment of philosophy, which now appears to be something incomplete.[19]

Nevertheless, we may discover in Valéry two reasons why Leonardo, the possessor of a "scientific mind," can never truly be considered a scientist. The first is that Leonardo's mind is far too universal to become narrowly specialized. This assertion will, of course, surprise only those who are not completely familiar with Auguste Comte, the apostle of positivistic science, who continually called for an *esprit d'ensemble* while denouncing the blind particularism that limited monopolistic scientists to their specialties. Or, as Valéry might put it, the urge to specialize inhibits their ability to draw analogies and their capacity for "imaginative logic." The second reason for Leonardo not being a scientist is simply that he always remains a painter. But could we say, with Valéry, that if Leonardo substitutes "painting for philosophy," he also replaces science with philosophy?

Let us now examine Leonardo's painting. First, to paint like Leonardo requires not only a well-trained hand, but also an educated eye capable of discerning underlying structures in what appears to be merely visible accidents:

To paint, for Leonardo, was an operation that demanded every form of knowledge and almost all scientific disciplines: geometry, dynamics, geology, physiology. A battle to be portrayed involved a study of vortices and clouds of dust, and he refused to depict such phenomena before observing them in a scientific spirit, with eyes that had been impregnated, so to speak, with the understanding of their laws.[20]

Although laws and causes may be important in science, they are not always operative when it comes to painting. And yet what is common to both Leonardo's painting and science is their aim: that of discovery. But which science? We might even go a step further and say that painting *is* a science whose fulfillment lies in the reproduction of appearances. In other words, painting is a science of the sensuous, or what Merleau-Ponty calls the "flesh of the world." The purpose of such a science is not to explain but to reproduce, to present something to the eye rather than the mind. Painting allows us to see what we have never seen before, precisely because we see more by means of words and concepts than through the senses. The sensuous—the glory of appearing—must rehabilitate our senses and express itself in opposition to our perceptual habits. Painting teaches us really to perceive. Now, if we are to continue this line of argument, we might say, as Klee did, that "painting does not represent the visible, it makes visible." This claim has served as the byword for all modern art since the time of Impressionism. Herbert Read, in his *History of Modern Painting*, invoked it as the only principle of unification, and thus intelligibility, linking the extraordinary stylistic diversity so characteristic of modern art.[21] But let us examine this point further. Klee would certainly not admit, as did Leonardo, or at least Valéry's Leonardo, that painting is a science. Conversely, Leonardo would not agree with Klee in his claim that painting returns to a universal matrix. At this point we should therefore further consider just how science finds its fulfillment in painting. This would seem to be in basic contradiction with the idea of a science that results in making. But perhaps not, since painting is also a type of constructing, is often associated with assemblages, and requires both conceptual and material artifacts. Even in Leonardo's time reconstructing appearances called for a theory of light and shadow. And for Leonardo, shadow is just as real as light: "I treat shadows, and say in this connection that every opaque body is surrounded and has its surface clothed with shadow and lights, and to this I devote my first book."[22]

This immediately draws our attention to the object of Leonardo's science. The representation of light and shadow undoubtedly requires the conceptual tools inherent in geometrical optics. Consequently, Leonardo deals with light and shadow in accordance with strict optical laws. But the very fact that he conversely interprets light in the same terms as shadow clearly indicates that he is intrigued not by the substance but by the phenomenon, not by the nature of things but by their appearances. The nature of light, he notes, is splendor; the nature of shadow, obscurity. What kind of nature could that be, if not the sensuous itself! Leonardo focuses on the visibility of things, that is, not on their essences but on their qualities and forms. Thus his concern with shadows: "Shadow is the expression of bodies and their shapes."[23]

The subordination of a scientific instrument to a science of the sensuous can also be observed in Leonardo's use of perspective. For many of his contemporaries, the problem of the third dimension was indeed a problem of geometry: How does one render on a two-dimensional surface an imaginary section through the pyramid of visual rays joining the object and the eye of the perceiver? Unlike many of his contemporaries, Leonardo was dissatisfied with a purely artificial solution to this problem. He rather chose to combine a natural perspective with the commonly accepted artificial perspective, thus taking into account the natural sphericity of the human eye, and providing a more faithful rendition of the appearance of the object in question.

The actual production of art, however, requires more than merely rendering forms. For things are given to us with sensible qualities that interfere with their absolute spatial relationships and observable outlines. Thus Leonardo distinguishes and applies three kinds of perspectives: 1) linear perspective; 2) chromatic perspective, or the compensation for the change of color according to spatial recession; and 3) the perspective of effacement, or the dimunition of contour definition according to distance. The latter two forms of perspective are most commonly known as aerial perspective. And Leonardo defines its use in a passage that is quite reminiscent of Cézanne's ingenious play with blues: "Therefore you should make the building which is nearest above the wall of its natural color, and that which is more distant make less defined and bluer."[24]

Undoubtedly Leonardo never completely dispenses with linear perspective, nor with traditional modes of composition. According to Wölfflin, the pyramidal disposition of figures in *The Virgin of the Rocks* and *St. Anne and the Virgin* represent a decisive moment in the history of classicism.[25] Leonardo in fact advanced further than many of his contemporaries in experimenting with aerial perspectives. He succeeded to a considerable degree in depicting the manner in which objects are enclosed in an atmosphere, and this was not seen in terms of a rational law of appearance, but rather as the very substance of appearing. The sensuous reveals itself within the enveloping atmosphere, and this revelation compels the painter to transcend the demands of linear perspective. Leonardo is fascinated by the ambiguity of the indistinct: values become opposed to colors, modulation to saturation, *chiaroscuro* to clarity, and *sfumato* to precision.

This inclination then leads to the infamous *non-finito*, which is neglected by Valéry as if it were merely an immaterial and meaningless failure provoked by Leonardo's bold experiments. And of course, the reason Leonardo discontinued the *Battle of Anghiari* could simply have been that the dessication of colors rendered it technically impossible to complete. We should not, however, in any circumstances comprehend *non-finito* as mere failure! It is rather a constraint imposed upon Leonardo by his own enterprise, that is, the celebration of the sensuous, of the glory of appearing. Is it necessary to master the sensuous in order to celebrate it? Yes, but it can never be absolutely mastered, and this incapacity is the homage one must pay to the sensuous. Leonardo pays this tribute, for example, when he suggests that young artists seek landscape designs in amorphous stains and other natural shapes (*componimento inculto*). He is primarily a painter because he realized that the true painter always remains a novice, and that painting itself defies completion. In speaking of Leonardo we can invoke the names of Cézanne and Klee—they are all quite similar. We cannot, however, speak of Leonardo and Valéry in the same breath—they are quite different.

Should we follow Chastel, who pays little attention to ambiguity in Leonardo's works, in claiming that the triumph of *chiaroscuro* heralds the defeat of thought? I would prefer to say that there are two Leonardos: the constructor-scientist-technologist and the painter. The latter both assimilates and surpasses the former. Leonardo the painter searches for the bones of the world only to enjoy its flesh. He wishes to make painting identical with that flesh. And if this flesh is charged with affects, then he is also Freud's Leonardo. Or he would be if Freud had presented nature—Mother Nature—as appearing, rather than in the guise of an absent and desired human mother.

In concluding, we can turn to Valéry's "Note and Digression," where he writes: "I was charmed to the height of my senses by this Apollo."[26] But Leonardo is not merely an Apollo. There is something of the Promethean in his constructing, and something of the Dionysian in his painting. This painter is not a clear and motionless mirror of nature, he is inspired by nature to the point of being ravished by the Maenads of the *non-finito*. Would the later Valéry agree with this? That is difficult to say.

Notes

1. Paul Valéry, *Cahiers* (Paris: Centre National de la Recherche Scientifique, 1956–60).
2. Paul Valéry, *Oeuvres*, vol. 1 (Paris: Gallimard, 1957), pp. 1223–4; English translation, *The Collected Works of Paul Valéry*, trans. Malcolm Cowley and James R. Lawler (Princeton: Princeton University Press, 1972) vol. 8, p. 96. (All further references will be to English translation).
3. Paul Valéry, *Collected Works*, vol. 8, p. 13.
4. G.W.F. Hegel, *The Phenomenology of Mind*, trans. J. B. Baillie (New York: Harper & Row, 1967), pp. 229–40.
5. Paul Valéry, *Collected Works*, vol. 8, p. 8.
6. Paul Valéry, *Collected Works*, vol. 4, pp. 90–2.
7. Ibid., pp. 169–70.
8. Valéry, *Collected Works*, vol. 8, p. 13.
9. Valéry, *Collected Works*, vol. 8, p. 15.
10. André Chastel, *The Genius of Leonardo da Vinci* (New York: Orion Press, 1961), pp. x–xxv.
11. Valéry, *Collected Works*, vol. 8, p. 32.
12. Ibid., pp. 32–3.
13. Ibid., p. 10.
14. Ibid., p. 21.
15. Ibid., p. 38.
16. Ibid., p. 131.

17. Ibid., p. 134.
18. Ibid., p. 137.
19. Ibid., p. 146.
20. Ibid., p. 144.
21. Herbert Read, *A Concise History of Modern Painting* (New York: Praeger, 1959), passim.
22. Leonardo da Vinci, *Notebooks*, trans. Edward McCurdy (New York: Braziller, 1955), vol. 2, p. 953.
23. Ibid., p. 980.
24. Ibid., p. 880.
25. Heinrich Wölfflin, *Classic Art* (New York: Phaidon, 1959), pp. 33–4.
26. Valéry, *Collected Works*, vol. 8. p. 67.

Bibliography of Mikel Dufrenne

A. WORKS BY MIKEL DUFRENNE

I. Books

1947: *Karl Jaspers et la philosophie de l'existence.* Written in collaboration with Paul Ricoeur. Paris: Editions du Seuil.

1953: *Phénoménologie de l'experience esthétique.* 2 vols. Paris: Presses Universitaires de France. English translation: *The Phenomenology of Aesthetic Experience.* Translated by Edward S. Casey et al. Evanston, Ill.: Northwestern University Press, 1973.

La personnalité de base—un concept sociologique. Paris: Presses Universitaires de France.

1959: *La Notion d'a priori.* Paris: Presses Universitaires de France. English translation: *The Notion of the A Priori.* Translated by Edward S. Casey. Evanston, Ill.: Northwestern University Press, 1966.

1963: *Language and Philosophy.* Translated by Henry Veatch. Bloomington, Ind.: University of Indiana Press.

Le Poétique. Paris: Presses Universitaires de France.

1966: *Jalons.* The Hague: Martinus Nijhoff.

1966: *Les Categories ésthétique* in *Revue d'Esthétique*, No. 19, Special Number.

1967: *Esthétique et philosophie I.* Paris: Klincksieck.

1968: *Pour l'homme.* Paris: Editions de Seuil.

1974: *Art et politique.* Paris: Presses de la Cité (coll. 10/18).

1976: *Esthétique et philosophie II.* Paris: Klincksieck.

1977: *Subversion, perversion.* Paris: Presses Universitaires de France.

1979: Editor. *Main Trends in Aesthetics and the Sciences of Art.* New York: Holmes and Meier (reprint).

1981: *Esthétique et philosophie III.* Paris: Klincksieck.

L'Inventaire des a priori. Paris: Editions Christian Bourgois.

Editor with Dino Formaggio, *Trattato di Estetica.* Milan: Mondadori.

II. Articles and Reviews

1946: "Existentialisme et sociologie." *Cahiers Internationaux de Sociologie* (1), pp. 161–167.

1947: "Note sur la tradition." *Cahiers Internationaux de Sociologie* (2), pp. 158–69.

"Sociologie et phénoménologie." *Echanges sociologiques.*

1948: "Actualité de Hegel." *Esprit* (16), pp. 396–408.

"Dieu et l'homme dans la philosophie de Spinoza." In *L'Homme métaphysique et conscience de soi*, pp. 37–92. Neufchâtel: La Baconnière.

"Histoire et historicité. Un aspect de la sociologie de Marx." *Cahiers Internationaux de Sociologie* (3), pp. 98–118.

"La Philosophie de Jaspers." *Etudes germaniques*, March, pp. 64–79.

"Philosophie et littérature." *Revue d' Esthétique* (1), pp. 289–305. English translation: "Philosophy and Literature." In *In the Presence of the Sensuous: Essays in Aesthetics.*

1949: "La connaissance de Dieu dans la philosophie spinoziste." *Revue Philosophique de la France et de l'Etranger* (74), pp. 474–485.

"Heidegger et Kant." *Revue de Métaphysique et de Morale* (54), pp. 1–28. A review of Heidegger's *Kant und das Problem der Metaphysik.*

1952: "Coup d'oeil sur l'anthropologie culturelle américaine." *Cahiers Internationaux de Sociologie* (12), 26–46.

Ed., with Suzanne Bachelard. *Logique et philosophie des sciences*, by Paul Mouy. Paris: Hachette.

1953: "Un livre récent sur la connaissance de la vie." *Revue de Métaphysique et de Morale* (58), pp. 170–187. A review of Georges Canguilhem's *La connaissance de la vie.*

1954: "Bréve note sur l'ontologie." *Revue de Métaphysique et de Morale* (59), pp. 398–412.

"Intentionalité et esthétique." *Revue Philosophique de la France et de l'Etranger* (79), pp. 75–84. English translation: "Intentionality and Aesthetics." In *In the Presence of the Sensuous: Essays in Aesthetics.*

'La mentalité primitive et Heidegger." *Les Etudes Philosophiques* (9), pp. 284–306.

Review of *Introduction a l'esthétique*, by Maurice Nédoncelle. *Revue Philosophique de la France et de l'Etranger* (79), pp. 130–131.

1955: "Les aventures de la dialectique ou les avatars d'une amitié philosophique." *Combat*, 29 September 1955.

"L'Esthétique et le concept du Beau." *Institut propédeutique de l'Université du Vietnam.*

"L'Expérience esthétique de la nature." Brussels: *Revue Internationale de Philosophie* (9), pp. 98–115.

"Signification des a priori." *Bulletin de la Société française de la Philosophie* (9), pp. 97–132.

1956: "Bilan de carence de la sociologie." *Cahiers Internationaux de Sociologie* (21), pp. 128–137.

1957: "A propos de Pindare." *Revue d'Esthétique*, pp. 166–173.

"Valeurs et valeurs esthétiques." *Atti del III Congresso Internazionale de Esthetica* 3–5 September 1956, pp. 145–148.

Review of *Commentaire sur le Banquet de Platon*, by Marcilio Ficino (Paris: Les Belles Lettres, 1956), *Revue d'Esthétique* (10), p. 210.

Review of *La Littérature européene et le Moyen-Age Latin*, by Ernst Curtius.

1958: "Expérience esthétique et jugement esthétique." *Il Guido Estetica*, pp. 79–82. Padova: Edizioni della Rivista de Estetica.

1959: "Le parti de l'homme." *Esprit* (27), pp. 113–124. English translation: "The Role of Man in the Social Sciences." *Philosophy Today*, 1960, pp. 36–44.

1960: "Mythe, science et éthique du sexe." *Esprit* (28), pp. 1702–1710.

"La sensibilité généralisatrice." *Revue d'Esthétique* (13), pp. 216–226. An article in memory of Raymond Bayer.

1961: "The Beautiful." In *In the Presence of the Sensuous: Essays in Aesthetics*.

"De l'expressivité de l'abstrait. *Revue d'Esthétique* (14), pp. 210–215.

Review of *De l'esthétique à la métaphysique*, by Jean-Claude Piquet. *Revue d'Esthétique* (14), pp. 110–112.

"La critique de la raison dialectique." *Esprit* (29), pp. 675–692.

Review of *Esthétique contemporaine*, by Guido Morpurgo-Tagliabue. *Revue d'Esthétique*, (14), pp. 392–393.

1962: "Maurice Merleau-Ponty." *Les Etudes philosophiques* (17), pp. 81–92.

1963: An article in *Les philosophes français d'aujourd'hui par eux-mêmes*, pp. 395–400. Paris: Centre de Documentation Universitaire, 1963.

"Gaston Bachelard et la poésie de l'imagination." *Les Etudes philosophiques* (18), pp. 174–187.

Review of the *British Journal of Aesthetics*. *Revue d'Esthétique* (16), pp. 101–107.

Review of *Actes du IVième Congrès international d'Esthétique* (Athens, 1960). *Les Etudes philosophiques* (18), p. 343.

Review of *L'Inspiration*, by François Heidseick's, *Revue d'Esthétique* (16), pp. 110–112.

"La mort de Giraudoux n'aura pas lieu." *Revue d'Esthétique*, (16), pp. 81–86.

"La Terre, le temps, et les Dieux." *Revue d'Esthétique* (16), pp. 203–210.

1964: "The Aesthetic Object and the Technical Object." *Journal of Aesthetics and Art Criticism* (23), pp. 113–122.

"L'apport de l'esthétique à la philosophie." *Algemeen Nederlands Tijdschrift voor Wijsbeerte en Psychologie* (56), pp. 235–240.

"Critique littéraire et phénomenologie." *Revue Internationale de Philosophie* (18), pp. 192–208. English translation: "Literary Criticism and Phenomenology." In *In the Presence of the Sensuous: Essays in Aesthetics*.

"Mal du siècle? Mort de l'art?" *Revue d'Esthétique* (17), pp. 190–214. English translation: "Mal du siècle? Death of Art?" In *In the Presence of the Sensuous: Essays in Aesthetics*.

Participation in a discussion entitled "Le possible" at the Société Française de la Philosophie. Reported in the *Bulletin de la Société française de la Philosophie*, 58, no. 4, pp. 129–151. Paris: Armand Colin, 1964.

"Formalisme logique et formalisme esthétique." *Annales d'Esthétique*, Athens.

1965: "Les a priori de l'imagination." *Archivo di Filosofia* (Surrealismo e simbolismo), pp. 53–63. Padua: Cedam. English translation: "The A Priori of Imagination." In *In the Presence of the Sensuous: Essays in Aesthetics*.

"Existentialism and Existentialisms." *Philosophy and Phenomenological Research* (26), pp. 51–62.

"Wittgenstein et la philosophie." *Les Etudes Philosophiques* (20), pp. 281–306.

1966: "L'A priori comme monde." *Annales de l'Université de Paris*, pp. 1–15.

"L'art est-il langage?" *Revue d'Esthétique* (19), pp. 1–42.

"A New Approach to Novelty." *Pacific Philosophy Forum*, February, pp. 78–81.

"Wittgenstein and Husserl." Lecture given at Johns Hopkins University. Published in *Jalons*, 1966, pp. 188–207.

Participation in the following discussions: (1) La lutte pour les droits de l'homme; (2) Conventional rights and right conventions; (3) Le phénomène de la "Reconnaissance universelle." Published in *Le fondement des droits de l'homme* (Florence: La Nuova Italia, 1966).

1967: "A Priori et philosophie de la nature." *Filosofia* (18), pp. 723–736. English translation: "The A Priori and the Philosophy of Nature." *Philosophy Today*, Fall 1970, pp. 201–212. Reprinted in *In the Presence of the Sensuous: Essays in Aesthetics*.

"La philosophie du neo-positivisme." *Esprit* (35), pp. 781–800.

"Structure et sens: La critique littéraire." *Revue d'Esthétique* (20), pp. 1–16. English translation: "Structure and Meaning: Literary Criticism." In *In the Presence of the Sensuous: Essays in Aesthetics*.

1968: "L'anti-humanisme et le theme de la mort." *Revue internationale de Philosophie* (22), 3–4, pp. 296–307.

"Syntaxe et sémantique dans l'art." *Rivista di Estetica* (13), pp. 161–177.

1969: "Phénoménologie et ontologie de l'art." *Les sciences humaines et l'oeuvre d'art* (Brussels: La Connaissance).

1970: "L'art et le sauvage." *Revue d'Esthétique* (23), pp. 241–254.

"L'art abstrait"; "Le Beau"; "L'esthétique"; "L'oeuvre"; Le Public"; "Le style." In *Encyclopedia Universalis*, Paris.

"Structuralism and Humanism." In *Patterns of the Life-World: Essays in Honor of John Wild*, pp. 290–297. Evanston, Ill.: Northwestern University Press.

1971: "L'année 1913." In *Les Formes esthétique de l'oeuvre d'art à la veille de la première guerre mondiale*, edited by L. Brion-Guerry, pp. 25–57. Paris: Klincksieck.

"L'art conceptuel." *Revue d'Esthétique* (24), pp. 91–93.

"Esthétique et structuralisme." In *La philosophie contemporaine*, edited by R. Klibansky, pp. 97–101. Florence: Là Nouva Italia.

1972: "Aesthetik der Abbildung." *Philosophische Perspektiven*, Frankfurt, IV.

A discussion on the "Critic and the Lover of Art" with R. K. Elliott in *Linguistic Analysis and Phenomenology*, edited by Wolfe Mays, pp. 128–136. Lewisburg, Pa.: Bucknell University Press.

"Questionari le riposte." *BN Strutturalismo e critica del Film* 3–4, March–April 1972.

"Comment peut-on aller au cinéma?" *Revue d'Esthétique* (26), pp. 371–382. English translation: "Why Go to the Movies?" In *In the Presence of the Sensuous: Essays in Aesthetics*.

"On the Phenomenology and Semiology of Art." In *Phenomenology and Natural Existence: Essays in Honor of Marvin Farber*. Albany: State University of New York Press.

1974: "L'art de masse existe-t-il?" *Revue d'Esthétique* 10/18 (903).

"Création et engagement politique." *Revue Internationale de Philosophie* (109).

"L'Esthétique." In *Enciclopedia Italiana*, Rome.

"Phénoménologie et esthétique." *Actes de Congrés de Phénoménologie*, Montréal.

Preface to *La Pensée cosmologique d'Etienne Souriau*, by Luce de Vitry-Maubrey. Paris: Klincksieck, 1974.

"La Crise de l'art," "Oeuvre et non-oeuvre," "Du style." *Encyclopedia Universalis*, Paris.

1975: "Après le structuralisme." In *La philosophie française contemporaine*. Bologna: Editions Forni.

"Ecriture, peinture." *Revue d'Esthétique* (Coll. 10/18).

"L'Esthétique de Paul Valéry." In *Sens et Existence*. Paris: Editions du Seuil.

"Esthétique et Science de l'art." In *Tendances actuelles des sciences humaines*. UNESCO, the Hague: Mouton & Co.

"La Poésie: Où et pourquoi." *Revue d'Esthétique* 3–4, pp. 10–40.

1976: "L'Imaginaire." In *Esthétique et philosophie II*. Paris: Klincksieck, 1976. English translation: "The Imaginary." In *In the Presence of the Sensuous: Essays in Aesthetics*.

"Le jeu et l'imaginaire." In *Esthétique et philosophie II*, pp. 133–150. Paris: Klincksieck, 1976.

"L'oeuvre et le public." In *Esthétique et philosophie II*, pp. 273–288. Paris: Klincksieck, 1976.

"Doutes sur la 'libidiné.'" *L'Arc* (64), pp. 13–27.

"Peindre, toujours." *Revue d'Esthétique, Peindre* (Coll. 10/18), pp. 3–42. English translation: "Painting, Forever." In *In the Presence of the Sensuous*: Essays in Aesthetics.

"Les Metamorphoses de l'Esthétique." *Enciclopedia Italiana*, Rome.

"Valéry's Leonardo." Presented at the *Stony Brook Studies in Philosophy* ("Leonardo and Philosophy"), 1976. Reprinted in revised form in *In the Presence of the Sensuous: Essays in Aesthetics*.

"The Phenomenological Approach to Poetry." *Philosophy Today*, Spring 1976, pp. 12–19. Reprinted in *In the Presence of the Sensuous: Essays in Aesthetics*.

"Vers l'originaire." In *Esthétique et philosophie II*, pp. 85–98. Paris: Klincksieck, 1976.

1977: *Actualité* "Les Malassis à Montreuil." *Revue d'Esthétique*, pp. 409–411.

"Sur la Création." *Diotima* (5), pp. 84–89.

1979: "Le Champs de l'esthétisable." *Revue d'Esthétique* (3–4), pp. 131–143.

1980: "La couronne d'herbes." *Revue d'Esthétique* (3–4), pp. 96–117.

"La peinture à l'oeuvre et l'enigme du corps." *Revue d'Esthétique* (3–4), pp. 355–359.

"Le système contre la liberté." *Raison Present* (55) pp. 165–168.

"Sartre and Merleau-Ponty." In *Jean-Paul Sartre: Contemporary Approaches to His Philosophy*, edited by Hugh J. Silverman and Frederick Elliston, pp. 309–320. Pittsburgh: Duquesne University Press.

"Venir au jour." In *Textes pour Emmanuel Levinas*, pp. 105–110. Paris: Editions Jean-Michel Place.

1981: "Du signifiant au référent." *Revue d'Esthétique* (2), pp. 71–81.

"Note sur les sciences humaines." In *Fenomenologia e scienze dell'uomo*, 1981, pp. 123–131.

1982: "Comment voir l'histoire?" *Esprit* (6), pp. 45–52.

"Le Jour se léve." In *Fenomenologia e scienze dell'uomo II*, pp. 35–39.

"La Région Nature." In *Fenomenologia e scienze dell'uomo II*, pp. 19–33.

Review of *Mikhail Baktine*, by T. Todorov. *Revue d'Esthétique* (3), pp. 166–168.

1983: "La Profondeur comme dimension de l'objet ésthétique," *Diotima*, No. 10, pp. 9–16 (1982).

B. TEXTS CONCERNING DUFRENNE.

(*Note*: The Festschrift entitled *Pour une esthétique sans entrave: Mélanges Mikel Dufrenne*, Paris: U.G.E., 1975, will be referred to as *Mélanges*.)

Allen, David G. "Aesthetic Perception in Mikel Dufrenne's Phenomenology of Aesthetic Experience." *Philosophy Today*, Spring 1978, pp. 50–64.

Aufhauser, Marcia. Review of *The Phenomenology of Aesthetic Experience*. *Journal of Philosophy*, 30 January 1975, p. 49.

Barilli, R. *Per un'estetica mondana*, pp. 271–298, 323–328. Bologna: Mulino, 1964.

Beardsley, Monroe C. *Aesthetics from Classical Greece to the Present*, pp. 271–272, 395–396. New York: Macmillan, 1966.

Berg, John. "Towards a Phenomenological Aesthetics: A Critical Study of Mikel Dufrenne's Philosophy with Special Reference to a Theory of Literature." Dissertation, Purdue University, 1978.

Brisson, Marcelle. "De la perception sauvage à l'utopie." *Mélanges*, pp. 33–50.

Casey, Edward S. Translator's introduction to *The Notion of the A Priori*, Mikel Dufrenne, pp. xviii–xxviii, Evanston, Ill.: Northwestern University Press, 1966.

―――. Translator's foreword to *The Phenomenology of Aesthetic Experience*, by Mikel Dufrenne, pp. xv–xlii, Evanston, Ill.: Northwestern University Press, 1973.

―――. "L'Imagination comme intermédiare." *Mélanges*, pp. 93–114.

Cauquelin, Anne. "Mikel Dufrenne: portrait chinois." *Mélanges*, pp. 21–32.

Charles, Daniel. "Mikel Dufrenne et l'idée de la nature." *Mélanges*, pp. 73–88.

Clement, Catherine B. "Séminaires." *Mélanges*, pp. 61–64.

Cohn, Robert Greer. *Modes of Art*. Saratoga, Ca: Amma Libri. 1975.

Coleman, Francis J. "A Phenomenology of Aesthetic Reasoning." *Journal of Aesthetics and Art Criticism*, vol. 25, Winter 1966.

Dayan, Maurice. Review of *Pour l'homme*. *Revue de Métaphysique et de Morale* (25), January–March 1970, pp. 115–117.

Delhomme, Jeanne. "D'un nouvel a priori." *Mélanges*, pp. 89–92.

Dumery, Henri. "Il n'y a pas de feu enfant." *Mélanges*, pp. 65–72.

Feezel, Randolph M. "Mikel Dufrenne and the Ontological Question in Art: A Critical Study of *The Phenomenology*." Dissertation, State University of New York at Buffalo, 1977.

———. "Mikel Dufrenne and the World of the Aesthetic Object." *Philosophy Today*, Spring 1980, pp. 20–32.

Figurelli, Roberto. "La notion d'a priori chez Mikel Dufrenne." *Mélanges*, pp. 133–142.

———. "Por una estética fenomenológica: Introducão á obra de Mikel Dufrenne," *Textos SEAF* 3, No. 4, pp. 44–57 (1983).

Formaggio, Dino. "Mikel Dufrenne, la natura e il senso del poetico." In *Fenomenologia e scienze dell' uomo*, 1982, pp. 7–18.

Franzini, Elio. "Natura e poesia. Su un inventario degli a priori di Mikel Dufrenne." In *Fenomenologia e scienze dell'uomo*, 1982, pp. 67–90.

Gillan, Garth. "Mikel Dufrenne: The Mythology of Nature." *Philosophy Today*, Fall 1970, pp. 168–169.

Gilson, E.; Langan, T.; and Maurer, A. *Recent Philosophy: Hegel to the Present*, pp. 396–401. New York: Random House, 1966.

Kaelin, Eugene F. *An Existentialist Aesthetic*, pp. 359–385. Madison: The University of Wisconsin Press, 1962.

———. *Art and Existence: A Phenomenological Aesthetics*. Lewisburg, Pa: Bucknell University Press, 1970.

Lyotard, Jean-François. "A la place de l'homme, l'expression." *Esprit* (7), 1969.

———. *Discours, figure*, pp. 291–295 and passim. Paris: Klincksieck, 1971.

Magliola, Robert R. *Phenomenology and Literature: An Introduction*, pp. 142–173. West Lafayette, Ind.: Purdue University Press, 1977.

Matei, Dimitri. "Du Transcendental à l'ontologie dans l'explication de l'expérience esthétique." *Philosophie et Logique* (23), January–March 1979, pp. 67–82.

———. "Originile artei," in *Les Origines de l'art*, Bucharest: Medidian, 1981.

Morawski, Stefan. *Inquiries into the Fundamentals of Aesthetics*. Cambridge: MIT Press, 1974.

Morpurgo-Tagliabue, Guido. *Esthéique contemporaine*, pp. 460–468. Milan: Marzorati, 1960.

Pascadi, Ion. "La science, la philosophie et l'art sous le signe de l'homme." *Mélanges*, pp. 129–132.

Piquet, Claude. "Esthétique et phénoménologie." *Kant-Studien* 47 (1955–56): 192–208.

Ricoeur, Paul. "Philosophie, sentiment et poésie." *Esprit*, March 1961, pp. 504–512.

————. "Le Poétique." *Esprit*, January 1966, pp. 107–116.

————. Preface to *The Notion of the A Priori*, by Mikel Dufrenne, pp. ix–xvii. Evanston, Ill.: Northwestern University Press, 1966.

Robert, Jean-Dominique. Review of *Pour l'homme. Archives de Philosophie* (32), October–December 1969, pp. 681–683.

Saison, Maryvonne. "Mikel Dufrenne: Imaginaire et anarchie." *Mélanges*, pp. 11–20.

Sallis, John. "Constitution in Mikel Dufrenne." *The Modern Schoolman* (47), January 1970, pp. 169–175.

Sansot, Pierre, "En revenant de la rue Rosa-Bonheur." *Mélanges*, pp. 51–60.

Silverman, Hugh J. Review of *The Phenomenology of Aesthetic Experience. Journal of Aesthetics and Art Criticism* (33), no. 4, Summer 1975, pp. 462–464.

————. "Dufrenne's Phenomenology of Poetry." *Philosophy Today*, Spring 1976, pp. 20–24.

Spiegelberg, Herbert. *The Phenomenological Movement: A Historical Introduction*, 2d ed., vol. 2, pp. 579–585. The Hague: Martinus Nijhoff, 1965.

Taminiaux, Jacques. "Notes sur une phénoménologie de l'expérience esthétique." *Revue Philosophie de Louvain* (LV), 1957, pp. 93–110.

Tertulian, Nicolas. "En relisant la *Phénoménologie de l'expérience esthétique.*" *Mélanges*, pp. 115–128.

Van Droogenbrock, J. Review of *Pour l'homme. Revue Philosophique de Louvain* (68), Fall 1970, p. 124.

Vasquez, Adolfo Sanchez. *Estetica y Marxismo*, vols. 1 and 2. Mexico: Editiones Era, 1970.

Zéraffa, Michel. Review of *Les'Inventaires des a priori. Revue d'Esthétique* (3), 1982, pp. 168–170.

Name Index

Subject Index